Also by Jack Cashill

Unmasking Obama: The Fight to Tell the True Story of a Failed Presidency

Barack Obama's Promised Land: Deplorables Need Not Apply

Untenable: The True Story of White Ethnic Flight from America's Cities

ASHLI

The Untold Story of the Women of January 6

Jack Cashill

BOMBARDIER
BOOKS

Published by Bombardier Books
An Imprint of Post Hill Press
ISBN: 979-8-88845-775-7
ISBN (eBook): 979-8-88845-718-4

ASHLI:
The Untold Story of the Women of January 6
© 2024 by Jack Cashill
All Rights Reserved

Cover Design by Joel Gilbert

Post Hill Press
New York • Nashville
posthillpress.com

Published in the United States of America
1 2 3 4 5 6 7 8 9 10

Table of Contents

Research Notes and Acknowledgments

On January 11, 2021, I submitted an article to what continues to be one of my favorite publications. The article was titled: "President Trump Takes a Hit for the Team." For the first and only time, the editors edited me for content—in this case, by removing my concluding paragraph:

> It seems somehow providential that the people's protest at the "People's House" occurred on the Epiphany. If we the people refuse to apologize, refuse to back down, refuse to submit, January 6 may one day be celebrated as a mid-winter 4th of July.

I understood the editor's prudence. The FBI was already rounding up dissidents. For the next two or three years, I watched as others did the heavy journalistic lifting on January 6 and followed them closely: Julie Kelly, Jim Hoft, Darren Beattie, Joe Hanneman, Nick Searcy, and Lara Logan among others. During this period, the reportorial beat on which I focused involved the only people less popular in the nation's courts and newsrooms than the J6ers, namely Derek Chauvin and his colleagues in Minneapolis. As I discovered in researching this book, these cases overlapped in ways I had not anticipated.

Providence intervened in the fall of 2023. I woke up one morning with the word "Ashli" in the forefront of my brain. I emailed Julie Kelly on October 17. "Do you know if anyone is working on a book about Ashli?" I wrote, "I'm looking for a new project and still simmer when I think about January 6." Julie replied, "Hi Jack, I don't but might be a good project?"

In that same email, I mentioned that the final chapter of my most recent book, *Untenable: The True Story of White Ethnic Flight from America's Cities*, takes place on January 6, 1993. In large part a memoir, the book deals with the death of my police detective father who fatally shot himself on an earlier January 6. That last chapter is titled, "Epiphany."

Within days of this exchange, my agent, Alex Hoyt, called and asked if I had any book ideas in mind. I said, yes, absolutely. He liked the idea as did our publisher, Anthony Ziccardi of Post Hill Press. I got to work. There was much to learn and quickly.

I live in Kansas City. A few weeks after getting approval, Melody Krell, the fabulous Mel K, came here for a conference. Although I had been on Mel's show many times, we had not met. Through Mel, I also met Ann Vandersteel. They both proved helpful in introducing me to the people whose blessing I needed to proceed. At the top of that list was Micki Witthoeft, Ashli's mom. When Micki agreed to cooperate, I was halfway home.

Rather than speculate on what Ashli Babbitt might have thought about the many issues roiling America in the years leading to January 6, 2021, and beyond, I chose to flesh out the larger story by speaking with women who survived the day. To start, I turned to the site, American Gulag, which tracks the progress of the J6ers through the judicial system. I selected eight living women whose cases each revealed some distinct facet of our current justice system.

To clear the next hurdle, I turned to one of my favorite co-conspirators, Susan Daniels, a licensed private investigator from Ohio. Susan not only volunteered to find contact information for these women but also to make the initial contact. Also helpful in this outreach were Lara Logan, Liz Collin, and Cara Castronuova.

Fortunately, I was able to establish a cooperative relationship with all eight of the living women profiled. These women had been through the wringer. Two of them were in prison at the time I was writing. I supplemented our conversations with other interviews they had done, media accounts, court documents, and the like. For simplicity's sake, I used endnotes on this external material but not for the information derived from my direct communication with the women.

The tenth woman I feature, Rosanne Boyland, was also killed on January 6. Working through intermediaries, I had hoped to communicate with her family but was not able to link up. For Rosanne's story, I have to give credit where it is due—MSNBC's Ayman Mohyeldin. His five-part podcast was a gold mine of useful information. Mohyeldin ended up alienating family members and likely made them gun-shy about working with the media, but his research was indispensable. Despite his biases, even he began to see the injustices endured by J6ers and their families.

Kudos to one of my other favorite co-conspirators, Joel Gilbert, not only a gifted filmmaker but also the designer of my book covers, this one included. And a major shout-out to my wife, Joan, the rare university professor willing to be seen with a dissident like me.

Finally, though, a word of gratitude for the thousands of J6ers and family members whose sacrifices have stirred many an American out of their slumber.

1

1789

On April 30, 1789, president-elect George Washington woke to the sounds of artillery fire from a nearby fort, only coincidentally named Fort George. Washington had to smile recalling that what he was hearing was a salute. There had been gunfire enough these many years, beginning in 1770 when British troops fired on a crowd of boisterous patriots in the streets of Boston, striking eleven, killing at least five, and creating the Revolution's first martyrs.

Later that April day, Washington arrived at Federal Hall in New York City. There he was greeted by both houses of Congress, and at 2 p.m., he was sworn in as the first president of the United States. In the inaugural address that followed, Washington paid homage to that "Almighty Being who rules over the Universe." Washington elaborated, "No People can be bound to acknowledge and adore the invisible hand, which conducts the Affairs of men more than the People of the United States."

In that same year, 1789, in Paris, a caucus of increasingly radical deputies from the National Assembly met in a former convent. In the days to come, the deputies added new members from the commercial elite and formed the Society of the Friends of the Constitution. The group became better known by the name of the convent in which they met, "The Jacobins."

In 1791, the National Assembly drafted the "Declaration of the Rights of Man and the Citizen."[1] Although democratic in its concept, one clause would forever distinguish this declaration from America's founding documents: "The source of all sovereignty resides essentially in the nation. No body, no individual can exercise authority that does not expressly proceed from the latter."

By contrast, the Declaration of Independence argues that men "are endowed by their Creator with certain unalienable Rights, that among these are Life, Liberty and the pursuit of Happiness."[2] The elevation of the nation over the individual would set the French revolutionaries on a statist, collectivist, godless path that inevitably led to their undoing.

While Jacobin-led mobs were dictating justice in the streets of Paris, here at home the separate states were peacefully deliberating on a Bill of Rights, one crafted by the very first Congress to protect the citizen's God-given freedoms. In 1791, Congress ratified ten of the proposed twelve amendments, the first of which remains the most essential: "Congress shall make no law respecting an establishment of religion, or prohibiting the free exercise thereof; or abridging the freedom of speech, or of the press; or the right of the people peaceably to assemble, and to petition the Government for a redress of grievances." The Second—"the right of the people to keep and bear arms shall not be infringed"—guaranteed the First.

In France, the revolutionary government was quickly consumed by the anti-Christian chaos it helped create. America, however, endured and prospered. In recent decades, however, America has developed its own increasingly faithless elite, one that eerily mimics the French Jacobins. Thinking themselves wiser than the God that humbled the nation's founders, these new Jacobins have set out to "fundamentally transform" America in their own light.

How this class evolved is a subject for another day, but its existence is hard to deny. In late 2023, pollster Scott Rasmussen conducted an extensive survey comparing the attitudes of the "elite" to those of ordinary citizens. Rasmussen defined the elite as those having a household income of at least $150,000, one or more graduate degrees, and an urban residence.

Although the results were startling across the board, the response to one question stands out. Rasmussen asked whether the United States "provides too much individual freedom, too much government control, or is the balance about right?" A stunning 47 percent of the elite said "too much freedom." Among the elite with Ivy League educations, an ominous 57 percent said "too much freedom." Among ordinary citizens that figure was 16 percent.[3]

Although not a perfect match with the French original, "Jacobin" serves as a useful shorthand for Rasmussen's "elite" and their fellow travelers. Despite their vast ideological divergence from ordinary citizens, these people hold enormous power. To the Jacobin club in Washington belongs every elected Democrat, some elected Republicans, much of the intelligence community, and most of the administrative state. Jacobin clubs in Hollywood and Silicon Valley exercise nearly monopolistic control over their respective industries. Jacobins rule higher education and increasingly, through their fully owned teacher unions, the public education establishment. Jacobins control the health care industry, almost every major newsroom, and most corporate boardrooms. Increasingly, they have wormed their way into strategic positions in the military.

The Jacobins have moved well beyond the liberalism that once defined the American Left. Most pay lip service to the progressivism they use as bait to attract the woke among their intersectional ranks—the blacks, the browns, the greens, the gays, the lesbians, trans, the feminists, the Muslims, and any other "marginalized" group willing to make noise in the street. But for club members in the know, the ultimate goal is power, global power. Having transcended the nation-state, they ally themselves with Jacobin elites throughout the world.

For the French Jacobins to succeed, the *ancien regime*—the old order headed by the king and the nobility and buttressed by the aristocracy and the clergy—had to fall. For the globalist Jacobins to succeed, nationalist America has to fall. Historian Victor Davis Hanson crystalized this class's way of thinking: "We are morally superior to the old America. This is a new America, and that gives us the right to use any means necessary to achieve a morally superior end."[4] The old America—grounded in faith, family, Judeo-Christian morality, property rights, and the freedoms enshrined in the US Constitution—stands in the way of the Jacobins' "new America," the cornerstone of a "new world order."

On January 6, 2021, the patriots of the old order came to Washington. Had Rasmussen surveyed them, the percent who believed they had "too much freedom" would have been close to zero. On that wintry day, in that hostile city, they were not about to sacrifice the freedoms they did have without at least making a statement. More attentive than the rest of us, they understood just how indifferent to the rule of law were the people with the power to enforce it.

Through their control of the newsrooms, Congress, and the White House, the Jacobins were confident they could write the history of that memorable day. The British thought much the same in 1770 when they dismissed the "Boston Massacre" as "the incident on King Street." The British were wrong. They underestimated the moral power of martyrdom. Even today, schools throughout America are named in honor of the first patriot to fall on King Street, a black man named Crispus Attucks, and not even homeschooled students know where King Street is.

To put some authority behind the headlines, in June 2021, the Democrat-controlled House authorized a "Select Committee to Investigate the January 6th Attack on the United States Capitol." All Democrats and two Republicans voted their approval. To no one's surprise, the committee's final report, issued in December 2022, proved to be as partisan and as gutless the people who commissioned it.

For all the fury of their rhetoric, the Jacobins could not disguise one inarguable fact: in responding to January 6, they unleashed their own reign of terror, the greatest mass injustice against American citizens since Japanese internment. If resistance to that terror has a face, it is that of Ashli Babbitt, an intrepid patriot and, like Crispus Attucks, an enduring martyr. This is her story and that of the other gallant women of January 6.

2

Dark to Light

On January 6, 2021, and on the days leading up to it, they came to Washington, DC, from all across the nation, just about every state of that nation—or so the DOJ boasted. They came in the thousands, tens of thousands, hundreds of thousands. Some came alone. Others came with their husbands, their boyfriends, their mothers, their fathers, their sons, their daughters, their political compadres. Their destination was the "March to Save America." Organizing the rally was a group called "Women for America First," headed by the mother-daughter team of Amy and Kylie Jane Kremer.

Unlike the women who descended on Washington four years prior to protest the inauguration of President Trump, the women of January 6 did not come as *women*. They came as Americans, as patriots, as defenders of the Republic. They did not wear pink hats. They wore MAGA hats. Their issues were indistinguishable from those of the men in their lives—the rule of law, free and fair elections, the preservation of constitutional rights. They brought no laundry list of special needs like, say, "reproductive rights." They understood that no one was challenging their right to reproduce. Many had reproduced abundantly.

There was not a single celebrity in their midst, no Ashley Judds, no Gloria Steinems, no Madonnas threatening "to blow up the White House."[5] These were Hillary's "deplorables," in the flesh, a whole heaping basket of them, "irredeemable" to the last woman. On average, they had less formal education than the pussy hat-wearing women of 2017, but, as shall be seen, they knew more and conformed less. If proof were needed, few among them flew to Washington. Nearly a year into COVID mania, they were much more likely than their liberal sisters to resist pointless restrictions, especially those imposed by the airlines.

That said, the petite thirty-five-year-old Ashli Babbitt had little choice but to fly. She and her husband, Aaron, lived in greater San Diego. On the morning of January 5, Ashli kissed Aaron good-bye and headed off to Washington, proudly wearing her "Trump 2020" mask lest anyone mistake her affections or her destination. "Nothing will stop us," Ashli tweeted on January 5, "they can try and try and try but the storm is here and it is descending upon DC in less than 24 hours…dark to light!"[6]

Sitting next to Ashli on the plane was a young journalist named Will Carless, who, as of this writing, mans the "extremism" desk at *USA Today*. On January 7, he posted an unusually thoughtful message on Twitter. Two days earlier on the DC flight, Ashli had helped him with his carry-ons as he took the middle seat. "It's a little sappy, but situations like this should remind us that there is more beyond politics. The person sitting next to you on a flight, even if they're wearing a mask you disagree with, is still a person."[7]

Having fasted and prayed, Rebecca Lavrenz, a great-grand-mother twice Ashli's age, decided she would drive by herself to DC from Colorado Springs. So why not? "Driving twenty-five hours to our US Capitol in January of 2021," she would write, "to stand with 100s of 1000s of fellow patriots who also agreed that something just wasn't right in the 2020 Presidential Election was not a tough decision."[8] Former US Marine Yvonne St Cyr drove even farther. On New Year's Day, Yvonne and her husband, Troy, left their home in Boise, Idaho, on a thirty-five-hour, mid-winter trek to Washington, DC.

Driving, as fifty-one-year-old Sara Carpenter knew, did not insure privacy, at least if you lived in the northeast corridor and depended on your E-ZPass. In the early morning hours of January 6, Sara, a retired NYPD cop and single mom, left her home in Queens for the four-hour trip to DC. She hoped to learn more about election fraud. She would learn a good deal more than that.

On the night of January 5, Rosanne Boyland, thirty-four, and her friend Justin Winchell left the Atlanta suburb of Kennesaw, Georgia, for the district, a drive of ten or so hours. They were psyched. En route, Justin sent Rosanne's dad, Bret Boyland, a text saying, "This is Justin, this is my number. I'm riding up with Rosanne. In case you have any trouble getting a hold of her through her phone, you got my number too."[9]

A mother of eight, Rachel Powell, forty, left her home in western Pennsylvania, met up with a friend en route, and drove together with him to the nation's Capitol. Victoria White, thirty-nine, a mother of four, made the drive from Rochester, Minnesota, with her seventeen-year-old daughter and two friends. Victoria had never been to Washington before.

Armed with a large sign reading, "We The People Take Back Our Country," on one side and, "The Children Cry Out for Justice" on the other, forty-nine-year-old Christine Priola, an occupational therapist for the Cleveland Metropolitan School District, rode in with like-minded patriots on a chartered bus from Willoughby, Ohio.

Lisa Eisenhart, fifty-six, a travel nurse, met up with her son Eric in Nashville and drove from there to DC. Like many of the protestors, Lisa believed the election had been stolen. She and Eric wanted to make sure their grievances were heard. "This country was founded on revolution," Lisa told a reporter just before driving back on January 7.[10]

An MD as well as a lawyer, Dr. Simone Gold, fifty-five, flew to Washington from Tampa with her significant other/ bodyguard John Strand. Dr. Gold spoke in Tampa on the issue of medical freedom, and she had permits to do the same in Washington on January 5 and 6. An outspoken critic of the nation's COVID regime, she did not readily surrender her right to speak freely. "We cannot live with this spider web of fear that's constricting our country," she would later tell Tucker Carlson.[11]

The ten women profiled above represent less than 1 percent of the protestors hunted down by the FBI in the most sweeping series of arrests on American soil since the notorious Palmer Raids of a century ago. Although many more men were arrested than women, the actions of these women are more or less representative of the whole. None of these women were armed. None were accused of anything more violent than a hand slapped or an elbow bumped. Only one was accused of vandalism, and that charge involved the use of a cardboard tube to break a window. And yet of the ten, eight would be arrested and six, to this point, imprisoned. The only two who escaped the Potemkin justice of the DC courts escaped though death.

On average, the men would fare worse in court, but the women fared worse in and around the Capitol. For a mix of reasons, police seemed to single out females for personal punishment. It was as though the very presence of these women at the Capitol offended the natural order of things.

The very passion of these women seemed to provoke the police. One officer, for instance, consciously shoved an unnamed elderly woman clad in American flag gear back-first down a half dozen concrete steps. Police officers hit Rachel Powell with a baton, grabbed her, threw her down, and sprayed her with a toxic substance. "My whole body was on fire," said Rachel.[12] A DC Metropolitan Police Department (MPD) lieutenant beat Victoria White bloody. A female Capitol Police (USCP) officer savagely thrashed the lifeless body of Rosanne Boyland. A male USCP lieutenant callously shot and killed the unarmed Ashli Babbitt.

More than three years after the Department of Justice launched these mass arrests, many questions remain unasked, let alone unanswered. The inquiry begins with the question of why did thousands of otherwise law-abiding women "storm" the Capitol and ends with the question of why did two of those women never return home. "This government murdered my daughter," said Ashli's mom, Micki Witthoeft, and she will not rest until the perpetrators—plural—are brought to justice.

3

CommonAshSense

Ashli Babbitt did not shy from risk. Having been deployed multiple times to hot spots like Iraq and Afghanistan, Ashli had seen more of life and death than all but a handful of journalists. On her Twitter page, under the handle "CommonAshSense," Ashli defined herself in a way that few Americans would think to criticize: "#veteran #America #libertarian #2A #KAG. I [love] my dude, my [dog], & above all my country. Flag, Flag, #Freedom." The hashtag 2A, of course, refers to her support of the Second Amendment. #KAG appears to mean "Kick Ass Girl."

And yet one major media article after another denied Ashli agency for her actions. This denial has been routine in the reporting on J6 females. From the media's perspective, these women had fallen prey to male masterminds, none more seductive than Donald Trump. A review of their histories, however, shows that none of them fell for Trump the way leftists did for Barack Obama. There was no swooning, no talk of a "messiah," no empty chants along the lines of, "Yes, we can." Several admitted to disliking Trump initially and warming up to him only because he championed one or more of their causes. "Trump's not going to save us," Yvonne St Cyr told her husband, Troy, before the 2020 election. "We're here to save ourselves."[13]

As the media saw things, these women were also vulnerable to the peddlers of "conspiracy theories," especially those involving election fraud, COVID, or the elusive QAnon. Indeed, in its first article on Ashli, the *New York Times* ignored her own self definition and defined her in its own light, "Woman Killed in Capitol Embraced Trump and QAnon."[14]

In reality, QAnon was one minor tributary among the many conservative communications streams. Most people who "followed" QAnon did so the way they might follow a daily horoscope or the interpreted musings of a Nostradamus. Some believe the Q team to be a white-hat crew of intelligence insiders fighting the good fight against a globalist cartel, but no two people seem to agree on what QAnon is.

The major media don't know and don't really care to know. In its initial article on Ashli, the *Times* satisfied itself with the unsourced claim that QAnon "has asserted that the 2020 presidential election was stolen by an elite Satan-worshiping cabal, and that it was up to ordinary people to reinstate Mr. Trump."[15] In fact, the Q phenomenon does have a strong association with a conspiracy, real or imagined, known as "Pizzagate." This reputed high-level ring of pedophiles involves, most prominently, John Podesta, Hillary Clinton's 2016 campaign chair.

The Left, of course, ridicules Pizzagate, and the respectable conservative media dare not even mention it, but before readers dismiss it, they might watch the movie *Out of Shadows*.[16] Among the people featured in the film is Liz Crokin, a veteran reporter and columnist who sacrificed any career ambitions she might have had to report on child sex trafficking.

Said Crokin, "I was basically embraced by the mainstream media until I started reporting on Pizzagate." Her deconstruction of the coded language in the Podesta emails obtained by Wikileaks could make a media fact-checker sweat. "I'd be willing to debate anyone who thinks Pizzagate has been debunked," said Crokin. She is dismayed that "there has not been one single investigation into any of it."

No doubt, prominent Democrats had been behaving badly in the run-up to the 2020 election. Anthony Weiner, Harvey Weinstein, and Hunter Biden come quickly to mind. None, however, proved more dangerous to the existing order than celebrity pedophile and Jacobin prince, Jeffrey Epstein. After years of being protected, Epstein was arrested in 2018. His secrets intact, he died in jail soon after in an incident that vaguely resembled a suicide. Although Epstein's client list remains more closely guarded than Barack Obama's SAT scores, the story of his child trafficking is well enough known.

Less well known is the saga of Keith Raniere, in the words of the *New York Daily News*, the "pedophile leader of the creepy, woman-branding sex cult."[17] Just a week before the November 2020 election, Raniere was sentenced to 120 years in prison. Among other diabolic acts, Raniere had sex with minors, created and distributed pornography with their images, and forced the girls to have abortions if they became pregnant.

Given the timing of his sentencing, the media downplayed Raniere's relationship with Sara and Clare Bronfman, the youngest daughters of the late Seagram's chair and Democratic megadonor, Edgar Bronfman. A recipient of the

Presidential Medal of Freedom from President Bill Clinton in 1999, Bronfman supported Hillary in the 2008 campaign before backing Barack Obama in the general election.

Those were the circles in which high-profile Democrats ran. Malia Obama interned with Harvey Weinstein. Bill Clinton logged frequent flyer miles on Epstein's "Lolita Express." Hillary Clinton intimate Huma Abedin married Anthony Weiner. A few years earlier, Hollywood gave child rapist Roman Polanski a standing O and an Oscar. In 2020, Barack Obama did a one-on-one interview with Bronfman's granddaughter, Hannah Bronfman, a reputed "influencer." A month prior, Hannah's aunt Clare was sentenced to eighty-one months in prison for her role in Raniere's sex trafficking ring. Actress Allison Mack was sentenced to two years in prison for her involvement after accepting a plea deal in 2019.

A child star, Mack may herself have been groomed. As revealed in the explosive five-part 2024 Max series, *Quiet on Set: The Dark Side of Kids TV*, Hollywood has long been a hotbed of pedophilia. The show focuses on Nickelodeon and its disgraced producer, Dan Schneider. Not surprisingly, Schneider was a friend of the Obamas. In 2012, an election year, he produced a show on the long-running series *iCarly* that featured Michelle Obama and her "Joining Forces" initiative. Network president Cyma Zarghami was paraphrased as saying that the episode was "in no way a political statement."[18] Of course not.

In a blistering April 2024 takedown of his Democrat allies, liberal provocateur Bill Maher addressed "Quiet on Set" and explored the reason why the Jacobins tolerated allies like Schneider whose run at Nickelodeon lasted twenty-five years. "We're so tribal now," said Maher, "The Left will overlook [pedophilia] if the guy from the wrong party calls it out."[19]

To prove his liberal credentials, I should add, Maher used a phrase more vulgar, much more, than "pedophilia."

In light of this background, the media's eagerness to tar anyone who addressed the pedophilia issue with the "QAnon" brush says more about the media than about the person tarred. If one googles "Liz Crokin," for instance, the first item that appears after her Wikipedia page is a CNN article from 2022 headlined, "Trump Poses with QAnon, Pizzagate Conspiracy Theorist at Mar-a-Lago."[20]

In the summer of 2023, *Sound of Freedom*, a film about real-life Department of Homeland Security (DHS) agent Tim Ballard's efforts to stop child sex trafficking, proved to be a box office hit. The film's success surprised the media. Critics were anticipating a dud. Disney, after all, had sat on the finished product for five years before selling the rights back to the producers.

The film's marketability was not the issue for Disney. The film's message was. As Maher detailed, Disney's history with the sexual abuse of minors was as bad as Nickelodeon's. Explained *Time*, the film became "mired in controversy over criticisms that it features misleading depictions of child exploitation and plays into right-wing conspiracy theories associated with the QAnon movement."[21] The fact that the film was made before anyone even heard of QAnon only made the Jacobins more anxious. Those "theories" suddenly seemed less fanciful.

To kill the pedophile issue, the media compulsively ridiculed it. True to form, CNN headlined its post-J6 profile of one protestor, "Yvonne St Cyr lost faith in organized religion, the medical establishment, the government and other institutions. She began following QAnon."[22] That headline reflected CNN's obsession, not Yvonne's. Yvonne followed QAnon the way a Democrat follows MSNBC, just more skeptically. If ever investigated, Pizzagate might prove to be no more substantial than Russiagate, but the *New York Times* got a Pulitzer for Russiagate.

The fact that women typically care more about child trafficking than men is a tribute to their natural role as nurturers. Even though she was only vaguely aware of QAnon, Christine Priola campaigned against child trafficking. For her efforts, she was tagged in a *Daily Mail* headline as a "female QAnon fanatic."[23] What triggered the *Daily Mail* was the sign Christine carried at the Capitol reading, "The Children Cry Out for Justice."

The women's attachment to Trump on this issue is not idle. He famously kicked Jeffrey Epstein out of Mar-a-Lago. As president, he took the child trafficking issue seriously, claiming in July 2023 that under his leadership, the US did "more than any administration in history to combat human trafficking."[24] He made this claim after hosting a screening of *Sound of Freedom* at his New Jersey golf club.

The active struggle to ridicule conservative media precedes QAnon by decades. In 1995, for instance, the Clinton White House produced a mind-boggling 332-page report documenting what its authors called the "communication stream of conspiracy commerce." When the document surfaced in January 1997, the *Washington Post* described its thesis as follows, "A cabal of right-wing extremists had figured out how 'fantasy can become fact' by advancing rumors about Whitewater and Clinton's personal life through a 'media food chain' that starts in ideological journals and ultimately finds its way onto the front pages of mainstream U.S. newspapers."[25]

In January 1997, the Clinton White House was crying foul because *Newsweek* did a cover story on Paula Jones. Jones was the Arkansas woman who accused then governor Bill Clinton of exposing himself and asking for sex. The Clintons denied the allegations, blaming them on the internet's "crazy, right-wing sources."[26] Those right-wing sources proved to be not so crazy. The Jones accusation set in process a sequence of events that led to Clinton's impeachment.

For the Jacobins, the emergence of the internet was a classic black swan event, unexpected and hugely consequential. In time, their media would come to think the way the Clinton White House did in 1995. They would treat almost all stories emanating from the Right as "crazy," if not altogether fake. Those stories they could not ignore, they would recruit their spurious fact-checking agents to "debunk" or "discredit." Through omission and falsification, journalists would turn what had once been a potable, if not exactly pristine, "mainstream" into what recovering liberal Dave Rubin called, justifiably, "a river of bullshit."[27]

4

Deplorables

In fact, many conspiracy theories were afloat in the years leading up to January 6. The Jacobins launched most of those that mattered. With Trump's emergence in 2015, these theories flowed in seemingly endless streams, one theory more easily disproven than another. Now shaping news to confirm audience biases, corporate media were not at all inclined to share stories that did not.

Former *Times* op-ed editor James Bennet confirmed as much in a stunning December 2023 *Economist* article headlined, "When the New York Times Lost Its Way." In June 2020, Bennet ran a well-argued editorial by Republican Sen. Tom Cotton of Arkansas calling for the use of federal troops to help suppress the George Floyd riots. The powerful woke contingent at the *Times* responded by calling for Bennet's head, successfully as it turned out.

"The *Times*'s problem," wrote Bennet, "has metastasized from liberal bias to illiberal bias, from an inclination to favour one side of the national debate to an impulse to shut debate down altogether."[28] Although an ardent anti-Trumper, Bennet conceded a critical point in understanding January 6: "For now, to assert that the *Times* plays by the same rules it always has is to commit a hypocrisy that is transparent to conservatives, dangerous to liberals and bad for the country as a whole."[29]

Ashli Babbitt was only twelve when Bill Clinton was impeached. His many crimes and misdemeanors played no part in her formation, especially given the apolitical nature of her family life. During her years in the military, she barely followed the news. A close airman friend, interviewed by the FBI in April 2021, confessed to not knowing Ashli's political views "as she was not political." He did know, however, that she had voted for Obama. He also expressed frustration at "media portrayals of Babbitt as being associated with white nationalists, which was not accurate."[30] Hoping to find some seditionist dirt on Ashli, FBI agents opened an investigation on her the day after her death. They had no luck. As her friend told the interviewer, Ashli "loved her family and loved her country."

In returning to civilian life in 2017, and running a business in a state as oppressive as California, Ashli's eyes began to open. By this time, thanks to the internet and social media, not to mention talk radio, America had the world's most robust alternative media. Ashli could fully inform herself without ever once watching CNN or reading the *New York Times*. It was activists like Ashli who gave Republicans/conservatives the edge in just about all political knowledge surveys.

Conservative/libertarian activists in the Ashli Babbitt mold are particularly well schooled in civics and American history. Rachel Powell, mother of eight, drove for hours in the George Floyd summer of 2020 to help protect Union Civil War monuments from desecration. Lisa Eisenhart attended a "Back the Blue" rally in Nashville. Rebecca Lavrenz, the great-grandmother from Colorado, drove to Washington "to reconfirm the covenant which was set forth in the year 1620 by our pilgrim forefathers." Or as Dr. Simone Gold told Tucker Carlson, "My fight was the Constitution."

Conservative activists know their Constitution and revere it. As lovers of liberty, the women profiled, to a person, had no alliance with any movement that would deny citizens their equal rights. At day's end on January 6, they were horrified to hear themselves and their compatriots defamed as white supremacists. "Conspiracy theorist," they could live with. "White supremacist," they could not.

The Jacobins had been cultivating this theme from the moment Donald Trump declared for the presidency. In June 2015, while discussing illegal border crossers, Trump said in his wonderfully artless way, "They're bringing drugs. They're bringing crime. They're rapists. And some, I assume, are good people." The word went out to the media: feel free to distort.

The media needed little prompting. At an August 2016 campaign rally, Democratic vice presidential candidate Tim Kaine casually repeated what had by then become a standard media talking point. "The thing that amazes me is the depth of his trash-talking with Latinos," said Kaine, "saying all Mexicans are rapists and going after Latino immigrants." In a rare honest moment, even PolitiFact was forced to concede Trump had said "nothing that even approached such a contention."[31]

Not to worry. For the population that pulled its news from the major media, the odd positive fact-check mattered little. Trump was a racist. Everyone agreed. In 2017, the fight over the removal of the Robert E. Lee statue in Charlottesville, Virginia, gave the media another chance to distort the record. Here, they led their audiences to believe that Trump called the neo-Nazis and white nationalists involved in that day's dustup "very fine people."

For the next two years, the Jacobins repeated this lie, no one more often or more passionately than Joe Biden. Biden routinely ignored Trump's earlier comment, "I'm not talking about the neo-Nazis and the white nationalists. They should be condemned totally." In April 2019, he launched his presidential campaign on the tailwinds from this lie. After showing a stunningly dishonest video about Charlottesville, Biden excoriated Trump for his imagined racist sympathies.

No major candidate has ever begun a presidential campaign with a more divisive and slanderous opening gambit than did Biden. Claiming that Trump's racism motivated him to run, Biden insisted, "We are in the battle for the soul of this nation." He warned that if Trump were reelected, "he will forever and fundamentally alter the character of this nation, who we are, and I cannot stand by and watch that happen."[32]

This series of slanders convinced the Left that Trump and his supporters were—as Hillary Clinton reminded America in her "basket of deplorables" speech—"racist, sexist, homophobic, xenophobic, Islamaphobic, you name it."[33] The ten women profiled in this book were all opinionated. The media dug through as many of their social media postings as they could find, but no racist tropes turned up. Race was a nonissue for these women as it was for the great majority of J6ers. Ashli Babbitt complained about illegal immigration, but who in San Diego didn't?

Washington, DC, is an overwhelmingly Democratic city. For the six years preceding January 6, 2021, its residents consumed a steady stream of leftist media libeling Trump as racist. When his supporters descended on the Capitol, more than a few police officers imagined themselves at war with neo-Nazis and white supremacists and responded in kind.

In the wake of that event, President Biden continued to spread this monstrous propaganda. "The violent, deadly insurrection on the Capitol nine months ago," he said in October 2021, "it was about white supremacy, in my opinion."[34] Unchastened, he has made white supremacy the focus of his 2024 campaign.

Echoing the themes of Biden's libelous propaganda, journalists set their sights on Ashli Babbitt. Their goal was to smear Ashli with the taint of racism lest anyone speak of her as a martyr. Fewer than twenty-four hours after Ashli's death, the *New York Times* took the lead. "A dead or injured white woman—even the illusion of one—has always been a powerful symbol on the far right," wrote Seyward Darby, "a rallying cry for people to stand up and act to preserve their contorted notions of honor, liberty and purity."[35]

"Hold my beer," said *Time* magazine's Vera Bergengruen a few days later as she raised race-baiting to the level of cringe. "Babbitt's emergence as a martyr for many of the different groups that made up the pro-Trump mob is no surprise," wrote Bergengruen. "White women's deaths have long been leveraged for propaganda, from the 19th century Klu [*sic*] Klux Klan to the militia movements of the 1990s to Donald Trump's 2016 presidential campaign, which often invoked their killing at the hands of undocumented immigrants."[36] At the time these very white females were mainstreaming this toxin—and misspelling "Ku Klux Klan"—neither knew that a black man named Michael Byrd had pulled the trigger.

5

Undaunted

In the Netherlands, they call it "Dolle Dinsdag" or, in English, "Crazy Tuesday." That was the day in 1944 that the Dutch took to the streets in celebration believing that the Allies had liberated their country from Hitler's grasp. In the Jacobin Thunderdome, Crazy Tuesday came on a Friday, October 7, 2016. That was the day the *Washington Post* dropped the infamous *Access Hollywood* tapes. In newsrooms and boardrooms and teachers' lounges across America, the enemies of Donald Trump celebrated, convinced that they had been liberated from their own imagined Hitler.

"When you're a star, they let you do it. You can do anything…. Grab 'em by the pussy. You can do anything," Trump was heard telling television host Billy Bush on this eleven-year-old tape.[37] Democrats popped corks and RINOs stampeded for the exits. "I am sickened by what I heard today. Women are to be championed and revered, not objectified," said Republican House Speaker Paul Ryan. Ryan promptly withdrew from a campaign appearance with Trump the following day in his home state of Wisconsin. That same Saturday, RNC Chairman Reince Priebus hit Trump with a sobering assessment. "I'm hearing," said Priebus, "that you can either withdraw or you can lose in the biggest landslide that's ever been had."[38]

Trump stood firm, and the rest is history. He understood his female supporters better than the RINOs did, better than the pollsters did, and much better than the media did. Writ large, they were a far hardier crew than their female counterparts on the left or in the GOP's squishy middle. That Trump had been divorced twice, married three times, and filed for bankruptcy six times did not alienate his base. If anything, it made him more relatable. What they saw in Trump was a man whose life had been as messy as the subject of a Hank Williams song but who, praise the Lord, had seen the light or at least something like it.

Modern journalists did not know Hank Williams from Serena Williams. Cosseted from birth and college-bred, they knew little of the struggles that define life in flyover country, the kind of struggles that find their outlet in country western music—poverty, loneliness, joblessness, heartbreak, addiction, D-I-V-O-R-C-E. Unlike many activists on the left, however, the women of the right respect the idea of marriage, of family, of faith, of country. They have no interest in revolution. If anything, they want restoration. They live their lives believing in a Judeo-Christian world order even if they do not always live up to its expectations.

On first learning of Ashli Babbitt's death, the media attacked her much as they had Trump. Aware that the fatal shooting of an unarmed female veteran would undermine the saga, already in play, of law enforcement's heroic battle to "save democracy," journalists promptly shared the imperfections of her life. Their collective goal was to deny Ashli martyr status—by any means necessary.

The *New York Times* set the tone. Within a day of the shooting, a trio of *Times* reporters had dug up just about every seemingly wayward blip in Ashli's adventurous life. Yes, she had been divorced, married twice, fallen into debt, and once gotten into an altercation with a former girlfriend of her second husband, Aaron Babbitt. These enterprising reporters had managed to retrieve the complaint filed by the girlfriend and quote it extensively—all of this within twenty-four hours of Ashli's being shot and killed.

What the reporters overlooked was the ability of women like Ashli to overcome adversity. There was a good deal to overcome. Born to an unmarried mother in 1985, Ashli caught a break as a toddler when Roger "Rocky" Witthoeft came into her mom's life. Rocky and Micki would have four children together, all of them boys. The rough and tumble Ashli adapted well. Micki refers to her as the "quintessential big sister."

As the only girl in a family of five children, Ashli grew up as something of a tomboy in Lakeside, California, a "rodeo town" of about twenty thousand people twenty or so miles inland from San Diego. Coming of age at a time when the state was still the stuff of dreams and songs, Ashli lived the archetypal life of a young Californian—swimming, riding horses, playing water polo and soccer, doing gymnastics.

San Diego has a long history as a military town, and Ashli fell under that influence. She was particularly close to her maternal grandfather, Anthony Mazziott, a Navy vet who helped raise her when she was a little girl. Sixteen when Islamic terrorists attacked the World Trade Center and the Pentagon, Ashli redoubled her commitment to join the military. Once she turned eighteen, she did just that and would spend the next fourteen years in the Air Force, either on active duty, as a reservist, or in the Air National Guard.

While on active duty, Ashli met the man who would become her first husband, Tim McEntee. "She was a baby when they married," said Micki. "They helped each other through some really hard times." Their separate deployments put a strain on the marriage, but they maintained "love and friendship," added Micki, even after the marriage dissolved.

In 2015, a defense department publication caught up with Senior Airman Ashli McEntee as she was about to leave on her eighth deployment, this time to "an undisclosed location in Southwest Asia." She had previously been deployed to Iraq and Afghanistan. As a veteran of overseas missions, Ashli served as something of a mentor to young airmen on their first deployment. "The newer airmen have been coming to us and asking about the living conditions, the weather, the gear, the schedule, how we work as teams, the hours we work," Ashli told the interviewer. "As we have a large amount of first timers deploying with us, I think we can offer comfort and knowledge."[39]

While still in the National Guard, Ashli started working at the Calvert Cliffs Nuclear Plant in Maryland on a security detail. It was there she met Aaron Babbitt, a bearded man as brawny and gruff as Ashli was cute and petite. Micki was thrilled when the couple returned to San Diego County and purchased a pool supply company. "I have been blessed to have two good sons-in-law," said Micki.

Ashli and Aaron married in June 2019.

"Ashli was not radicalized," said Micki. "She was activated."

Micki and her family had several years to watch Ashli transform from passive citizen to outspoken protestor. "My sister was 35 and served 14 years—to me that's the majority of your conscious adult life," Ashli's younger brother Roger Witthoeft told the *Times*. "If you feel like you gave the majority of your life to your country and you're not being listened to, that is a hard pill to swallow. That's why she was upset."[40]

Even the *Times* reporters conceded that Ashli was no shrinking violet. "You guys refuse, refuse to choose America over your stupid political party, I am so tired of it," they quoted her as saying in a video message addressed to California politicians, both Democrat and Republican. "You can consider yourself put on notice. Me and the American people. I am so tired of it, I am woke, man, this is absolutely unbelievable."[41]

For Rosanne Boyland, the activation came quicker than it had for Ashli. The thirty-four-year-old Rosanne fit no one's stereotype of a "Young Republican." In fact, as the election of 2020 approached, she had not yet voted for any candidate in any election. This was due in no small part to the ten-year probation she was serving for drug dealing. Nor did Rosanne fit the stereotype of a drug dealer. She grew up in a stable two-parent, middle-class home in Kennesaw, Georgia, with two caring parents and two loving sisters.

Rosanne had issues her family could not wish away. In her twenties, she had developed cervical cancer. Being unable to give birth came as a blow to a woman who loved children, her nieces in particular. She had a weight problem as well, one that the COVID lockdowns only aggravated. In that final year, her social life revolved around the Atlanta Triangle Club, a space set aside for recovery meetings. It was there she met Justin Winchell, the fellow with whom she would travel to DC on the night of January 5, 2021.

In 2020, stuck at home with her mother during the lockdowns, Rosanne grew increasingly passionate about a new cause, the Trump campaign in general and QAnon in particular. Although her father, Bret Boyland, never saw Rosanne happier than when she was able to vote, her sisters, both liberals, believed her political passion to be simply a new addiction. Older sister Lonna and younger sister Blaire were convinced that QAnon filled the void in her life that drugs once did. "Rosanne was a victim," Lonna told MSNBC's Ayman Mohyeldin, "surrounded by some bad people who had convinced her into believing something that wasn't real."

Friend Nicholas Stamathis had a different take on Rosanne's recovery. "She got clean and sober and stopped blaming other people for her problems and got real conservative," Stamathis told the Associated Press. "Making fun of liberals together, we bonded over that a lot."[42] The AP preferred the story line offered unwittingly by Rosanne's liberal relatives, "Family: Trump Supporter Who Died Followed QAnon Conspiracy." Journalists could not get enough of QAnon—whatever it was.

As her friends knew better than her family, Rosanne did not die for the QAnon conspiracy. She died in the pursuit of truth. Her sister Blaire, while rooting through Rosanne's diary, unearthed her motive for traveling to Washington on January 6. "It looks like she was kind of doing some research about election fraud. So she has a couple politicians' names written down," Blaire would later reveal. "And she just says, 'Hear the evidence…Correct false statements…Demand a vote on decertification.'"

Rosanne knew what her sisters knew, but she knew more. Her post in July 2020, six months before she died, contained a core truth that eluded her sisters—"Crazy how the internet can not block child trafficking, but can block those who talk about it." That reality did not discourage Rosanne. It motivated her. In her final post on Parler the day before she died, Rosanne shared her refreshingly upbeat view of the world: "I want to say thank you to everyone involved in this movement. My family thinks I'm crazy, but I'm heading up from Atlanta to be shoulder to shoulder with my true brothers and sisters."

In their pursuit of the truth, Ashli and Rosanne found common cause with millions of other "patriots." It's the word they use, and it's an apt one. Despite what everyone has told them, even their family members, these patriots remained passionately committed to the idea of America as embodied in the Constitution and as preserved by its historic Judeo-Christian culture.

In male circles, to espouse these values did not raise eyebrows. Most men voted for Trump. As a rule, they tend to be more politically aware. Everywhere and always, men have performed better on political knowledge tests than women, just as conservatives outperform liberals. Among the more popular hypotheses is that women are more risk-averse than men and thus, on tests, are less likely to "guess under conditions of uncertainty." The women who were risk-averse, however, did not come to Washington on January 6. Those who did go left behind friends and family too locked into their own media to understand.

Like Rosanne and Ashli, Rebecca Lavrenz, the great-grandmother from Colorado, had educated herself against the feminist grain. A pioneer, always ready for adventure, Rebecca was taking classes on the US Constitution in 2020 while liberal women were sheltering in place, watching *Law and Order* reruns. The daughter of two teachers, her father a teacher of history and government, Rebecca became a nurse but never forgot sitting as a student in his classes, learning about the beauty of limited government.

Like her mom, who after starting her family chose to leave her teaching career, Rebecca left her nursing career to raise and homeschool her four children. She taught them the values of family, liberty, and limited government that she learned from her parents. It has helped enormously through her ordeal that all of her children and grandchildren have held firm to these same values.

Rebecca's husband had died five years prior. A passionate believer in the covenant of marriage, she had refused to give up on their marriage even though there were difficulties. Although separated from her husband for stretches, she was with him at the end and spoke at his funeral.

Ashli, Rosanne, and Rebecca were not unusual among female J6ers in the unevenness of their lives. As shall be seen, all the J6 women profiled here traveled roads riddled with speed bumps. Navigating these roads seems to have made them more savvy than their cloistered feminist sisters, more suspicious of the whims of self-righteous elites, more willing to believe their own eyes and ears. In the year 2020 especially, they had a much keener nose for truth than the women who masked their senses literally and figuratively.

Yvonne St Cyr had a rougher young life than most of the J6ers. She grew up in a turbulent household in small-town Idaho, her alcoholic father splitting when she was five. During her adolescence, she knocked around from house to house. By her senior year of high school, Yvonne had married, divorced, and given birth to a child. Along the way, she also had two abortions.

"The Marine Corps saved my life," Yvonne told CNN. "It was a dad I didn't have." CNN did a useful, if slanted, profile on Yvonne for a series called *Assault on Democracy*. For some reason, they labeled Yvonne "the believer." A much more appropriate title would be "the searcher." The true believers inhabited the newsroom of CNN. The destructive nonsense they believed and professed just in the year 2020—on COVID, on George Floyd, on Hunter Biden—could fill a library.

Yvonne served eighteen years in the Marines. By the time she met her husband, Troy, in the Marines, she had four children. They married and had a son. Despite her many medals for good conduct, Yvonne slipped into drug use and was discharged for the same in 2005. "Yes, for the haters, I was kicked out," said Yvonne in a later interview, "but I still took an oath and I still love my country."[43] After her court-martial, she and Troy left South Carolina for Idaho where they rebuilt their lives.

When the 2016 primaries rolled around, Yvonne threw her support behind Dr. Ben Carson. Initially at least, she was not a Trump fan, at one point posting a "Stop Trump" meme. She did appreciate, however, Trump's patriotism and his love for the military and eventually warmed up to him. As someone who understood the horrors of abortion, Yvonne welcomed his embrace of the pro-life movement, however strategic.

In her search for meaning, she, too, stumbled on the film, *Out of Shadows*. "What I really believe," Yvonne told CNN, "Donald Trump—President Trump—was trying to show us and Q team is that we are the ones that are responsible, we have to take control back."[44]

Rachel Powell, "a very granola, very crunchy" mom from western Pennsylvania was still another J6er who defied easy categorization.[45] Raised by a mother who worked at a local shop and a plumber stepfather, Rachel grew up on "the really bad side" of Fresno. As a child, carjackers held her at gunpoint while they kidnapped her stepfather before releasing him several hours later. Understandably weary of Fresno, the family moved to West Sunbury, Pennsylvania, when Rachel was fifteen. She married young and had the first of her eight children when she was sixteen. She separated from her husband just three years before her brush with destiny.

In 2016, Rachel did not support Donald Trump for president. "Trump makes me uncomfortable as a presidential candidate," she posted on Facebook, linking to a piece about his lack of civility. "What disturbs me is that so many people support this type of person." A libertarian at heart, she gradually came to respect Trump as president. What turned her away from a life that centered on organic foods and toward one of political activism, however, was not Trump, and it was not QAnon. It was something much more central to her life, namely a quest for freedom from irrational government dictates.

Like many of these women, Lisa Eisenhart lived a childhood out of a Dickens novel. Raised in East Chicago, Indiana, Lisa watched her home life collapse around her at three when her parents divorced. Unfortunately, divorce did not stop her father from abusing her on his occasional visit. Lisa's mother married again only to divorce again when Lisa was fifteen. Her own domestic life mirrored that of her mother's. The father of her two boys was sufficiently abusive to her and her sons that Lisa fled with them to a battered woman's shelter in Dalton, Georgia.

It was there that Lisa, a single mother, began to take control of her life. With support from a local church, she enrolled in Dalton College, graduating in 1994. For the next twenty-five years, Lisa worked as a registered nurse and raised her two sons. Not a mere follower, Lisa, like many of these women, had willed herself through a turbulent early life and emerged as a strong-minded and independent patriot. "I'd rather die as a 57-year-old woman than live under oppression," Lisa told a reporter for the *London Times* on January 7, 2021. "I'd rather die and would rather fight."[46]

Victoria White's life was as far from storybook as Lisa Eisenhart's. Abandoned by her mother as a baby, Victoria lost her father at age four to a sudden heart attack. An older sister took over at this point. The unknowing Victoria called the sister "mom" until another sister wised her up years later. Her early adult life was as unstable as her childhood. She endured a ten-year relationship with a "severely violent" man whom she left after a nearly fatal beating. "I should have died," said Victoria, "but I didn't." She takes solace in the fact that this man was not the father of any of her "four beautiful girls."

Christine Priola did not meet her biological father until she was about twenty-one. Her own marriage was rocky as well, sufficiently so that she was awarded full custody of her daughter, then aged seven. A liberal as a young woman, Christine realized at one point that she knew almost nothing about the issues of the day. In the course of her self-education, she rediscovered Catholicism. In her faith, she finally grasped "what life should really be."

At twenty-one, Sara Carpenter had an unexpected encounter with destiny. When her car broke down in lower Manhattan, two undercover cops emerged out of nowhere and rescued her from a knife-wielding thug. That incident alerted the Queens native to the potential nobility of a police career. Although her real passion was painting, Sara signed up for the NYPD. Nine years later, she put in for retirement. Says Sara, "I did not like who I was becoming." Her last day was scheduled to be September 12, 2001.

September 11 intervened. Although off duty that day, Sara headed reflexively to Ground Zero where she would spend the next month. Toward the end of that month, having seen far too much, she found herself unable to stop crying. The NYPD had little choice but to put her on medical leave. In the confused and confusing years that followed, Sara got pregnant by a man not fit to be a father.

Broke and depressed, Sara thought seriously of making an appointment with Planned Parenthood. Always open to both sides of an argument, she turned to Mother Teresa for an alternative opinion. The three-word quote she found saved her son's life and her own soul. Said Mother Teresa, "Abortion is terrorism." Sara had seen terrorism enough for a lifetime. She would not contribute to its spread. To compare January 6 to 9/11 as Kamala Harris and others have done, is, in Sara's informed opinion, blasphemous.

Dr. Simone Gold knew something of terror as well, if not in her own life, certainly in her father's. He had survived the Holocaust. Taking advantage of America's freedom, he prospered as a physician on Long Island where he raised his family.

Like the other women, Dr. Gold, the mother of two, endured her own share of heartbreak along the way, including a 2010 divorce from businessman husband Larry Gold. In the year 2020, the two hospitals that employed her dismissed her for daring to tell the truth about COVID. In her world, to challenge the orthodoxy *du jour* was to declare oneself an apostate. In the year 2020, anti-Semites did not generate a fraction of the hate that America's "Karens" did.

Hate was in the air during COVID mania. Dr. Gold caught a major dose of it when Nancy Pelosi called the January 6 protest a "white supremacist raid on this Capitol." Pelosi's libelous quote appeared in a *Time* magazine article shamelessly titled, "'Hate Never Disappears. It Just Takes a Break for a While.' Why the U.S. Capitol Attack Makes Holocaust Remembrance Day More Important Than Ever."[47] Friends who stuck with Gold during her COVID protests started pulling away. Why, they asked, was their friend associating with Nazis? They took Pelosi seriously.

As a side note, Pelosi profiled the mass of protestors as white supremacists based on the arrest of *one* man wearing a sweatshirt that read "Camp Auschwitz." Robert Keith Packer had been arrested twenty-one times before January 6. Despite his record and his turbulent time inside the Capitol, he received an unusually light prison sentence of seventy-five days. "It seems to me that he wore that sweatshirt for a reason. We don't know what the reason was because Mr. Packer hasn't told us," said the judge.[48] For his part, Packer took offense at being called a white supremacist and threatened to sue Pelosi.

6

Red Pill

In 2020, Rosanne Boyland's references to "red pills" and "rabbit holes" disturbed her well-meaning sisters. Although the "red pill" concept had been floating around for more than twenty years—and the "rabbit hole" for more than 150—few understood either.

In his 2023 biography of Elon Musk, Walter Isaacson felt the need to explain the meaning of these concepts. The "rabbit hole," of course, is a plot device in Lewis Carroll's 1865 classic, *Alice in Wonderland*. The "red pill" serves a corollary function in the 1999 movie *The Matrix*. A hacker named Neo learns from his would-be mentor, Morpheus, that he has been living in a virtual, computer-generated world designed, says Morpheus, "to blind you from the truth."

Morpheus offers Neo a choice of two pills. "You take the blue pill," he says, "and the story ends. You wake in your bed and believe whatever you want to believe." If Neo takes the red pill, Morpheus promises to show him "how deep the rabbit-hole goes." He adds, "Remember—all I am offering is the truth, nothing more."[49] The fact that the color of the pill aligned with the color of the more conservative states on electoral maps helped make the metaphor popular on the right.

As Isaacson suggests, Musk took his red pill in May 2020 when a COVID-manic California tried to shut down production at Tesla's Fremont plant just as it was about to gear up. Musk was outraged. "Give people back their goddamn freedom," Isaacson quotes him as saying.[50] Once red-pilled, Musk made a series of moves that left Isaacson, an establishment liberal, confused. Most prominent was Musk's purchase of Twitter. Musk's reckless embrace of free speech, Isaacson feared, would encourage right-wing conspiracy theorists.

Isaacson was much more comfortable with Musk in his "fanboy and fundraiser for Barack Obama" phase. Similarly, for those friends who knew Ashli Babbitt in *her* Obama phase or Dr. Simone Gold in her "middle of the road" days or Rosanne Boyland in her apolitical phase, their sharp right turns were mystifying. The blue-pilled failed to understand the red pill's residual effect. Once the newly red-pilled realize they have been deceived about one thing, they begin to question everything. In the year 2020, the consumption of red pills rivaled that of ivermectin. In both cases, COVID was the driver.

No one has documented the red pill effect more thoughtfully than Naomi Wolf. Former consultant to Bill Clinton and Al Gore, and onetime poster girl for third-wave feminism, Wolf explained her apostasy in her essential 2022 book, *The Bodies of Others: The New Authoritarians, COVID-19 and the War Against the Human*. Observing from the inside, Wolf revealed what happened to "my people, my tribe, my whole life, the progressive, right-on, part of the ideological world" during the COVID reign of terror.

It wasn't pretty. "It was as if these communities were in the grip of a collective hallucination," Wolf writes, "like the witch crazes of the sixteen and seventeenth century." She continues, "Whole understandings and belief systems were abandoned overnight. Intelligent, informed people suddenly saw things that were not there and were unable to see things that were incontrovertibly before their faces."

Following Anthony Fauci proved far more destructive than following QAnon. As quickly became obvious during that deeply polarized year of 2020, the educated Left proved much more fearful of COVID than did the hard-knock Right. Throughout that year, it was not unusual for conservatives, when assembled, to regale each other with tales of masked bicyclers or mountain climbers or even swimmers. "The real agenda," said Dr. Simone Gold, "was to shift us to a people that would accept government control over our daily lives."[51]

These observations were not just anecdotal. "Americans were "riveted and captured by fear," said Gold. Democrats were especially fearful. A survey done by Franklin Templeton-Gallup during the last six months of 2020 confirmed just how divided Americans had become on this critical issue. In the survey, some thirty-five thousand Americans were asked their assessment of COVID, a subject that had dominated the news cycle since the beginning of the year.

The most revealing indicator came in response to the question: "What percentage of people who have been infected by the coronavirus needed to be hospitalized?" The Democrats that responded proved scarily clueless. Some 41 percent believed that 50 percent or more of those who contracted COVID would end up in the hospital. Another 28 percent said that 20–50 percent of COVID sufferers would be hospitalized.

The correct answer was 1–5 percent, an answer that Republicans were nearly three times as likely to get right. In sum, 69 percent of Democrats were deeply misinformed about a subject of critical importance, and 41 percent were grotesquely misinformed. This mass delusion was obvious to anyone who cared to see, but given their control of the health science complex, the Jacobins encouraged its spread. Simultaneously, they projected this delusion onto the opposition.

A case in point: During roughly the same period as the Gallup survey, researchers R. Kelly Garrett and Robert Bond performed a longitudinal study focused on political knowledge. The National Institutes of Health endorsed the resulting paper titled, "Conservatives' Susceptibility to Political Misperceptions." Unable to say that conservatives knew less than liberals, the authors took solace in the belief that conservatives were "worse at distinguishing truths and falsehood."

The reason the Right failed to distinguish between the false and the true, the authors argued, was "that the most widely shared falsehoods tend to promote conservative positions, while corresponding truths typically favor liberals." The authors' confirmation bias flirted with parody, but that was not the most chilling part of the report. That honor belonged to the authors' unapologetically fascistic solution. "These results," they insisted, "underscore the importance of reducing the supply of right-leaning misinformation."[52]

What leftists know about the 2020 election and the events of January 6 is as delusional as what they knew about COVID. Anxious about their own ignorance, they respond to alternative information by shutting it down. Ashli had a perfectly apt name for COVID, the "controla virus." She and other J6ers may not have had PhDs, but they had been red-pilled well before Naomi Wolf.

"We are being hoodwinked. The sheep need to wake up," Ashli posted on social media. A sign on the door of her and Aaron's pool supply business captured the take of most J6 protestors. It declared the business a "mask free autonomous zone, better known as America." Another sign read simply, "If you need to wear a mask outside, I'm not sure we can help you."[53]

Throughout 2020 and into 2021, Ashli's tweets show that COVID restrictions were a driving force in her activation. On January 3, she retweeted a post about newly sworn-in congresswoman Marjorie Taylor Greene refusing to wear a face mask. Closer to home, on that same day, Ashli retweeted a video showing an organized anti-mask protest at a California grocery store.[54]

Rebecca Lavrenz, the great-grandmother from Colorado, refused to wear a mask under any circumstance. As a nurse, she knew the masks were "ridiculous," but more to the point, she did not like the idea of people "taking away her liberties." In 2020, she sought out people like herself willing to go maskless in a grocery store even at the risk of being kicked out. Through these new affiliations, she got involved actively in politics and worked her precinct on behalf of Donald Trump. "I knew I had to do something," said Rebecca. "Politics are local." Unabashedly Christian, she prayed long and hard before deciding to make the twenty-five-hour drive by herself to DC. She wasn't about to fly on airlines that treated its healthy passengers like tubercular patients.

"God put us on this planet for a purpose and to make a difference for good!" Rebecca would write. "YOU have a part to play, so take courage and do that which God leads you to do, not only here with your finances but in your own sphere of influence. All of us working together CAN and WILL make a difference!!" She closed with a quote from Anglo-Irish statesman Edmund Burke, "All it takes for evil to prevail is for good men to do nothing."[55]

Yvonne St Cyr lived ten hours farther from Washington than Rebecca, but she was not about to fly either. On December 8, 2020, she was arrested at an anti-mask rally in Boise at the Central District Health Department. She refused to cover her nose and mouth, she said, because "I have a right to breathe oxygen." This was not something QAnon told her.

Yvonne's defiance of Idaho's lawless COVID restrictions did not sit well with the local apparatchiks. As CNN matter-of-factly reported, Yvonne "was placed under citizen's arrest by a staff member."[56] COVID awakened the inner fascist of the American Left. After January 6, many would channel this newfound enthusiasm into the gleeful hunt for J6ers.

The red pill Rachel Powell took was labeled COVID as well. Adamant that she would not wear a mask, Rachel found herself banned from local farmers' markets in western Pennsylvania where she sold her cheese and yogurt. Just weeks after January 6, she made the mistake of giving an interview to Ronan Farrow. He traced her resistance to the "misinformation" and "conspiracy theories" about COVID that were being spread by Trump and others.[57] The cosmopolitan Farrow wrote this in January 2021. When Naomi Wolf spoke of her fellow "tribe" members caught in "the grip of a collective hallucination," she had man-boys like Farrow in mind.

"One good thing about this whole CV crisis is that I suddenly feel very patriotic," Rachel posted on Facebook in May 2020. Outraged by the restrictions, she added, "It isn't to [sic] late to wake up, say no, and restore freedoms." Soon after, she posted a short video shot outside a shuttered local gym. "Police need to see there's people that are citizens that are not afraid of you guys showing up in your masks. We're going to be here banded together, and we're not afraid of you," said Rachel, adding, "Maybe they should be a little bit afraid."

Living in Rochester, Minnesota, the home of the Mayo Clinic, Victoria White felt like she was living in a medical police state, one in which citizens were encouraged to snitch on dissenting neighbors like herself. "I would go above and beyond not to comply," said Victoria. She took the restrictions more personally than most as she believes the lockdown led to her brother's suicide. "It was absolute hell," she said. "We couldn't mourn."

Ohio's Christine Priola wore a face mask early on, but the more research she did, the more wary she became of COVID mania. The constant pressure from the media and government to compel all citizens, even the healthy, to isolate themselves was a "big red flag" for her. The inequity of the government response troubled Christine as well. Abortion centers were open, but not churches. Celebrities and politicians could host parties, but not the average Joe. The authorities leaned on doctors to recommend certain drugs and avoid others and tried to silence those who disagreed.

Christine couldn't recall any of the media-approved doctors recommending the obvious, namely "get regular exercise and fresh air, eat a healthy diet, and take vitamins to boost our immune systems." Her attempts to inform others met stubborn resistance and caused friction with some friends and family.

For those J6ers who lived in liberal strongholds like New York City, COVID resistance took a heavy toll on personal relations. "I tried to educate my family about COVID," said

Sara Carpenter. "'Stop it,' they yelled. They'd get furious with me." At times, Sara felt as if she were living in a "parallel universe." Like Rosanne Boyland and others, she was growing estranged from her own family, so much so that she skipped Thanksgiving dinner.

On the question of COVID, Dr. Simone Gold was having comparable problems with her own mother. "She definitely thought I was wrong," said Gold. "Because to accept that I'm right, you have to accept that everyone is lying to you…how scary and sad is a world where everyone's lying to you?"

No female quite defied the profile of a J6 protestor the way Dr. Gold did. "She is 5'8" but looks shorter; she's 57 years old but appears much younger," wrote Joel Stein in an unfriendly article in the *Financial Times*.[58] Simone graduated from medical school at twenty-three and headed to Stanford where she picked up a law degree. As a career choice, she stuck to emergency medicine. If there was a profile she fit, it was that of the hip, rootless Californian. Although her background could not have been more different from that of Ashli Babbitt or Rachel Powell, the red pill she swallowed looked much the same.

Dr. Gold's transformation from a reliable liberal Jewish Democratic voter to something else was triggered by, of all people, Barack Obama. "I hated Obama," she told Stein. "You looked at [Obamacare], and it was crap. You didn't get to keep your doctor. And then the media didn't say anything about it. So I started to hate the media." What attracted her to Trump was his open disdain for Obamacare. Like Trump, too, she objected to the lockdowns, but she was free from the political restraints that tempered Trump's resistance.

In March 2020, Los Angeles's Cedars-Sinai hospital installed tents outside its emergency room to handle the anticipated COVID overflow. Dr. Gold responded by posting a video showing there was no overflow. The tents were pure theater. In May 2020, she recruited some six hundred physicians to sign an open letter to Trump protesting the lockdowns.

"The downstream health effects…are being massively under-estimated and under-reported. This is an order of magnitude error," Gold's letter read. The letter detailed the spike in calls to suicide hotlines, the curtailment of routine screening for diseases like stroke and cancer, the documented aversion to hospitals by people who needed urgent care.

"The millions of casualties of a continued shutdown will be hiding in plain sight," the letter continued, "but they will be called alcoholism, homelessness, suicide, heart attack, stroke, or kidney failure. In youths it will be called financial instability, unemployment, despair, drug addiction, unplanned pregnancies, poverty, and abuse."[59]

Dr. Gold could not have been more right, but the lockdowns persisted, particularly in California. In November 2020, weeks *after* the election, California tightened the screws on its COVID rules, putting more than 94 percent of its population in the most restrictive tier. Citizens were required "to wear a mask whenever outside their home, with limited exceptions."[60]

In a foreshadowing of what would happen after January 6, the heavily indoctrinated Californians felt empowered to monitor and report on their fellow citizens. "Random people became citizen cops preventing you from living your life doing ordinary things," said Gold. "I was watching Nazism unfold."[61] As the daughter of a Holocaust survivor, she insisted she was "not using hyperbole."

California's insanely arbitrary COVID rules disqualified anyone who willingly honored them from ever mocking

QAnon. On a given day, one could park at the City of Hermosa Beach but only for fifteen minutes. At Big Rock, Maritime Rocks beach access was closed, but at Escondido Creek, beach access was open. Venice and Cabrillo fishing piers remained closed, but the Malibu Pier was open while the Santa Monica Pier had just begun phased reopening. Every day, some bureaucrat had to recalibrate all the openings and closings of California beaches. "Our response to COVID-19 has and will continue to lead with data and science," Gov. Gavin Newsom insisted at the time.[62] Californians Simone Gold and Ashli Babbitt did not take him seriously. No patriot did.

The California regulations called to mind San Marcos president Esposito as much as they might Stalin or Mao. In Woody Allen's 1971 film *Bananas*, his character, Fielding Mellish, helped liberate this fictional Latin American country. Upon taking power, rebel leader Esposito issued orders to the citizens of San Marcos so wonderfully daft, they now seem almost prescient. "From this day on, the official language of San Marcos will be Swedish," said *el Presidente*. "In addition to that, all citizens will be required to change their underwear every half-hour. Underwear will be worn on the outside so we can check.

"Furthermore," added Esposito, "all children under 16 years old are now…16 years old!"[63] At least those kids got to go to school. Public schools in California remained shut down through the 2020–2021 school year. When schools reopened in the fall of 2021, Gov. Newsom required all students to be masked and all eligible students vaccinated.[64]

The self-destructive force of Newsom's dictates alarmed responsible parents throughout the state. And with good cause. In December 2023, the Policy Analysis for California (PACE), shared a summary of COVID's after effects: "Student achievement in California has not rebounded after the precipitous declines of the COVID-19 pandemic, with English language arts (ELA) and math scores remaining well below prepandemic levels."[65]

Dr. Gold saw all of this coming. Alarmed by the hysteria, she promptly organized a group called America's Frontline Doctors. In July 2020, the group traveled to Washington for a two-day summit that covered, among other subjects, the effectiveness of hydroxychloroquine (HCQ). While in DC, she secured a meeting with then vice president Mike Pence and held a press conference live-streamed by Breitbart News on the steps of the Supreme Court. Within eight hours, the video of the press conference had been viewed seventeen million times.

Despite the fact that the president of the United States, an HCQ advocate, tweeted out the video, Facebook, YouTube, and Twitter felt empowered to pull it. Big Pharma and its allies/clients within the health establishment could not afford to let HCQ establish itself as an effective remedy to COVID.

The FDA claims that "available treatment for COVID-19 does not preclude the FDA from authorizing a vaccine to prevent COVID-19,"[66] but Gold disagreed. "To race the vaccines through as an emergency use vaccine," she said, "the law requires there be no other treatment option."[67] It is hard to conjure an alternative explanation for the government's tyrannical reaction to the doctor-approved use of proven safe drugs like HCQ and ivermectin.

Joel Stein of the *Financial Times* was interviewing Gold during her rise to infamy in the summer of 2020. As he explained to his readers, Dr. Gold preferred to meet in person, but he was "nervous." When she suggested they meet outdoors, he consented. Upon learning that she would not wear a mask, however, he "ultimately was too afraid" to meet her. In 2020, with craven journalists like Stein scaring citizens into submission, the Jacobins sensed the election was theirs for the stealing.

7

Jacobin Justice

In one of the many ironies of January 6, Ashli Babbitt was better trained to deal with civil disturbances in Washington than were the Capitol Police. Ashli spent most of her Air Force career doing police work. While on active duty, she guarded the gates at bases in, among other hellholes, Iraq and Afghanistan. Later, while in the National Guard, she was assigned to the 113th Security Forces Squadron known as the "Capitol Guardians." Operating out of Joint Base Andrews, the unit served as a ready response force for the District of Columbia.[68] On January 6, 2021, these units were not ready to respond.

Needing to undermine Ashli's potential as a martyr, journalists tended to cite her credentials with a quiet smirk. In turning against the police, they implied, it was she who betrayed her profession and her country. As shall be seen, Ashli never resisted the Capitol Police. If anyone betrayed anyone, it was the Capitol Police who betrayed Ashli and her fellow J6ers. The protestors came to DC as backers of the Blue. The Blue, at least some of them, never got that memo.

To understand the breakdown, a useful place to start is an extraordinary article published by *Time* magazine in February 2021. The author, Molly Ball, laid out in exquisite detail what the article's headline described as "The Secret History of the Shadow Campaign That Saved the 2020 Election."[69] The word "saved" is misleading. "Rigged" would be more accurate.

At the time, the Yale-educated Ball was *Time*'s national political correspondent and a political analyst for CNN. As of this writing, she's the senior political correspondent for the *Wall Street Journal*. Ball knows her way around the corridors of power, certainly the Jacobin wing. In May 2020, Henry Holt and Co. published Ball's book, *Pelosi*, described by the publisher in a flurry of superlatives as a "riveting inside account of the unprecedented rise to power and unmatched political legacy of the first woman Speaker of the House."

In assembling what a cynic might call the "Ball Dossier," its author claimed "access to the group's inner workings." By "group," Ball referred to an unlikely "cabal"—her word—of "left-wing activists and business titans." Their shared goal was to deny President Trump reelection. Ball interviewed dozens of those involved and reviewed "never-before-seen documents." There is no reason to doubt her research. What needs to be questioned is her motive. Not since James Comey's *A Higher Loyalty* has an author spent so much effort making a plot so boldly nefarious seem somehow noble.

Aligned against these powerful interests were President Trump, a handful of Trump insiders, and millions of red-pilled Americans. Activists like Ashli Babbitt could not comprehend the scope of the opposition, but they could sense the control it had over the nation's discourse. Particularly worrisome was the response of the government and the media to the often violent protests spawned by the death of George Floyd in Minneapolis on May 25, 2020.

One "conspiracy theory" traced to the Right is that the Floyd riots were orchestrated to enhance Democratic chances in November. Ball confirmed that the conspiracy was no mere theory. The organizers who led what she called "the racial-justice uprising" hoped to "harness its momentum for the election." Rioting, Ball all but boasted, was the leverage leftists used to keep the business interests in line.

"The summer uprising," Ball wrote, "had shown that people power could have a massive impact." Harnessing the numerical power of passive young whites and the active menace of young blacks and their Antifa allies, protest organizers brought America to its knees, in many places, literally. High on their success, "Activists," claimed Ball, "began preparing to reprise the demonstrations if Trump tried to steal the election."

By "steal" Ball meant "win." Potential rioters had been conditioned to believe that only election fraud could assure Trump victory. Well before the election, a coalition called "Protect the Results" had posted a map with some four hundred sites where protestors would assemble to protest the election results and, if history was a guide, not necessarily peacefully.

The business community, Ball revealed, "was engaged in its own anxious discussions about how the election and its aftermath might unfold." The rioters had alerted corporate America to the very real possibility of "economy-disrupting civil disorder" should Trump prevail. Not one to stand on principle, the US Chamber of Commerce partnered with the very activists who had orchestrated the summer's disorder. Together, they called for "the American democratic process to proceed without violence, intimidation or any other tactic that makes us weaker as a nation."

From the Jacobin perspective, "any other tactic" meant a Trump challenge to what they knew would be millions of disputed votes. In general, corporate honchos never had much use for Trump. They needed little arm twisting to make, in Ball's words, "a sort of implicit bargain…to keep the peace and oppose Trump's assault on democracy."

Ball mentioned "George Floyd" once in her article and then just offhandedly. Like others who exploited his death, she had little interest in the person and no interest in the Minneapolis police officers sacrificed to assure a favorable outcome in November. Sacrificing the innocent was a Jacobin tradition. During the French Revolution, the Jacobins derived their power from their ability to manage the Parisian mobs. To satisfy the mob's bloodlust, they imposed a state of revolutionary justice on France untethered to any traditional sense of Judeo-Christian morality. "Liberty, equality, fraternity or death," wrote Charles Dickens in *A Tale of Two Cities*, summarizing revolutionary France's reign of terror—"the last, much the easiest to bestow."[70] In the summer of 2020, Derek Chauvin and his colleagues experienced the distilled essence of Jacobin justice.

There had been outbreaks of mob justice throughout American history, but only in 2020 did America's elites lend their imprimatur to mob violence. "If you're able to," then senator Kamala Harris tweeted in June 2020 in the wake of the Minneapolis riots, "chip in now to the [Minnesota Freedom Fund] to help post bail for those protesting on the ground in Minnesota." Those needing bail were not arrested for "protesting." Among other wanton acts of violence, they burned down a police station.[71]

During the very days Chauvin was on trial in 2021, California congresswoman Maxine Waters traveled to Minnesota. There, Waters told the angry crowds, "We're looking for a guilty verdict." She then specified what was to happen if Chauvin were acquitted. "We got to stay on the street. And we've got to get more active, we've got to get more confrontational. We've got to make sure that they know that we mean business."[72]

Knowing the consequences of a not guilty verdict, the frightened jury hastily convicted Chauvin. On the occasion of his conviction, Nancy Pelosi looked heavenward and muttered through her designer face mask, "Thank you, George Floyd, for sacrificing your life for justice." She then praised the "millions of people who came out for justice," omitting the billions of dollars in damage those millions of people caused.[73]

As with so much else that happened in 2020, the Floyd death was stage managed for maximum effect. Although the amateur video of Floyd's final moments was shown by every TV station in America, Minnesota attorney general Keith Ellison suppressed the officers' body cam video. Only when ordered by a judge did Ellison release the footage to the public. In the seventy-five days between Floyd's death and the video's release, Jacobin operatives in and out of media spun an anti-police, anti-America narrative that had hardened into dogma. In the days after January 6, they would use similar tactics to spin an anti-Trump, anti-MAGA narrative.

In Minneapolis, the body cam footage told a more accurate story than the street-side video. Viewers learned that it was a black police officer, Alex Kueng, who arrested Floyd. "I can't breathe Mr. Officer! Please. Please! Aaaaaah," said Floyd before Chauvin even showed up on the scene. When the four officers tried to load Floyd into the patrol car, he moaned repeatedly, "I want to lay on the ground." A friendly onlooker named Charles shouted at Floyd, "Bro, you about to have a heart attack and shit, man. Get in the car." Charles was right. Floyd was about to have a fatal heart attack, and there was nothing the officers could have done to stop it once he refused to leave with them peacefully.[74]

Attorney General Ellison, whose coziness with the Nation of Islam cost him the DNC chair, purposely suppressed this video. The calculation in leftist circles was that a true picture of what happened on May 25 would rob the moment of its emotional power. Floyd, after all, had complained he couldn't breathe while standing. In fact, he made the same complaint a year earlier during an Oxycontin bust.

To preserve the party line, Ellison not only suppressed the body cam footage, but he also allowed the autopsy report to be corrupted. In truth, Minnesota authorities knew from day one that Chauvin did not "murder" Floyd. Not until 2023 did the Floyd story blow up and only then for people who cared to know. In a 2023 deposition for a sexual harassment suit, Amy Sweasy, a former Hennepin County prosecutor, told of how she spoke with Hennepin County medical examiner Andrew Baker the day after Floyd's death.

Sweasy testified under oath that she called Dr. Baker the day after Floyd's death to ask him to perform the autopsy. Baker called later that same day to report "there were no medical findings that showed any injury to the vital structures of Mr. Floyd's neck. There were no medical indications of asphyxia or strangulation." This was not surprising. Chauvin was using a maximum restraint technique (MRT) featured in training materials prepared by the Minneapolis Police Department. Ellison suppressed this fact too.

By the day after Floyd's death, Baker knew the risks involved in telling the truth. Sweasy continued, "He said to me, 'Amy, what happens when the actual evidence doesn't match up with the public narrative that everyone's already decided on?' And then he said, 'This is the kind of case that ends careers.'"

Baker chose to preserve his career. In August 2021, a memorandum surfaced that memorialized a November 2020 conference between Dr. Roger Mitchell, then the Washington, DC, chief medical examiner, and several Minnesota state prosecutors. It detailed Mitchell's effort to coerce Baker into including neck compression in his diagnosis of Floyd's death.

As noted above, Baker conducted an autopsy on May 26 that showed no physical evidence of asphyxiation. Toxicology reports would also show that Floyd had ample amounts of fentanyl and methamphetamines in his system, the latter of which aggravated what Baker called Floyd's "very severe underlying heart disease." Without a diagnosis of asphyxia, however, the state could not accuse Chauvin of murder. This is where Mitchell came into play.

A well-connected black political activist, Mitchell boasted of his involvement in Baker's diagnosis to the state attorneys. As he told them, he had called Baker more than once in the days after Floyd's death, criticizing his initial report and threatening to slam him in a *Washington Post* op-ed. The conniving Mitchell showed Baker a way out of the jam. According to the memorandum, "Mitchell said neck compression has to be in the diagnosis." Sure enough, on Monday, June 1, one week after Floyd's death, Baker's office released a report that began, "Cause of death: Cardiopulmonary arrest complicating law enforcement subdual, restraint, and *neck compression*."[75] (Italics added.)

With a stroke of the pen and the complicity of the prosecutors, Baker turned four innocent cops into murderers and justified the self-destructive social revolution that followed. As shall be seen, Mitchell's DC office would play a comparable role in enabling the mass injustice that would follow January 6.

To the Jacobins, truth no longer mattered. America's deplorables had come to expect them to lie. For the past five years, mainstream journalists had lied about so much of consequence—from Russia collusion to COVID's origins to Floyd's "murder" to Hunter's laptop to the "Big Guy's" dementia—the once "mainstream" media had lost all sway over half of America.

That half included the great majority of America's active and retired police, including Sara Carpenter. Sara fit no one's preconception of a Republican activist. Nor was she the only cop there to support the president. After a summer in which police were assaulted and humiliated with near impunity by leftist mobs, law enforcement officers rallied to President Trump's cause in record numbers.

In New York City, for instance, although Trump received only 18 percent of the popular vote in 2016, in 2020, one NYPD union after another endorsed him. "In the New York City PBA, Mr. President you earn the endorsement and you've earned this endorsement," said Police Benevolent Association president Patrick Lynch. "I'm proud to give it." Paul DiGiacomo, the president of the NYPD's Detectives' Endowment Association, explained why his union endorsed Trump: "There was only one person at the time supporting us and that was President Trump. There was no one else out there in the political world praising or doing anything for the police. They left us no choice."[76]

In the summer of 2020, one local police officer after another would be sacrificed to protect Jacobin interests. Starting in the winter of 2021, a winter that has not yet ended, hundreds of J6ers would wake to the sound of their jailer's commands, a reminder to patriots everywhere that Jacobin interests must not be threatened again.

8

Molotovs Rollin'

As president, Joe Biden would be mocked for saying, "Even Dr. King's assassination did not have the worldwide impact that George Floyd's death did."[77] Oddly, this was the rare occasion on which Biden proved more accurate than his critics. In April 1968, no one was prepared for King's assassination. The rioting that followed in America's cities, Washington, DC, most prominently, was heartfelt and largely spontaneous.

There was nothing spontaneous about the George Floyd riots. As the Ball Dossier makes clear, leftist organizers worldwide were waiting for a useful spark. The shooting death of "black jogger" Ahmaud Arbery in Georgia in February 2020 had potential, but organizers chose not to bite. As they knew, Arbery was no more a jogger than Michael Brown was a "gentle giant" or Trayvon Martin a little boy with Skittles. The video was ambiguous. The three ordinary Joes involved in the incident represented nothing institutional or systemic. Besides, it was February. Organizers could not count on a mass turnout in the winter.

Based on recent trends, the year 2020 promised many more "victims." With roughly twenty thousand anticipated arrests each day in America,[78] and with a projected 2 percent of those arrests meeting resistance, the nation's cell phone warriors would have some four hundred daily opportunities to record something resembling police brutality. Takedowns, after all, are never pretty. Of course, this imagery only mattered if at least one cop were white and the perp black, but this kind of interaction was, unfortunately, not unusual.

In 1968, rioting worked against the Democratic Party's interests. Presidential candidate Hubert Humphrey secured only 42 percent of the popular vote against George Wallace and winner Richard Nixon, both of whom promised a return to law and order. The year 2020 was different. In 2020, rioting was part of the calculus. George Floyd was no Martin Luther King, but King died at a time when journalists still felt some obligation to the truth.

The organizers of the riots planned for Washington, DC, on May 29, four days after Floyd's death, had a more immediate goal than those in Minneapolis and elsewhere—discrediting Donald Trump. The very first protestors on that Friday afternoon showed up at the White House gates. They demanded that Trump resign. The fact that Floyd died in a liberal city in a Democrat state mattered not at all. The Jacobins had long ago convinced their minions that these killer cops had merely heeded Trump's epic dog whistles.

As if on cue, protesting soon turned into rioting. At 7 p.m., anxious Secret Service agents ushered the president and his family into an underground bunker. The rioting resumed on Saturday and grew more serious. Rioters tried to push through security barriers, damaged a half-dozen Secret Service vehicles, and threw bricks, rocks, fireworks, bottles, and other objects at Secret Service personnel. In some instances, they kicked, punched, and threw bodily fluids at the officers. By Sunday morning, sixty of the officers had been injured.[79]

At the *New York Times*, reporters focused the drama on Trump. No matter what he did, it was wrong. The May 31 headline read, "As Protests and Violence Spill Over, Trump Shrinks Back." The "empathy" he had expressed for Floyd, heavyweight reporters Maggie Haberman and Peter Baker insisted, "was overshadowed by his combative threats to ramp up violence against looters and rioters."

The reporters took issue with Trump's plan to designate Antifa as a terrorist organization. Antifa, they reminded their readers, was a movement, not an organization. "Moreover," they wrote, unaware of how naive this would sound after January 6, "American law applies terrorist designations to foreign entities, not domestic groups."

The reporters found a Trump supporter, Dan Eberhart, who told them, "Trump is far more divisive than past presidents. His strength is stirring up his base, not calming the waters." A Trump backer he may have been, but Eberhart was also the head of a private equity firm and the CEO of a drilling services company. The business interests cited in the Ball Dossier were getting the message—in the words of one rioter who scrawled it on the front of a high-end restaurant—"THE RICH AREN'T SAFE ANYMORE!"

Not content with breaking windows at the US Chamber of Commerce, rioters set the building on fire. "We're trying to recover as best we can from what transpired last night and then tonight it's supposed to be the same thing, so we'll probably be back tomorrow, doing the same thing," a wary chamber staffer told the *Times* as he painted over the graffiti. Outrage was not an emotion the victims of the riots were allowed to express. That sentiment was reserved for the rioters.

The reporting had a whiff of Monty Python about it. *Times* reporter Shawn McCreesh quoted a young black protestor as saying, "I think it's nice that people are still coming out to push for change." McCreesh immediately followed this bromide with the observation that "a Chevy Suburban on I Street was in flames" and that the crowds were "smashing windows and trying to wreck as much as they could."

Amid the carnage, organizers managed to get their point across. "We want charges. We want convictions. No more acquittals. We want these people to be held accountable."[80] This was Jacobin justice at its purest. In Minneapolis, these demands would rattle the jury pool, but in Washington, they rattled the business lobbies. In the years ahead, Trump would have no better chance of securing justice in the district than Chauvin and his colleagues did in Minneapolis.

The rioting and protesting in Washington would last for days, weeks even, but its climax came on Monday night, June 1. To show the media he was not a "shrinking" president, tweeting away madly as Washington burned, Trump and a small entourage walked to the historic church of St. John's, the "Church of the Presidents." Rioters had set it on fire the night before. There, Trump defiantly held up a Bible. After about fifteen minutes, he returned to the White House.

The otherwise faithless media took umbrage at the president's seeming blasphemy. "Protesters Dispersed with Tear Gas So Trump Could Pose at Church," read a *New York Times* headline.[81] Feasting on false information, Democratic leaders were as quick to denounce Trump as were the media. Senator Kamala Harris claimed to have "watched as President Trump, having gassed peaceful protesters just so he could do this photo op, then he went on to tear gas priests who were helping protesters in Lafayette Park." Asked House Speaker Nancy Pelosi, "What is this, a banana republic?"[82]

Pelosi was righter than she knew. A nation in which mobs ran rampant and truth no longer mattered deserved the "banana" designation. She and Harris, however, were wrong about everything else. A report by the Interior Department inspector general disproved their wild-eyed claim that Trump had the crowd gassed for a photo-op. The protestors were removed hours earlier, read the report, "to allow a contractor to safely install anti-scale fencing in response to destruction of Federal property and injury to officers that occurred on May 30 and May 31."[83] Trump's church visit had not even been planned at that time. The whole story—tear gassing priests?—was just another trickle in the "river of bullshit."

Watching the rioters in Washington or in scores of other cities, the women of January 6 did not see themselves. They saw mindless, masked young people whose cause was too dubious, whose response was too violent, and whose goals were too subversive to respect. The J6 women refused to let the media gaslight them into thinking Floyd a saint and the ensuing mayhem "mostly peaceful."

If the J6 women did not know for sure, they sensed that the protests had been organized around a contrived cause. They could not help but see that the corporate media, locally and nationally, sympathized with the rioters. Journalists did not hesitate to scold the police for using tear gas or firing rubber bullets or making mass arrests. In the months and years after January 6, the media would use all manner of verbal jiujitsu to deny the obvious, namely that the "justice" dished out to the J6ers, either on the scene or in the courts, was far harsher than that applied to the Floyd protestors.

On July 30, 2021, for instance, the Associated Press ran an article headlined, "Records Rebut Claims of Unequal Treatment of Jan. 6 Rioters." Readers were apparently not expected to get beyond the headline. If they did, they saw the "hypocrisy" that James Bennett of the *Times* admitted was now "transparent to conservatives."

"Dozens" of Floyd rioters may have been convicted and sent to prison, but their crimes dwarfed those of the J6ers.[84]

A DOJ report from September 24, 2020, set a baseline for federal offenses.[85] As of that date, some eighty Floyd rioters had been charged "with offenses relating to arson and explosives." No J6er was charged with either offense. The J6ers, at their worst, broke windows. They set no fires, overturned no cars, toppled no monuments, sprayed no graffiti.

Fifteen Floyd rioters were charged with damaging federal property, but that damage included the $2 million in hard costs resulting from the months-long siege on the federal courthouse in downtown Portland. Not to be outdone, the largely peaceful protestors in Minneapolis destroyed the Third Precinct police station, totaled it. The *New York Times* editorial by Sen. Tom Cotton that led to Bennet's termination offended leftist sensibilities simply by documenting the outrages of the Floyd rioters. Wrote Cotton:

> Outnumbered police officers, encumbered by feckless politicians, bore the brunt of the violence. In New York State, rioters ran over officers with cars on at least three occasions. In Las Vegas, an officer is in "grave" condition after being shot in the head by a rioter. In St. Louis, four police officers were shot as they attempt-

ed to disperse a mob throwing bricks and dumping gasoline; in a separate incident, a 77-year-old retired police captain was shot to death as he tried to stop looters from ransacking a pawnshop.[86]

Despite the rampant violence, state and local authorities were even more lenient than the feds. A record review by UK's left-leaning *Guardian* found that the "vast majority" of charges were "dropped, dismissed, or otherwise not filed." In Dallas and Philadelphia, more than 95 percent of citations were dropped, in Houston 93 percent, in San Francisco 100 percent. Even for felonies like looting and assault, local authorities dropped the majority of charges.[87]

The injustice in the courts flowed from the imbalance in the newsrooms. Writing less than eight months after January 6, the Associated Press reporters so loaded their language as to make it useless even as propaganda. The J6 protestors engaged in a "riot," indeed in an "insurrection." The "mob of Trump supporters" was "whipped up by the former president's lies about the election." By contrast, Floyd protestors participated in "demonstrations for racial justice." These demonstrations "were largely peaceful calls to address racial inequality and police brutality."

As shall be seen, the real lie was that President Trump was lying. He believed everything he said, and he was almost assuredly right. The provable lie is the one that President Joe Biden told about Floyd on the occasion of Derek Chauvin's conviction: "It was a murder in the full light of day, and it ripped the blinders off for the whole world to see the systemic racism the Vice President just referred to—the systemic racism that is a stain our nation's soul."[88]

Not a word of what Biden said is true. The heavily drugged Floyd, a chronic felon, suffered a massive coronary as he struggled to resist arrest. His death in a liberal city was indicative of nothing, not police brutality, not systemic racism. The arresting officer was black, his colleagues white and Asian. The restraint used on Floyd was standard. When the protests "occasionally turned violent" that violence cost insurers as much as $2 billion, all for a cause as counterfeit as the money Floyd was arrested for passing. Even with the most inflated accounting, January 6 caused only about $2 million of damage, a good chunk of that the result of law enforcement's promiscuous use of toxic sprays.

Lisa Eisenhart waded through the pepper spray as she walked into an open Capitol on January 6. The word had spread throughout the crowd on the southwest side of the Capitol that the members of Congress had been evacuated, and "they were letting people in." Still, as a caution, Lisa's son, Eric Munchel, urged Lisa to put on her bandana. "It's going to get spicy," he said. After thirty years as a registered nurse, Lisa was undaunted. There was little she had not seen or experienced.

Wary of potential attacks from Antifa, the fifty-seven-year-old Lisa and her son were wearing tactical gear. This was not illegal nor irrational. Lisa had gone out the night before wearing the gear for safety reasons. If Trump supporters behaved themselves, she knew that BLM/Antifa activists often did not. After a self-organized, self-declared "Million MAGA March" in Washington on November 14, 2020, leftist agitators openly attacked stragglers as they were walking to their hotels, knocking one man unconscious. "Why are you guys letting this happen?" a Trump supporter asked a Metro DC officer who failed to intervene.[89]

Thugs ran free in the anarchic streets of Washington. In late August 2020, Sen. Rand Paul and his wife were assaulted upon leaving a Trump speech at the White House. Reluctant to report leftist violence, the Associated Press headlined the story, "Sen. Paul Complains about 'Angry Mob' Encounter after RNC."[90] Paul had no need to fabricate. Three years prior, his Trump-hating neighbor attacked the senator on his lawn, fracturing five of his ribs. As with most inconvenient news, the major media "de-amplified" the tales of these increasingly routine attacks.

Through her own channels, however, Lisa watched and prepared, but the idea that she and Eric had come to the Capitol to initiate violence, let alone stage an insurrection, she considers "preposterous." As her charging document notes, "The record contains no evidence indicating that, while inside the Capitol, Munchel or Eisenhart vandalized any property or physically harmed any person."

If Lisa had followed the case of Urooj Rahman, she would have had some reason to be hopeful about her sentencing. In the early morning hours of May 30, 2020, Rahman drove with her friend and fellow attorney, Colinford Mattis, to a police precinct in the Clinton Hill section of New York City. There, after encouraging others to do the same, Ms. Rahman threw a Molotov cocktail through the window of an empty NYPD patrol car, setting it on fire. She and Mattis were arrested and spent a few days in jail before being released to home confinement. By contrast, Lisa Eisenhart was held in pre-trial detention for eleven weeks, six of them in the DC hellhole.

In November 2022, a federal judge sentenced Rahman, the thirty-something daughter of immigrant Pakistani parents, to fifteen months in prison. "She was the primary caretaker of her aging mother," a pair of weepy *New York Times* reporters observed. Judge Brian Cogan sounded almost apologetic for having to sentence Rahman. "You are a remarkable person who did a terrible thing on one night," Cogan told her. Praising her lifetime of hard work, he explained that hers was one of the most difficult sentences he ever had to impose. Being the "instigator," Rahman received a longer sentence than Mattis, who got twelve months.[91]

There was, however, much the *New York Times* did not report about this "remarkable person." The day before the attack, Rahman and Mattis exchanged a series of menacing texts in which Rahman boasted of her scores. "Set a police car on fire," she said in one text. "My rock hit someone. A cop of course," she wrote in another, this one capped with a smiley face. "Molotovs rollin'," she wrote in still another text. "I hope they burn everything down" she enthused. "Need to burn all police stations down and probably the courts too."[92]

Unfortunately for Lisa and Eric, Rahman's sentencing had no predictive value. At the *New York Times*, editors chose not to notice the disparity in a coldhearted article headlined, "'Zip Tie Guy' and His Mother Get Prison Terms in Jan. 6 Riot."[93] The *Times* summarized their offense as follows, "A Tennessee man and his mother were sentenced to prison on Friday for seeking to intimidate lawmakers by marching with matching tactical vests and carrying zip tie-style handcuffs." That's about it. Lisa got two-and-a-half years, twice what Urooj Rahman got for firebombing a police car. Eric was sentenced to nearly five years, four more years than Mattis got for aiding and abetting Rahman. Unequal treatment? No. That's just another Trump lie.

9

The Rigging

In the months, years even, leading up to the November 2020 election, Ashli Babbitt's mom, Micki, regrets that she did not pay closer attention to what Ashli was saying. Throughout conservative America there was a growing wariness about the upcoming election. Ashli's unease was a barometer. She was a Cassandra in a nation grown deaf.

The more a conservative activist knew, the more anxious that activist became. The media delighted, for instance, in finding a former customer of Ashli's pool service business who quit using her business over a political argument he admits to having started. "I brought it up, I think, about a political race that had just happened and Ashli absolutely went off," the anonymous source told CBS 8 in San Diego. The station ran this hit piece just two days after Ashli had been shot and killed under the headline, "Local Man Fired Ashli Babbitt after Political Rant over the Telephone."[94] That Ashli worried more about her country than her business offended Jacobin sensibilities. Females especially were expected to honor the party line.

Those women who knew anything about Democratic attorney Marc Elias were particularly worried. Ashli may not have known him by name, but she had seen his handiwork in the 2018 midterms. "I'm so tired of it," she tweeted weeks after that election, "all they want to do is talk about trump and sling hateful rhetoric around but what in the actual hell are they doing?"[95]

Ashli had reason to be frustrated. As the November 2018 election approached, things were going swimmingly in President Donald Trump's America. The GDP was up 5.2 percent from 2017. The unemployment rate declined to a forty-nine-year low of 3.8 percent. Inflation had increased only 2.49 percent year-to-year. The murder rate fell nearly 6 percent, the second straight year of decrease after a wild spike under Obama. No new wars had been launched, and the American death count in Afghanistan had fallen to 3 percent of its peak eight years prior.

Yet despite all the good Republican news, the Democrats captured forty-one seats in the House, their biggest gain in a midterm since the post-Watergate bloodbath of 1974. The Republicans held the Senate, but barely, and they had only nine seats at risk. The Democrats surged, Ashli knew, because all the media wanted to report was "hateful rhetoric" about Trump.

Lacking a real Watergate, the Jacobins had created one. To be sure, the Watergate inquiry in all its tentacles was very nearly as corrupt as Robert Mueller's investigation of Trump's imagined collusion with Russia. At the heart of Watergate, however, there was a real crime. With Russiagate, only the accusers were guilty, and their crimes were seditious beyond Nixon's imagination.

In November 2018, most Americans did not know how specious were the charges against Trump. It would be six more months before Special Counsel Robert Mueller broke leftist hearts everywhere with his much anticipated report. There was no collusion with Russia. None. So stunned were Democrats that to this day many refuse to believe Mueller's reluctant conclusion.

In November 2018, Democrats still believed Trump and Putin were BFFs, as did many independents and more than a few Republicans. In the four weeks before the 2018 midterms, the *New York Times* ran eight articles or op-eds on the Mueller investigation, all of them hopeful Trump would be brought low.

One of the more damning articles involved Trump's deputy attorney general, Rod Rosenstein, the John Dean of his administration. On September 21, the *New York Times* revealed that Rosenstein had volunteered in early 2017 to secretly tape President Trump "to expose the chaos consuming the administration." The end goal of the conspirators was to invoke the Twenty-Fifth Amendment and have Trump removed from office as unfit.[96]

Placing a story in the *Times* about a plot that imploded more than a year prior was just another day on the job for the conspirators. Their insiders, "insisting on anonymity," allowed the *Times* to put the pieces of the story together just in time for the midterms. For those *Times* readers worried that Trump might fire the treacherous Rosenstein and kill the Mueller investigation, the *Times* ran a follow-up op-ed to reassure them. The author, Asha Rangappa, was a former "F.B.I. special agent focusing on counterintelligence investigations" and a Jacobin princess if there ever were one.

Asha's life experience could not have been more different from Ashli's. The daughter of Indian immigrants—the father an anesthesiologist, the mother an accountant—Rangappa followed the new silk road from Princeton to a Fulbright sojourn in Colombia to Yale Law School to the FBI for a quick cup of coffee and on to Yale University's Jackson Institute for Global Affairs. Her sex and ethnicity surely opened doors for her along the way.

Not to worry about Rosenstein, wrote Rangappa, "The F.B.I. has already collected hundreds of thousands of pages of evidence in the form of documents, interviews, electronic surveillance and foreign intelligence shared by our allies that are stored in the F.B.I.'s tamper-proof system and cannot be destroyed." She concluded her op-ed with this final reassurance, "The wheels of justice are already in motion, and it would take someone willing to take a fall for the president to try to stop it."[97]

In her op-ed, Rangappa speculated that—"if Congress changes hands"—Republican Devin Nunes would lose his control of the House Intelligence Committee. Nunes had been a nuisance. It was he and his team of investigators that uncovered the funding source for the infamous Steele Dossier, the foundational piece of the Russia collusion hoax. Incredibly, it was not until October 2017 that the *Washington Post* finally reported what Nunes had discovered, namely that the DNC and the Clinton campaign commissioned the Steele Dossier.[98]

Bitter about being scooped, *New York Times* reporter Maggie Haberman tweeted on the day the *Post* broke the story, "Folks involved in funding this lied about it, and with sanctimony, for a year."[99] Haberman was referring to the cutout on this scam, Perkins Coie attorney Marc Elias. With the blessing of Hillary Clinton and the DNC, Elias pulled off the most comprehensive dirty trick in the history of American politics.

In the 1972 reelection campaign of President Nixon, youthful campaign aide Donald Segretti made the phrase "dirty tricks" part of the American political lexicon. Segretti's mischief included sending embarrassing letters under the names of Nixon's political rivals. Although his dirty tricks had little effect on the election's outcome, Segretti served four and a half months in prison. For Elias's black magic, the Democrats tasked him with managing their legal apparatus in advance of the 2020 presidential election.

Elias did not disappoint. The convenient arrival of COVID gave him and his crew a rationale for dismantling the safeguards against voter fraud in state after state. Federalist editor in chief Mollie Hemingway tells this dispiriting story well in her excellent book, *Rigged.* "At the drop of a hat," she marvels, "America's electoral system went from irredeemably corrupt and broken in 2016 to unquestionably safe in 2020."[100]

It was unsettling that thirty-nine states changed their election laws prior to the 2020 election. It was unconstitutional that many of them did so without legislative approval. Article I, Section 4, of the Constitution specifically entrusts the state legislatures with responsibility for prescribing the "Times, Places, and Manner" of elections for federal office. In several states, however, the courts and election administrators exploited the media-driven COVID panic to assume this right for themselves. The Republicans responded with lawsuits, but the courts could not or would not respond in a timely fashion.

The Ball Dossier put its uniquely perverse spin on Republican efforts to protect the integrity of the election. "The President spent months insisting that mail ballots were a

Democratic plot and the election would be 'rigged,'" wrote Ball. "His henchmen at the state level sought to block their use, while his lawyers brought dozens of spurious suits to make it more difficult to vote—an intensification of the GOP's legacy of suppressive tactics." Ball's crude retelling—henchmen?—reflects the general tenor of media reporting during this period. COVID-skeptics like Ashli watched this madness from afar and could only assume that it was being orchestrated to assure the victory of the hapless Biden.

Aware of the skepticism, Elias and his public relations arm had a major task in front of them. In 2005, through his work as co-chair of the Commission on Federal Election Reform, former president Jimmy Carter came down hard against almost every change Elias and cronies would pass off as reform. "Fraud occurs in several ways," Carter and his fellow commissioners concluded. "Absentee ballots remain the largest source of voter fraud." They cited many of the ways in which voting is vulnerable to manipulation. Blank ballots get intercepted. Citizens at group sites like nursing homes are intimidated. Vote buying schemes escape detection. Early ballots go unsecured. "Third party" registration drives enlist noncitizens and other ineligible people. These problems were not theoretical. The commission cited case after case in which these practices had occurred and even affected outcomes.[101]

In a lengthy 2012 article in the *New York Times*, Adam Liptak affirmed the liberal case against mail-in ballots. "On the most basic level," wrote Liptak, "absentee voting replaces the oversight that exists at polling places with something akin to an honor system." Moving beyond mere principle, Liptak cited numerous cases in which mail-in ballots denied citizens their due. "Votes cast by mail are less likely to be counted," he argued, "more likely to be compromised and more likely to be contested than those cast in a voting booth, statistics show." In addition to innocent errors, fraud was "vastly more prevalent" in mail-in voting than voting in person.

"Election administrators have a shorthand name for a central weakness of voting by mail," wrote Liptak. "They call it granny farming." He cited many of the problems the Carter-Baker commission did, the intimidation of the elderly and the easy purchasing of votes among them. Liptak gave the article's final word to a Yale law professor who reaffirmed that "all the evidence of stolen elections involves absentee ballots and the like."[102]

In 2020, with an unmarketable candidate heading the Democratic ticket, the Jacobins ignored all warnings and bet the granny farm on mail-in ballots. COVID gave them the excuse. The Ball Dossier laid out the game plan with stunning candor. Ball attributed Biden's election to "a well-funded cabal of powerful people, ranging across industries and ideologies, working together behind the scenes to influence perceptions, change rules and laws, steer media coverage and control the flow of information." With something resembling a straight face, she concluded, "They were not rigging the election; they were fortifying it."

In reading this Soviet-worthy propaganda, I am reminded of the scene in *National Lampoon's Vacation* when the adolescent Rusty Griswold sees his father, Clark, skinny-dipping in a motel pool with a nameless hottie. When Clark tries to explain that he was merely trying to place an order with a "swimming pool waitress," Rusty deadpans, "Do you think mom will buy it?" In 2020, informed moms across America weren't buying the Jacobin twaddle about "saving democracy."

The elites were still in denial about the exit polls showing that some 53 percent of white women had voted for Trump in 2016, including nearly two-thirds of white women without college degrees. Not knowing these women, the feminists chastised them. "What leads a woman to vote for a man who has made it very clear that he believes she is subhuman?" seethed L. V. Anderson at *Slate*. "Self-loathing. Hypocrisy. And, of course, a racist view of the world that privileges white supremacy over every other issue."[103]

It was that simple. White women were supposed to do what their betters told them. MAGA women, the Jacobin elites were shocked to learn, had minds of their own. In 2020, fearing an even more decisive beating, they abandoned whatever principles they might have had and called the abandonment "saving democracy."

Then still with Project Veritas, James O'Keefe did an excellent job of showing how the many gears of this "well-funded cabal" meshed. In late September 2020, Project Veritas went public with its research into industrial-strength "granny farming" in Minneapolis's large Somali community. Aiding the Project Veritas team were a few undercover journalists from within that community. They were alarmed by the Democrats' exploitation of their countrymen. Exploiting immigrant voters, it should be noted, is nothing new. Democrats have held a near monopoly on urban vote fraud since at least the mid-nineteenth century when Boss Tweed's Tammany Hall mastered the art of picking winners.

Tweed's power lay in his ability to control the Irish vote. "As long as I count the votes," Tweed was caricatured as saying, "what are you going to do about it?"[104] The *New York Times* of that era did not sit by idly. It was the *Times*'s reporting that led to Tweed's downfall. Unchastened, Tweed's successors in New York and other cities would stake out claims to ethnic groups newly arrived from Europe, from Puerto Rico, from the American South, from China, from Mexico. For the next century, mainstream journalists competed to expose the election fraud they saw.

As Democratic and media interests began to meld, however, journalists stopped seeing fraud. By 2020, they were scolding those who did see it. As the November election approached, the media would ignore Jimmy Carter's cautions and treat each Democratic vote as though Jesus Christ himself had notarized it.

In 2020 in Minneapolis, Project Veritas was serving much the same role as the *Times* did in 1870. Thanks to undercover video, Veritas captured several financial exchanges between harvesters and voters, but Veritas's biggest catch was a video shot by a harvester himself. The harvester was Liban Osman, an ally of Congresswoman Ilhan Omar and the brother of Jamal Osman then running for city council in an early special election.[105]

One video, posted on Snapchat, showed Osman sorting through a stack of ballots the way he might a roll of bills. "Two in the morning," he sang as he sorted, "still hustling." On camera, Osman boasted about a practice that would have made Boss Tweed blush. "Numbers don't lie. Numbers don't lie," said Osman. "You can see my car is full. All these here are absentees' ballots. Can't you see? Look at all these. My car is full."

Osman went on to explain a political philosophy as old as Tammany Hall. "Money is everything. Money is the king in this world," said Osman. "If you got no money, you should not be here, period. You know what I'm saying?" Osman did not expect the video to fall into enemy hands, but it did. A Project Veritas source was following Osman's Snapchat account and captured his video.

Through a variety of friendly channels, millions of Americans saw the Project Veritas videos. The chicanery they showed was too obvious and too consequential to ignore or defend. So the Jacobins enlisted their go-to fixers at the *New York Times*. In a September 29 article headlined, "Project Veritas Video Was a 'Coordinated Disinformation Campaign,' Researchers Say," reporter Maggie Astor led the attack.

According to Astor, researchers at Stanford University and the University of Washington concluded that the Veritas videos were "probably" part of a disinformation campaign.[106] To build a major story around the word "probably" would have been unthinkable just a decade earlier, but the *Times* was all in for Joe Biden.

Once Astor enlisted academia to validate a transparent falsehood, the lesser media, including the local media in Minneapolis, felt free to pile on. Reinforcing the deception was the Jacobin "fact-checking" apparatus. A typical headline, this one from *USA Today*, read, "Fact Check: No Proof of Alleged Voter Fraud Scheme or Connection to Rep. Ilhan Omar."[107] Apparently, the videos of the Somali harvesters at work did not meet the media's new evidentiary standards.

Thanks to social media, millions of Americans witnessed not only a flagrant vote fraud scheme but also a coordinated media campaign to bury the fraud. That campaign involved the Democratic Party, the major media, academia, the local media, and their "fact-checking" allies. Months later, Twitter got in on the game, permanently banning Project Veritas. In his book, *American Muckraker*, O'Keefe sums up media perfidy by quoting the "final, most essential command" of the "Party" in Orwell's *1984*, namely "to reject the evidence of your eyes and ears."[108]

In 2020, the Jacobins were that "Party." If its operatives were willing to play by Orwellian rules, the patriots in flyover country were not. As November 2020 approached, they could see what the conspirators were doing, if not the detail, at least the big picture. They did not need QAnon to tell them two plus two equaled four. The equation hadn't changed even if the Party said it did.

10

Thought Police

On the day before she died, Ashli Babbitt retweeted a post from @FJD1911. It read simply, "I'm a small fry and I'm being censored." The woman in question had only 244 followers, but that was enough for her to feel the pressure from above. It went that deep.

If they had yet to learn the infrastructure of oppression, conservatives across America—especially future J6ers—were aware that the social media companies were trying to silence them. "If they're going to take every legitimate means from us, and we can't even express ourselves on the Internet, we won't even be able to speak freely, what is America for?" asked Lisa Eisenhart.[109]

Censorious or not, social media remained the conservatives' best weapon. At the end, Ashli had more than six thousand followers on Twitter, not much by, say, Kardashian standards, but for a woman without a media megaphone, it was impressive. Ashli tweeted a lot. Social media was the Right's equivalent of the old Soviet *samizdat*, an underground network that allowed patriots to be heard when *Pravda* would not give them a voice. Leftists argue that the Right had Fox News in its corner, but on taboo subjects like COVID or George Floyd and, soon, election fraud, Fox played by very nearly the same rules as the other corporate media.

Before social media, Democrats could spend their whole lives without being exposed to conservative thought. Fox News was as easily avoided as Rush Limbaugh or Alex Jones. Social media changed the equation. Facebook, especially, allowed the individual to share an unwelcome news story with friends and family. This free exchange troubled the Left. A survey done by the nonpartisan Public Religion Research Institute found that liberals were three times more likely to "unfriend" a person for political reasons than were conservatives.[110] These numbers will not surprise conservatives.

The Jacobins well understood the danger that social media posed. "Trump's lies and conspiracy theories, the viral force of social media and the involvement of foreign meddlers," the Ball Dossier insisted, "made disinformation a broader, deeper threat to the 2020 vote." In her *Time* article, Molly Ball boasted about what would prove to be the most pervasive and coordinated censorship campaign in American history.

Ball traced the effort to silence conservatives to progressive operative Laura Quinn, co-founder of Catalist, a progressive data mining operation out of Washington. Quinn's work on a "secret project" convinced her that responding to conservative arguments online only amplified the conservative message. Quinn's solution, Ball wrote, "was to pressure platforms to enforce their rules, both by removing content or accounts that spread disinformation and by more aggressively policing it in the first place." If you can't debate them, silence them.

Ball told of a November 2019 dinner meeting at the home of Facebook founder Mark Zuckerberg. In attendance were nine people who identified as "civil rights leaders." Their idea of civil rights apparently did not include free speech, as they pushed Zuckerberg to restrict "election-related falsehoods." Among those present was Vanita Gupta. "It took pushing, urging, conversations, brainstorming, all of that to get to a place where we ended up with more rigorous rules and enforcement," Gupta proudly told Ball. For her efforts, Joe Biden made the Yale-educated Gupta associate attorney general.

Dr. Simone Gold was not a small fry, and she definitely felt the effects of the Jacobin censorship campaign. In late July 2020, after Dr. Gold held a live-streamed "White Coat Summit" on the steps of the Supreme Court with her fellow doctors, Facebook promptly removed the video. Before being pulled, the video was Facebook's top-performing post in the world. Twitter and YouTube soon followed suit. In promoting the effectiveness of hydroxychloroquine, much as President Trump was doing, Gold and her colleagues helped puncture the panic balloon. By July 2020, the Jacobins understood that panic was essential to their election plans. Without it, their efforts to loosen election restraints would seem as nakedly partisan as they actually were. "People told me they were going to keep this going until the 2020 election," said Dr. Gold of the COVID hysteria, "and I said, 'no way, that's impossible.'"[111] At the time, she knew her medicine better than she did her politics.

Reporter Joel Stein, who covered Dr. Gold's public life for the *Financial Times*, served unwittingly as a testament to the power of panic.[112] Stein refused to meet with Gold indoors. He scoffed at her idea that "the many vaccines I took, the masks, the sheltering in place" were "all a trick." He mocked her theories about vaccine side effects, "all of which are disputed by mainstream scientists." He laughed off her worries about "vaccine mandates," pitied her efforts to prescribe hydroxychloroquine, and proved the wisdom of Benjamin Franklin's timeless caution, "Those who would give up essential Liberty, to purchase a little temporary Safety, deserve neither Liberty nor Safety."

Unfortunately, Stein wasn't an outlier. COVID hysteria spread through America's newsrooms more rapidly than did the disease itself, and no nostrum could ease the contagion. Not surprisingly, the media turned that hysteria against Donald Trump and other dissidents like Dr. Gold. To question the shifting COVID orthodoxy and its high priest, Anthony Fauci, was to blaspheme.

One particular incident illustrates how deeply the Jacobins had penetrated the social media networks and how perversely they conspired to assure the desired outcome in the 2020 election. The story involves one James Baker, the general counsel of the FBI at the time he and other Bureau insiders were scheming to nail Trump for his alleged ties to Russia and Vladimir Putin. In 2018, Baker got nabbed leaking unauthorized information to the media. His forced resignation, however, did not stop Baker from appearing semi-regularly on CNN in segments with titles like "Ex-Top FBI Lawyer: Trump Coup Claim Is Preposterous."

Quietly, in June 2020, Baker took a new job, perhaps the most influential of his career—deputy general counsel at Twitter. As the "Twitter Files" revealed, Baker used his position at the company for no larger purpose than to derail the Trump campaign. One information exchange stands out. In early October 2020, Trump was treated for COVID at Walter Reed Medical Center. On October 6, Trump tweeted that he was doing well, adding, "Don't be afraid of COVID. Don't let it dominate your life."

This perfectly presidential bit of optimism could not be allowed to stand. A Bizarro World FDR, Biden encouraged fear among his supporters to justify mail-in ballots. Whether spontaneously or on command, Baker did Biden's dirty work. Less than an hour after Trump's tweet, Baker emailed Twitter's head of Safety and Trust, Yuval Roth, "Why isn't this POTUS tweet a violation of our COVID-19 policy? (Especially the 'Don't be afraid of COVID' statement)."

No friend of President Trump, Roth was baffled. "This tweet is a broad, optimistic statement," he replied incredulously to Baker. "It doesn't incite people to do something harmful, nor does it recommend against taking precautions or following mask directives (or other guidelines)."[113]

At a congressional hearing in 2023, Arizona representative Paul Gosar asked Baker, "Was it your understanding that the Twitter COVID-19 policy was people *should* be afraid of COVID?" Baker claimed he was new and unsure of Twitter's policies, but this exchange made clear the cold reality of Jacobin COVID policy.[114] Baker and his allies were willing to crash the economy, ruin lives, and, if need be, let people die to sustain a politically useful panic.

The women of January 6, and not just Dr. Gold, had good reason to distrust what they were being told. They knew they were being lied to, and, in broad form, they understood why. Rachel Powell of Pennsylvania put confidence in her own experience. Looking around her largely rural county, Rachel was not seeing the deaths the media were touting. She believed that public health officials were overstating the risks and not for health reasons. Two days after the 2020 election, Rachel posted on Facebook, "I won't get a vaccine either. I hear what you're saying about the whole world being in on the conspiracy as far as the corona virus goes."

Rachel did not know the operational details, but she was right. There was a conspiracy. For her, COVID was a "liberty issue," and her liberty was at risk.[115] From Simone Gold's perspective, "The real agenda was to shift us to a people that would accept government control over our daily lives."

That control was on full display in the final few weeks of the 2020 presidential race. Confident to a fault, the Jacobins asked America to accept the most flagrant disinformation campaign in anyone's memory. There was nothing spontaneous about it. On October 14, when they saw the *New York Post* headline, "Smoking-Gun Email Reveals How Hunter Biden Introduced Ukrainian Businessman to VP Dad," their apparatchiks were ready to roll.

The conspirators had known since December 2019 that this story might drop. That was when Mac Isaac alerted the FBI to a laptop Hunter Biden had abandoned at his computer repair shop in Delaware. Before handing it over, Isaac made a copy of its contents. Had he not done so, we would still be unaware of the role the "Big Guy" played in the Biden family's seamy global enterprises.

In an August 2022 interview with Joe Rogan, Meta CEO Mark Zuckerberg casually shared the inside scoop on how Facebook came to defuse the *New York Post* bombshell.[116] Fearing the story might break at any time, the FBI reached out to Facebook, Twitter, and other social media platforms well before the 2020 election and warned them of a potential Russian pre-election "hack and dump" operation. On the day the *Post* story broke, representatives from the FBI's Foreign Influence Task Force met with Facebook execs. As would later be confirmed at a House Judiciary subcommittee hearing, the FBI knew the laptop was, in fact, Hunter Biden's.

Zuckerberg did not need to have his arm twisted. He and his wife, Priscilla Chan, had already invested $300 million, in CNN's words, toward "enhancing access to voting in the United States." CNN failed to add that the Zuckerbucks enhanced access almost exclusively in Democratic districts.[117] Without protest from the FBI, Facebook promptly "deamplified" the *Post* story, dramatically reducing its circulation. On the same day the story broke, the FBI's Foreign Influence Task Force also leaned on Twitter. The Twitter people needed little persuasion—some 98 percent of their political donations went to Democrats. They were all in for Biden, and Twitter blocked not only the *Post* story but also the *Post* itself.[118]

At a House Judiciary Committee hearing, Baker was asked about his role in silencing the *Post*. To virtually every salient question regarding the laptop, Baker pleaded memory loss. "You were entrusted with the highest level of power at Twitter, but when you were faced with the New York Post story, instead of allowing people to judge the information for themselves, you rushed to find a reason why the American people shouldn't see it," said committee chair James Comer. "You did this because you were terrified of Joe Biden not winning the election in 2020."[119]

Curiously, the Ball Dossier made no mention of the election plot's master stroke—the recruitment of the fifty-one spooks. A May 10, 2023, report by the Select Subcommittee on the Weaponization of Intelligence filled in the details.[120] The plot was hatched on October 17, 2020, when Biden campaign advisor—now secretary of state—Antony Blinken contacted Michael Morell. Morell had served as acting director of the CIA under Obama. At Blinken's request, Morell began assembling the draft of a statement that would dismiss this epic October surprise as more of the same old Russian disinformation.

Morell had a motive. He was in the running for the post of CIA director. Needing a Biden win to secure it, Morell went to work lining up co-conspirators. "Thereafter," reads the subcommittee report, "Morell contacted several former intelligence officials to help write the statement, solicit cosigners, and help with media outreach." On October 19, Morell emailed Nick Shapiro, his former deputy chief of staff, asking him to place the statement in major publications. "On background," Shapiro was to tell reporters that Morell, in talking to Russian intel experts, "was struck by the fact that all of them thought Russia is involved here." In truth, Morell had talked to no Russian intel experts before organizing the draft.

Politico bit first, running a story on October 19 under the bold headline, "Hunter Biden Story Is Russian Disinfo, Dozens of Former Intel Officials Say."[121] As Morell testified to the House subcommittee, one major purpose of the statement was "to help Vice President Biden in the debate." In an October 19, 2020, email, Morell told former CIA director John Brennan he wanted to "give the [Biden] campaign, particularly during the debate on Thursday, a talking point to push back on Trump on this issue."

During the October 23 debate, when Trump played the laptop card, Biden countered with the Russia card as planned. "Look, there are fifty former National Intelligence folks who said that what this, he's accusing me of is a Russian plan," said a well-rehearsed Biden. "They have said that this has all the characteristics—four—five former heads of the CIA, both parties, say what he's saying is a bunch of garbage. Nobody believes it except him, his, and his good friend Rudy Giuliani."

In an estimate more conservative than many, Trump pollster John McLaughlin found that 4.6 percent of Biden voters would not have voted for Biden if they had known about the contents of Hunter's laptop. Even if those people had simply not voted, their absence at the polls would have handed several swing states to Trump.[122]

Kept purposefully in the dark, too many Americans chose to believe Biden and his co-conspirators. "On November 3, 2020, the American people went to the polls to elect the president of the United States with the false impression that Hunter Biden's laptop was Russian disinformation," the House subcommittee concluded three years too late. "The American people cannot get back the 2020 election."

When Ashli Babbitt went to the polls on November 3, she knew all about the laptop and the Jacobin plot to kill the story. So did the recently activated Rosanne Boyland. In her first ever vote, Rosanne voted for Donald Trump. The vote mystified her liberal relatives. "She was into this QAnon thing," her brother-in-law Justin Cave told MSNBC, trying to explain Rosanne's actions on January 6.

"The perpetrators and enablers need to be stopped," said Rosanne's sister, Lonna Cave, referring not to the operatives who rigged the election but to the Trump supporters who protested the rigging.

When Ashli and Rosanne and Rebecca and Rachel and Christine and Simone and Sara and Lisa and Victoria and Yvonne voted on November 3, 2020, they did so with muted optimism. They were sure Trump would do better than he had done last time. They all knew people who did not vote for Trump in 2016 but would in 2020, and almost none who would do the opposite. They would be proved right. Trump would beat his 2016 numbers by nearly twelve million votes.

Yet in the last few weeks of the campaign, Trump supporters saw—if their liberal friends and relatives refused to—just how ruthless was the opposition. They watched a massive story be deep-sixed in real time, right in their faces. This fraud was unprecedented in boldness and in scope. So, too, they feared, would be the fraud on Election Day. The real question is not why these women went to Washington on January 6. The real question is why the rest of us did not.

11

The Big Lie

On the night of November 3, 2020, Ashli Babbitt was glued to the television set in her Southern California home. At her home nearby, Ashli's mom, Micki Witthoeft, watched attentively as well. Although not nearly as political as her daughter, Micki had seen enough in 2020 alone to understand the depth of Ashli's passion. She and Ashli exchanged texts throughout the night.

In the early hours, things were looking good for President Trump. "Election night began with many Democrats despairing," Molly Ball acknowledged. "Trump was running ahead of pre-election polling, winning Florida, Ohio and Texas easily and keeping Michigan, Wisconsin and Pennsylvania too close to call."

Ashli and Micki were particularly encouraged, as was the president, with the results in Florida. In 2016, Trump had carried this swing state by just 1.2 percent. In 2020, he was running two points ahead of that. By 10 p.m. California time, the networks projected Trump the winner in Florida. These numbers augured well for neighboring Georgia where Trump had won by five points in 2016.

In Wisconsin, Trump was crushing the pollsters' projections. In the last week of the campaign, all the major polls had Biden up by double digits in the Badger State. The ABC News and *Washington Post* poll had him up by seventeen points.[123] If the skewed polling was a part of the plan to demoralize Republicans, it didn't work. The MAGA base had long since turned off the major media. Republican turnout in Wisconsin and elsewhere on November 3 took the Jacobins by surprise. Their analysts, conceded Molly Ball, "hadn't comprehended how much better Trump was likely to do on Election Day."

That said, Democrats in the know were less worried than the rank and file. Theirs, after all, was the party that spawned Boss—"As long as I count the votes, what are you going to do about it?"—Tweed. The Jacobin elite—in the party, in the media, in big tech, in the intelligence community, in the US Postal Service—had been working for months to buy time to count votes after Election Day. According to the Ball Dossier, Trump was trying to "spoil the election" by insisting that "mail ballots were a Democratic plot and the election would be 'rigged.'" To make their argument, Trump loyalists referred Democrats back to the warning issued by the Carter-Baker commission: "Absentee ballots remain the largest source of voter fraud."

Carter represented the Democratic Party of old. In 2020, there was a new understanding. "It was crucial for voters to understand that despite what Trump was saying," wrote the soulless Ball, "mail-in votes weren't susceptible to fraud and that it would be normal if some states weren't finished counting votes on election night." To prepare the public, the Jacobins launched a massive campaign across all platforms.

By Election Day, more than 70 percent of voters expected that they would not know the results immediately. "A majority," wrote Ball, "also believed that a prolonged count wasn't a sign of problems."

That majority did not include Ashli Babbitt or other conservative activists. At about 11 p.m. Pacific time, certain key states simply stopped counting votes. Micki could all but hear the sigh in Ashli's text, "They're going to steal it." Months earlier, Trump supporter and tech entrepreneur Patrick Byrne would not have thought it possible for the media to deny the nation's "vulnerability to mass election fraud." As he observes in his book, *The Deep Rig*, historically, all parties had expressed concern about election integrity.

In 2020, the Jacobins changed the rules. Byrne's analysts warned him early on to "watch for counting being shut down during the election." At the time, Byrne thought the idea preposterous. This practice may have been normative in Third World countries, but, Byrne wondered, "Whoever heard of counting getting stopped, in the middle of an election, in the United States of America?"[124]

Alas, the prediction of Byrne's analyst allies came true. The counting ceased in the middle of the night, if not everywhere, at least in the swing state metros where the Jacobins needed it to stop. The *Federalist* headline on Wednesday, November 4, summed up the planned mess: "Ballot Counting Is Delayed in These Six States with Legal Battles on the Horizon."[125] Confident that they would count enough votes to win, the conspirators put out the word that there would be no need for rioting. "They had spent so much time getting ready to hit the streets on Wednesday," organizer Mike Podhorzer told Molly Ball, "but they did it." The "they" were the Jacobin shock troops. The "it" was "not rioting."

Overlooked by the major media throughout the campaign was the role of the US Postal Service. On August 13, 2020, the National Association of Letter Carriers (NALC) endorsed the Biden-Harris ticket.[126] This was not surprising. What alarmed observers was the language NALC president Fredric Rolando used in making the endorsement. Yes, Biden was a "fierce ally and defender," but, more to the point, President Trump was a threat to the very existence of the Post Office.

"In 2018," Rolando told his three hundred thousand members, "legislative recommendations from the White House Postal Task Force report called for the revocation of collective bargaining rights by America's postal unions, massive cuts to services, and the potential privatization of the agency." Rolando wasn't through. "Since that time," he added, "we have continued to see the administration take steps outside of the public eye to undermine the Postal Service and letter carriers."[127] The American Postal Workers Union (APWU), which represented the remaining Post Office staff, also endorsed Biden, and, of the two unions, the APWU was the more radical.

"In the end," wrote Ball, "nearly half the electorate cast ballots by mail in 2020, practically a revolution in how people vote." The fact that the people handling the mail feared the loss of their jobs should Trump win went unmentioned in the Ball Dossier. It went unmentioned almost everywhere. In the media, Fox News included, the subject of postal interference was all but taboo.

Ashli Babbitt and other J6ers were paying attention, not just to reports of fraud by postal workers but to a thousand other accounts of irregularities. Their own information streams were serving up one instance after another of likely abuses. Patrick Byrne found himself at the center of this data flow.

"A self-organized digital army sprung into existence," Byrne writes. "Networks of volunteers in various states, self-organizing and diving in on various aspects of the Deep Rig: what people had experienced in polling stations, what they had been told by precinct workers, what polling observers had experienced." Many of these people had backgrounds in the military or law enforcement. Lawyers volunteered to research laws. No one asked to be paid. "It quickly became clear that the problem was not going to be turning up facts," writes Byrne, "it was going to be managing the tsunami of evidence that poured in."[128]

Mainstream journalists dealt with this flood of contrary evidence by reinforcing seawalls. On Saturday, November 7, the networks all declared Joe Biden the president-elect. In her essential book, *January 6*, Julie Kelly questions how the media came to this unanimous and simultaneous conclusion "despite wide-spread documented irregularities and flagrant violations of state election law; despite the fact that the validity of 70 million absentee ballots had not been thoroughly vetted by state officials; despite the filing of numerous lawsuits related to illegal ballot processing and counting; and despite the fact that recounts would undoubtedly be demanded in close swing states."[129]

The Jacobin shock troops got the word even before the media did. "Activists," wrote Ball, "reoriented the Protect the Results protests toward a weekend of celebration." Ball added, "The planned day of celebration happened to coincide with the election being called on Nov. 7." Only the naive thought the timing a coincidence. Celebrating, like rioting, was orchestrated in the Jacobin world.

As expected, the major media shamelessly killed inconvenient stories, and Big Tech "de-amplified" those that survived.

To keep the *samizdat* humming, Byrne and his allies found new platforms—in Byrne's case, the Telegram app—on which to post their evidence. Activists like Ashli hungrily consumed this news, but others, elected Republicans included, chose not to know.

To keep the GOP at bay, the Jacobins played the most reliable card in their deck. Even before Election Day, activists were "calling attention to the racial implications of disenfranchising Black Detroiters," Ball boasted. That strategy was not limited to Detroit. Just months after the Floyd riots, elected Republicans and their corporate donors shied from confrontation. They would rather concede a disputed election than wear the Scarlet R.

The Jacobins dealt in absolutes. By December 2020, the Brennan Center for Justice was pleased to declare the 2020 election "one of the most secure elections in our history." What helped make it secure, claimed the center, was that "the votes were counted in a timely manner." Abraham Lincoln knew the election results before he went to bed on election night 1860. One hundred and sixty years later, votes were still being counted a week or more after the election. No matter. In 2020, once-respected institutions felt free to reject the evidence of their eyes and ears.

As for Trump, the Brennan Center scolded him for unleashing "an onslaught of outlandish claims about widespread fraud in the election." Worse, the presumably racist Trump was "shamelessly targeting the votes of Black and Latino citizens in several cities."[130] In the real world, there was nothing "outlandish" about the claims of Trump and his allies. As to the "targeting" of ethnic groups, that was something Boss Tweed had mastered more than a century prior. Trump was just dealing with the damage.

For those wanting a deeper statistical analysis of the fraud, Byrne's book, *The Deep Rig*, is an excellent resource. For insight as to how individual states violated their own laws to assure a Biden victory, Mollie Hemingway's *Rigged* is a must-read. To insist, as the Brennan Center did, that the election was among the most secure in our history was to spit in the eye of concerned citizens.

Moving in lockstep as was their norm, the Jacobins in media and government quickly settled on a name to describe any protest against the election's legitimacy. "Among the thousands of falsehoods Trump has uttered during his presidency," claimed Melissa Block of NPR, "this one in particular has earned the distinction of being called the 'big lie.'"[131] In fact, this label wasn't "earned." It was bestowed.

President-elect Biden's flailing attempt to explain the origin of the phrase proved to be what soccer fans call an "own goal": "I think the American public has a real good, clear look at who they are," Biden said of US Senators Ted Cruz and Josh Hawley. "They're part of the big lie, the big lie."[132] In *Mein Kampf*, Hitler accused the *Jews* of creating the "big lie." The alleged lie was that General Erich Ludendorff, a nationalist political leader, was to blame for Germany's loss in the Great War. In effect, Biden had libeled Hawley, Cruz, and Trump as liars in the same spirit Hitler libeled the Jews as liars. Despite Biden's bumbling, the libel endured. Today, Googling "Trump" and "big lie" nets more than a million hits.

The real big lie was the one told by the Brennan Center and the nation's Jacobins, namely that 2020 was "one of the most secure elections in our history." The media preserved this lie by killing stories like those produced by Project Veritas, shaming would-be whistleblowers, and refusing to investigate the "tsunami of evidence" that inundated conservative media outposts.

Rachel Powell saw through the media smokescreen. Knowing how willing the media were to lie about COVID, she assumed they would lie about the election. "I'm sitting here thinking about how everyone has been so complacent during COVID," she posted the day after the election. "The government knows exactly how far you can be pushed because the population has been successfully tested."[133]

Lisa Eisenhart did not mince words. "The elections were obviously rigged."

Said Sara Carpenter, "I knew [the election] was stolen not because Trump told me. I knew it from my own experience."

The Jacobins ignored the warnings of the Baker-Carter commission and the concern expressed in 2012 by the *New York Times* that fraud was "vastly more prevalent" when votes are cast by mail. Discouraged, too, was any challenge to the unconstitutional changes in election law. All but taboo was any inquiry into the role of the United States Postal Service. In retrospect, this still shocks. The nation entrusted sixty million votes, with negligible scrutiny, to workers who were told their jobs hinged on the outcome of the election.

On election night 2016, Hillary Clinton's female supporters and a few Beta males crowded the Javits Center in New York to celebrate Hillary's pending, glass-shattering victory. By evening's end, the only thing shattered were the dreams of the faithful. "Hillary Clinton supporters cry as Donald Trump takes the lead in the presidential race," lamented CNBC.[134] Crying, in fact, was the theme of the week and not just at the Javits Center. Some three thousand miles away, Google employees cried and hugged each other at an all-hands meeting the Friday after the election. "I find this election deeply offensive, and I know many of you do too," said Google co-founder Sergey Brin over the sound of wailing. "It's a stressful time, and it conflicts with many of our values."[135]

Unlike her weepy counterparts in Jacobin America, NYPD vet Sara Carpenter actually had values, unchanging values. As was true for the other women of January 6, those values sustained her in times of stress. Her belief in God and country, like her commitment to freedom, never wavered. In a city like New York, however, there were not many people who cared enough to see what she saw. "They were oblivious," said Sara of her friends and even her fellow parishioners. After the election, with COVID mania still raging in the city, Sara grew increasingly isolated.

On Thanksgiving weekend, Sara made a pilgrimage to Washington, DC, that proved eerily portentous. An ardent pro-lifer, as were many of the J6 women, Sara retraced the steps of the annual March for Life from the mall to the Capitol and ventured to the National Shrine of the Immaculate Conception to pray. There, in the company of a priest, she was rousted by a police officer who threatened to arrest them both if they did not leave. "DC Police," the NYPD vet observed, "were not ordinary cops." Six weeks later, she would have her observation confirmed.

As for Ashli Babbitt, after the election of 2020, she wasted no time on tears. "It was not like the election happened and her life changed," her mother, Micki Witthoeft, explained. "Her life was so many things. She was a lover of life, a liver of life, all the joys that life had to bring." As testament to that spirit, Ashli and husband Aaron flew off to Cabo San Lucas in late December 2020. Even on vacation in Mexico, however, Ashli never forgot where her duty lay. "Above all," said Micki, "she very much considered herself a patriot."

12

Epiphany

All but unmentioned in the coverage of the Capitol protest was that the date, January 6, already had a name: the Feast of the Epiphany. This is the day Christians celebrate the arrival of the Magi at the creche of the baby Jesus, early evidence that the Jewish messiah had come for the salvation of all the world. In everyday English, the word "epiphany" has come to mean "an intuitive grasp of reality through something (such as an event) usually simple and striking."

Many of the people who showed up in Washington on January 6 had an epiphany of their own, a sudden, intuitive awareness that they had to be there. For Ashli Babbitt, the decision to attend the rally was impulsive, a last-minute inspiration. Sitting on the beach in Cabo with Aaron on Christmas Day, Ashli saw on her phone a notice about the upcoming rally. She felt the urge to see up close what she presumed would be Trump's last speech as president. Aaron, a Trump supporter but less engaged than his wife, had to stay behind to reopen the couple's pool supply business. "There was no planning leading up to it," said Aaron of Ashli's decision. "But when Ashli has her mind set, she's just going to do it."[136]

For Rosanne Boyland, the inspiration to attend came from Trump himself. "My president has asked me to come support him," she told her mom, Cheryl, in their last conversation. "And I've done so many stupid things in my life that I'm going to do something that I really believe in."

In Rochester, Minnesota, Victoria White and her friends made the decision to attend the rally a day or two before the event. They drove through the night in shifts to reach Washington on time. In New York City, as late as the day before the rally, Sara Carpenter had no plan to attend. Later on January 5, some grade school pals—among her few political allies in a hostile city—called Sara urging her to come on down.

Used to strange hours while with the NYPD, Sara figured she could leave in the early morning hours, grab a few hours of shut-eye in her car, attend the rally, and be back home that night to make sure her sixteen-year-old son was ready for school the next day.

On New Year's Day, Rebecca Lavrenz, the great-grandmother from Colorado, got a call from her son asking if she intended to attend the rally. Knowing his mom refused to fly because of mandatory masking, he hinted, "You know it's only a twenty-five-hour drive. You can make it in two days." Rebecca prayed about it and came to the conclusion, "You know what, I think God's telling me to go." And so she went, stopping at St. Louis for a single overnight stay.

On that same New Year's Day in Boise, Yvonne St Cyr came to a similarly impromptu decision. The strong-willed Yvonne told husband Troy she was driving to Washington whether he was coming or not. As Yvonne later explained, "If we don't have free and fair elections, we don't have freedom anymore."[137] Fortunately, Troy was able to take a week's leave from the landscaping business where he worked and accompany Yvonne on the three-day drive, the first half through the nation's most unforgiving winter countryside.

The lure of the "Save America" protest that day proved to be more powerful than anyone anticipated. The rally was held on the Ellipse south of the White House, what is known informally as the "President's Lawn." Secret Service officers at various checkpoints monitored a crowd that they had no reason to believe would be violent or overly large. Trump supporters never initiated violence, not even at the hundreds of locally organized "Stop the Steal" protests held around the country in the uneasy days after the election.

If conservative women beat liberal women on political knowledge tests, they beat them even more decisively on appearance. The common understanding among conservative men is that the women who show up at Trump rallies look a whole lot better than the women who show up to protest those rallies. The ten women profiled here tend to bear that thesis out. Absent among them was the anger that distorts the demeanor of so many female activists on the left, let alone the purple hair and nose rings. Then, too, despite whatever relationship troubles these women have had, they did not see men as the enemy. They still wanted to look good. Above all, on January 6, they wanted their dress to reflect their affection for their country and their support for the president.

Despite the weather, despite the limited expectations of success, the protestors seemed delighted to be among like-minded people on what seemed to them a historic mission. "There is a sea of nothing but red, white and blue patriots for Trump," Ashli told viewers on a live Facebook feed. "God bless America, patriots."

Said her mom, Micki Witthoeft, "I can see in that video that she was absolutely in her element, having a wonderful time."

Aaron agreed. From her texts he concluded, "She was having the best day of her life."[138]

Still images from that day capture Ashli in her gray knit Ocean Beach brewery cap, her light-brown hair streaming out from beneath it, framing a smile as wide as the Potomac. With a Trump flag worn cape-like over her black jacket and tied around her neck, central casting could not have found a more radiant avatar of American patriotism.

After a thirty-five-hour drive from Boise, Yvonne and Troy were enthused to be in Washington. The couple arrived on January 5 and stayed at a hotel in old town Alexandria that friends recommended. Wanting a spot as close to Trump as possible, the couple left Alexandria before dawn and rode the Washington Metro to the South Capitol station.

To their surprise, the Ellipse was already hopping when they got there. Fellow patriots, most in good spirits, many carrying American flags and Trump banners, had arrived before them and taken their places close to the stage. Others circulated around the Ellipse, and more kept pouring in. Storm Team4 meteorologist Chuck Bell had predicted a "windy and cold" day, and Yvonne came dressed for the occasion in a well-padded, white parka and a red-white-and-blue 2A ski cap. The forecast held true, if not by Boise standards, at least by those of Washington.

Rosanne Boyland seemed in her element that day as well. Justin Winchell sent her father, Bret, a final photo of Rosanne, walking along in a Mossy Oak brand dark hoodie, stylishly ripped jeans, and stars-and-stripes sunglasses. Rosanne had a big smile on her cherubic face, a "Save America" sign in one hand, and a Gadsden flag resting on her right shoulder.

Designed during the Revolutionary War, the Gadsden flag pictures on its yellow face a timber rattler poised to strike. Below it are the immortal words, "Don't tread on me." In a recent Ken Burns documentary on PBS, the narrator explains the careful thinking behind Benjamin Franklin's conception of the rattlesnake imagery. One doubts that Burns, an outspoken Trump hater, knew that the FBI had identified this historic imagery with the MAGA movement as a potential sign of "Militia Violent Extremism."[139]

Victoria White and her Minnesota friends thought nothing of the thirty-degree temperatures. She found a sea of happy, singing people. "There was a feeling of freedom again," said Victoria, who was pleased to be around people who did not care whether she wore a mask. Despite the cold, she was keen on having a good time and showing her support for the president. A photo from that day captures this striking thirty-nine-year-old mother of four looking determined amid a group of smiling friends in a fur-collared black coat with her red MAGA baseball cap and matching red sweater.

In her pink knitted cap and cool shades, the fur-trim hood of her black parka pulled up around her neck, Rachel Powell looked much too young and hip to be the mother of eight, but that's what this "very granola, very crunchy" forty-year-old Pennsylvanian was. Rachel had met up with new friend Kevin Lynn in Lancaster, Pennsylvania, on January 5, and they rode to the Capitol together to hear Trump speak.

The program began at 9 a.m. with various speakers including former New York City mayor Rudy Giuliani and Texas attorney general Ken Paxton. Trump was scheduled to speak at 11 a.m. Inexplicably late, he started at noon. The protest was quixotic, to be sure, but not foolish. More than one hundred House members were prepared to challenge the certification of the electoral college results scheduled that day. Impressively, a dozen senators had signed on as well. This was to be the most serious challenge to an electoral count in American history. As matters stood, Trump did not have enough votes in either the Senate or the House to thwart Biden's certification, but he hoped that a good turnout on his lawn and a subsequent march to the Capitol would stiffen the backbone of wavering congressional Republicans.[140]

That morning, Rebecca Lavrenz, keeping warm in a dark jacket with a white sweater offsetting her red-and-white scarf and white knitted cap, walked from her daughter's apartment just a few blocks away to the east side of the Capitol across from the Supreme Court, arriving about 10 a.m. Quite possibly America's best-looking great-grandmother, Rebecca had been a finalist in the Miss Iowa contest back in the day and actually won the "Miss Congeniality" award.

At the Capitol, Rebecca merged into a sea of patriots whose enthusiasm and high spirits impressed her. As she had come to pray, not to protest, she felt no need to go to the Ellipse, a goodly walk away. Seeing others who had come for the same reason, she made her way towards a platform where worship and prayer were being offered. As she approached, however, she had her own personal epiphany. "I had this huge presence of God on me," says Rebecca. "I couldn't even stand up. I started weeping and sat down on the curb. It lasted about ten minutes, and then it lifted."

Empowered by the experience, Rebecca joined the others on the platform. There she prayed publicly about the 1620 Covenant. More commonly known as the Mayflower Compact, this document was signed by forty-one men on the

Mayflower as it anchored off the coast of Cape Cod. The signers "solemnly and mutually, in the Presence of God and one another, covenant and combine ourselves together into a civil Body Politick, for our better Ordering and Preservation." This nation, Rebecca believes, was consecrated to the glory of God and the advancement of the Christian faith. Despite her experiences that day, or perhaps because of them, she believes that America will one day fulfill the covenant's promises.

On the very early morning trip in from suburban Cleveland, Christine Priola sensed a more somber mood among her compatriots than on the two earlier bus trips she had taken to DC to attend Trump rallies. In any case, Christine arrived too late to hear Trump speak. Dressed in a red Bebe coat with hood, blue leggings inscribed with "Make American Great Again," a bright-red jacket, and a red-white-and-blue scarf, Christine joined the festive crowds on the east side of the building.

At noon, President Trump began his speech at the Ellipse. He marveled at the size of the crowd, and this time there was no need for exaggeration. Dr. Gold estimates an easy million. "Many of you have traveled from all across the nation to be here," said Trump, "and I want to thank you for the extraordinary love. That's what it is. There's never been a movement like this, ever, ever. For the extraordinary love for this amazing country, and this amazing movement, thank you."

The crowd, Ashli and Rosanne and Rachel and Victoria among them, responded by chanting, "We love Trump." In the speech, Trump pinned his hopes on the actions of Vice President Mike Pence. "States want to revote," said the president. "The states got defrauded. They were given false information. They voted on it. Now they want to recertify. They want it back. All Vice President Pence has to do is send it back to the states to recertify, and we become president, and you are the happiest people." From the crowd's perspective, Pence was going to be the day's hero or its villain. Trump made the process seem much simpler than it ever could possibly be, but if he was deceiving anyone, he started by deceiving himself.

"If this happened to the Democrats," Trump continued, "there'd be hell all over the country going on. There'd be hell all over the country." About this, he was absolutely right. The Ball Dossier had promised protests, and maybe worse, at some four hundred sites if Trump prevailed. Trump, however, did not expect violence from his supporters. "You're the real people, you're the people that built this nation," he told them. "You're not the people that tore down our nation."

Trump soon followed with the speech's most quoted line—most quoted on conservative media, that is—"I know that everyone here will soon be marching over to the Capitol building to peacefully and patriotically make your voices heard."[141] As Naomi Wolf observed, this admonition "had been deleted from all of the news coverage that I read." Said Wolf, "Because of lies such as these in legacy media—lies which I and millions of others believed—half of our nation's electorate was smeared and delegitimized, and I myself was misled."

The House committee did much of the misleading. "The rioters were inside the halls of Congress," wrote committee chairman Bennie Thompson, "because the head of the executive branch of our government, the then President of the United States, told them to attack."[142]

Trump concluded his speech at 1:12 p.m., saying defiantly, "We fight. We fight like hell and if you don't fight like hell, you're not going to have a country anymore. So let's walk down Pennsylvania Avenue." Twenty minutes before the speech's conclusion, protestors had breached the weakly protected outer perimeter of the Capitol grounds. By the time any of the marchers reached the Capitol, they would have had no idea that there had ever been a protective barrier on its west side.

Dr. Simone Gold, wearing a long, black parka with fur cuffs and a fur-trimmed hood, left the Ellipse shortly before Trump finished. She then made the forty-five-minute walk with John Strand to the east side of the Capitol. "It was a happy, joyful day," she remembered. There were grandmas pushing baby carriages, groups literally singing "Kumbaya," and people of every race mixing peacefully together. Gold had a permit to speak on the Capitol grounds. Her subject was not the election but medical freedom. She was not "anti-vaxx," as the media insisted, but anti-mandate, whether COVID vaccines, lockdowns, or masks.

Aaron Babbitt is sure Ashli stayed to the very end of Trump's speech. Her mood was still upbeat. "We are walking to the Capitol in a mob," Ashli told the viewers on Facebook. "There's an estimated over three million people here today." The Federal Protective Service estimated that ten thousand to fifteen thousand people were walking toward the Capitol. Ashli surely overestimated the size of the crowd, but the feds underestimated it. Whatever the actual number, no one seemed overly worried. Marchers saw little police presence and no effort at all to discourage their march to the Capitol. At the Capitol itself, House and Senate members convened at 1 p.m.

Sara Carpenter came prepared for the cold in a dark-green anorak-style coat, black pants and boots, and, of course, a red MAGA baseball cap. Tired, cold, and hungry, she thought of leaving early, but as she sat in the parking garage, she got a call from the friend who had urged her to come. "C'mon, Sara," he said. "Let's walk to the Capitol. It's all so patriotic. It's going to be great."

Although not good in crowds, Sara couldn't resist and joined the march. "It was kids. It was dogs. It was wonderful," she said. As a former NYPD officer, she presumed the police would not let the marchers near the Capitol building, but unknown to her, the conspirators had other plans.

13

Setup

About fifteen minutes before Trump had concluded his speech, Mike Pence tweeted out a letter he had not cleared with the president. In the letter's opening, Pence would seem to have swallowed the "big lie." Wrote Pence, "After an election with significant allegations of voting irregularities and numerous instances of officials setting aside state election law, I share the concerns of millions of Americans about the integrity of this election."

Later in the letter, Pence affirmed the right of members of Congress to protest what was clearly a flawed election. "Given the voting irregularities that took place in our November elections and the disregard of state election statutes by some officials," wrote Pence, "I welcome the efforts of Senate and House members who have stepped forward to use their authority under the law to raise objections and present evidence."

These, however, were not the words that shaped history. Said Pence for the ages, "It is my considered judgment that my oath to support and defend the Constitution constrains me from claiming unilateral authority to determine which electoral votes should be counted and which should not."[143]

Pence did not come to this conclusion casually. He must have suspected, however, that had he sent the results back to the states for further adjudication, he might have launched a civil war. What he got instead was a largely peaceful protest. When news of Pence's letter circulated among the crowd, Rebecca Lavrenz, praying on the Capitol's east side, sensed the people becoming a little edgy and agitated. On the Capitol's west side, the action was already under way prior to Pence's tweet.

At least a half hour before Trump's speech ended, Ray Epps, a large man wearing a Trump hat and tactical gear, was captured on video herding what the MPD called an "ad hoc" group of protestors down Pennsylvania Avenue. "We are going to the Capitol," he shouted. "That's where our problems are." This particular group of protestors was not provoked by Trump's speech. They didn't stick around to hear it.[144]

The most visible of the January 6 provocateurs, Epps had been caught on video the night before urging an impromptu audience to go "*in to* the Capitol." Skeptical of his motives, those around him chanted almost as a chorus—"Fed, Fed, Fed, Fed." On January 6, Epps helped lead his set of marchers to the Peace Circle at the end of Pennsylvania Avenue and on to the Pennsylvania Pathway. There, the protestors faced two light metal barricades with only five USCP officers, two of them female, guarding the second, better-fortified set.

The protestors made their way easily to that second set. In the lead was Ryan Samsel, a young Pennsylvanian with a criminal past. For a few minutes, Samsel and the others jawed with the police. At this point, Epps approached Samsel, whispered something in his ear, and Samsel began to push hard against the barricade. Others joined in, and the barricade top-pled, knocking over a policewoman. In an unlikely gesture, Samsel helped her to her feet. This first breach occurred at 12:53 p.m.[145] Minutes later, a small crowd breached another lightly guarded barricade just to the south. The police offered no real resistance. At 12:58, a single individual pulled down the temporary fencing protecting the lawn and with it the signs saying, "area closed." The USCP closed off the area not because of the protest but because of the construction on the inaugural platform.

Within a few minutes, a crowd had gathered at the gates in front of the west plaza area of the Capitol. At the front of the crowd, giving directions, was the ubiquitous Epps. The Capitol Police manned the terrace above the crowd. At 12:59, a fifty-year-old Trump supporter from Pennsylvania named Benjamin Phillips, the father of two teenagers, collapsed and would soon die of natural causes. A minute later, Vice President Pence entered the House Chamber to convene a joint session to certify the electoral votes. Unaware of the disorder at the Capitol, Trump continued his speech on the Ellipse.

At 1:06, while Rep. Paul Gosar was challenging the certification of the Arizona vote, USCP deputy chief Eric Waldow ordered the "less lethal" team to open fire on the protestors now numbering about a thousand. Trump was still speaking at the Ellipse. The crowd that he allegedly incited to insurrection would not arrive at the Capitol for close to an hour.

Inexperienced with crowds of this size, the USCP began shooting a barrage of grenades, gas, and rubber bullets into the growing mass of protestors on the Capitol's west side. "That was a shooting gallery out there," said Stan Kephart, the use-of-force expert who reviewed the video footage for the *Epoch Times*. "There was no tactical reason for it at all."[146]

Early on, protestor Joshua Black was shot with a rubber bullet that lodged in his cheek. In violation of all norms, the police were shooting at head level. This bizarrely unprofessional attack from on high would last, on and off, for an hour or more. If the protestors grew restive and angry, it was not because of Pence's letter. It was because they were being targeted by an ill-trained and disorganized police force, at least some of whom were openly contemptuous of Trump supporters. Independent journalist Tayler Hansen had been covering riots in cities across the country throughout the summer of 2020. Having grown up in a police family, he came to the conclusions he did about January 6 with reluctance. "The cops created this mess," he said. "I have never seen police brutality like I saw that day."[147]

At 1:28, fifty-six-year-old father of five, Kevin Greeson, collapsed after a Capitol Police flash bang exploded in his face. Retired Marine Sergeant Victor Mellor captured the moment on his cell phone.[148] Greeson would soon die of cardiac arrest. By 1:30, the USCP had reestablished a police line on the west plaza and would hold it for about an hour. At 1:32, one officer was recorded objecting to the launch of smoke grenades: "It's just going to make it worse. Hey stop, hold." Protestors were picking up grenades and hurling them back behind police lines.

The mood was shifting. Epps was at the front lines communicating with individual protestors. At 1:38, Trump tweeted, "Please support our local police and law enforcement. They are truly on the side of our Country. Stay peaceful." At 1:49, a "riot" was declared. Those who stayed to the end of Trump's speech would not yet have arrived at the Capitol. A minute later, Capitol Police on the west plaza shot an errant round of gas that sent the maskless officers scurrying for cover.

At 1:59, on the east side of the Capitol, demonstrators overwhelmed the police by their sheer mass and made their way to the east steps. When the police retreated into the building, the crowd followed. Back on the Capitol's west side, an officer shoved protestor Derrick Vargo off the terrace railing twenty or so feet above the ground, "a serious crime" according to Kephart. Vargo, who had hoped to plant a Trump flag, was retreating when pushed. He was badly injured.

At 2:10, protestors managed to get by the police on the west side of the Capitol and began breaking windows. At 2:12, Epps texted his nephew boasting that he had "orchestrated" events at the Capitol. At 2:13, Trump tweeted, "I am asking for everyone at the Capitol to remain peaceful. No violence! Remember WE are the party of law and order." Meanwhile, on the west side, a body cam captured one officer lamenting, "We can hit them with a lot of pain compliance, but we're hitting innocent people. We're taking out one and getting ten angrier."

Said another, less thoughtfully, "We're shooting zombies."

Not until 2:24 did Trump express his disappointment in Pence, tweeting, "Mike Pence didn't have the courage to do what should have been done to protect our country and our Constitution." The House committee blamed Trump's tweet for the surge of protestors that soon followed. To sell this, they had to overlook a misfired round of CS gas that chased the maskless police officers from their defensive positions, forcing them back into the Capitol through the soon to be notorious tunnel. The crowd followed.[149]

For the next several hours, the behavior of the USCP and the MDP had to confound anyone who was looking for an overall strategy. The police defended some entrances as though the Capitol were the Alamo. At other entrances, the police ushered protestors in as if they were tourists and this just an ordinary Wednesday in January. The confusion may have been planned. USCP Chief Steven Sund was kept in the dark by the FBI and other intelligence agencies—possibly even by his own head of intelligence—about the potential for violence at the Capitol. As shall be seen, Sund's requests for assistance from the National Guard were denied before January 6 and inexplicably delayed during the siege. His officers were unprepared and overwhelmed. They were victims of an apparent setup as much as they were victimizers.[150]

14

Entrapped

Each of the ten women profiled in this book did enter the building, two only barely. Their respective experiences inside defy any kind of generalization. Lisa Eisenhart was one of the eight who survived. She and her son Eric Munchel arrived the night before and stayed at the Grand Hyatt hotel. Wearing a blue plaid jacket under her tactical vest and a red MAGA knitted cap, Lisa was not hard to spot in the crowd. Were it not for the vest, she would look like your average grandma at a kid's soccer game.

Not much of a Trump fan, Lisa skipped the rally on the Ellipse and hung around the Capitol listening to speeches. Eric wore an iPhone on his tactical vest and recorded their nearly forty-minute queue into the Capitol and their eleven minutes within. Ryan J. Reilly, the chief chronicler of an outfit known as the "Sedition Hunters," has the entire video posted unedited under the heading, "Zip Tie Guy Capitol Attack Video."[151] The video, however, shows something entirely unlike an "attack."

Eric started recording shortly before 2 p.m. The mood outside was largely festive, and the air was punctuated with frequent chants of "USA, USA." Eric walked protectively behind his mother, his hand on her backpack. To access the door, they had to climb up the steps under the scaffolding amid a crowd that stayed impressively patient and calm.

As they entered through an open door at 2:37 p.m., several police stood passively along the corridor. With Lisa in the lead, the two mounted the stairway to the Rotunda. The protestors milling about inside seemed excited to be there and, like Lisa and Eric, confused about what to do next. As they wandered, Lisa joined a male-heavy chant of "treason, treason," and grabbed a pile of zip ties sitting exposed on the side of a corridor.

As recorded, Lisa was heard telling her son, "We're going straight to federal prison if we go in there with weapons." Although both had concealed carry permits, neither brought their guns to Washington, an unusual display of prudence for would-be insurrectionists. As the court later acknowledged, Lisa "was not a member of any suspect group, did not do any advance planning, nor did she use force to enter the Capitol on January 6."[152]

For a few minutes, the pair followed a group of rowdy young men whom Eric repeatedly cautioned, "Don't vandalize anything, we aren't Antifa," and then, more forcefully, "You break shit. I break you." The viewer sees what Lisa saw, and that was a total absence of violence and vandalism. What they did not see or hear was the shooting death of Ashli Babbitt, which took place while they were in the vast building.

Looking for an exit, Lisa and Eric found their way to the gallery of the Senate chamber. There was little police presence in the chamber and none in the gallery. Lisa remembers thinking that this was where the Kavanaugh protestors were arrested, and she knew they got off with a wrist slap. She could live with that. A photographer made Eric infamous when he took a picture of him holding the zip ties while in the Senate gallery. This photo earned Eric the media designation "zip-tie guy" and went viral quickly.

On the following morning, Eric was contacted by the *London Times.* Unaware of any possible consequences, Lisa did the interview. "This country was founded on revolution," Lisa said defiantly. "If they're going to take every legitimate means from us, and we can't even express ourselves on the internet, we won't even be able to speak freely, what is America for? I'd rather die as a 57-year-old woman than live under oppression. I'd rather die and would rather fight."[153] The DOJ took issue with this quote and included it in its Memorandum Opinion. Implied was that Lisa's stirring defense of free speech was seditious. Also cited was Lisa's shout of "treason, treason."

Lisa remembered correctly about the Bret Kavanaugh hearings. Just two years earlier in that same Senate gallery, screaming women repeatedly interrupted an "official proceeding," the Senate vote to confirm Kavanaugh to the Supreme Court. More than once, Vice President Pence had to stop the vote and call for order. Fourteen protestors were arrested. Others were arrested for blocking hallways and Senate offices.[154] Two days earlier, nearly three hundred protestors were arrested at a US Senate building for unlawfully demonstrating. As NPR reported, "Most of those charged this week with disorderly conduct, crowding or obstructing paid fines of $35 or $50."[155]

At approximately 2:43 p.m., Rebecca Lavrenz entered the Capitol through the open East Rotunda doors. Said Rebecca, "I felt that if those doors opened I was supposed to go through." After entering, engulfed in a crowd, she climbed the east stairs and headed towards the Rotunda. For the next few minutes, the last few minutes of Ashli Babbitt's life, Rebecca walked around the Rotunda unaware of the tragedy unfolding nearby. She didn't yell, didn't shout, spoke to no one, and saw no violence.

Although no one told her to leave, at 2:51 p.m., she climbed down the stairs she had just ascended. Before leaving, Rebecca spoke to a police officer, but she has no clear memory of what they spoke about. She left the building ten minutes after walking in, not knowing that she would eventually be charged with four misdemeanors.[156]

Rebecca had lost touch with her son and grandson, who stayed outside the building on the west side. After leaving the Capitol, she milled about for a while amid her fellow patriots, the mood still largely joyful and jubilant. Upon realizing that the members of Congress had already left the building, Rebecca headed back to her daughter's house. When her daughter returned from a work assignment in Florida a few days later, the two of them drove back to Colorado together. In the interim, when someone suggested that Rebecca might be arrested, she responded with an incredulous, "No!"

Christine Priola entered the Capitol from the east side as well. Following the crowd, she walked in through open doors and milled about with her friends. During the twenty or so minutes she spent in the Capitol, she talked to a police officer or two looking for guidance but got none. She spent much of her time there admiring the architecture.

Wandering alone into the vacated Senate chambers, Christine was photographed with the sign reading, "The Children Cry Out for Justice." The one officer present was just watching people come and go. Not until Christine exited through the west side did she see the chaos outside the building or sense it. Getting sprayed by the police on the way out was the only real drama of her Capitol visit.

For Dr. Simone Gold, there was even less drama, at least until the police started shooting flash-bangs into the generally peaceful crowd. When the doors swung open from the inside, Dr. Gold sensed a surge of excitement sweep through the crowd of the sort one would feel at a sporting event. Video would show a protestor who had entered from the west side opening the East Rotunda doors. At the time, with a crowd between her and the doors, Dr. Gold had no idea how they opened. Two minutes later, the video captured Strand physically supporting her as they were both swept in all but involuntarily.

The two ascended the nearby staircase and were shoved along with the crowd wherever the crowd went. They had no idea how to get out. By chance, Gold and Strand soon found themselves in the spacious National Statutory Hall. Here, Gold tried to give her speech, but a police officer prodded her and Strand toward the Rotunda. In the Rotunda, Gold stood on the base of a statue to speak. Someone passed her a bullhorn, and several people came over to listen. Following her five-minute speech, she took questions.

A police officer then informed the small crowd that it was now possible to leave through the east doors. Gold and Strand thanked him for the info and headed towards the doors. Exiting was not easy, but they managed to squeeze their way through the incoming crowds and onto the Capitol steps. "In the moment," said Gold, "this was a big fat nothing." She and Strand left soon after for a speaking engagement in West Palm Beach on January 10. Still oblivious to the fallout from her day at the Capitol, she did not even mention January 6. It wasn't until a friend texted a photo of her on an FBI "most wanted" list that she realized how costly a big fat nothing could be.

Given her Queens upbringing and her years in the NYPD, Sara Carpenter had a more turbulent experience at the Capitol than Christine or Rebecca or Simone. Sara's entrance, however, was entirely peaceful. Someone told her the south Senate door on the west side was open, and a policewoman waved her in that direction. "They're letting everyone in?" Sara asked. They apparently were. Even before entering, however, she was disturbed by the lack of crowd control. No one was giving vocal commands or directing traffic. She wondered to herself, "Why are they letting this happen?" As a former cop, she felt the urge to step in and help out. "I was looking for police," she explained. "I was looking for them. That's what led me up the steps."

Not seeing anyone in control, she floated along with the crowd and found herself in the Rotunda. "It was so calm, so beautiful," said Sara. She took out her cell phone and shot video of the ceiling. The calm did not last. Suddenly, she heard a man yelling behind her. Wary of crowds, and at five-foot, four-inches, unable to see above them, Sara got caught up in a scrum and appears to have had something of a panic attack. She soon found herself in front of a row of police in tactical gear with a crowd of Trump supporters and/or provocateurs pushing her from behind.

"The cops were giving no vocal commands," said Sara. "I was waiting for them to act like cops." Sara is still not quite sure what happened in that encounter, but she felt like a trapped animal. When she confronted the police, one officer pushed her, and she pushed back.

The front end of this confrontation has not surfaced on video, but the climax has. Clearly upset, Sara yelled at the police, "I was at 9-11. I touched the bodies."

One of the officers, off screen, taunted her, "You're a fucking animal. You're a fucking animal."

Sara shouted back defiantly, "I'm a fucking animal." She then pulled off her MAGA cap, her dirty-blond hair streaming over her shoulders, and yelled, "I *am* a fucking animal." Now shaking a tambourine in their unseen faces, she yelled louder, "Do you hear me? Do you hear me in the back? You want a fucking animal?"[157]

Sara's street experience seems to have kicked in. "I have been in life threatening situations," she explained. "A tactic is to look crazy. It gets the other person off balance. Now you control the energy." At that moment, there is no disputing who controlled the energy, but Sara had no way to channel it. "I didn't know where to go," she admitted.

Sara got caught up in another scrum on the way out. Three officers surrounded her and started macing her. She remembers being pushed and nearly trampled. She grabbed a small Chinese woman by the hand and helped lead her out. In a surreal moment, a man handed her a wine bottle, saying it was Nancy Pelosi's. Sara was savvy enough to leave the bottle behind. A police officer she approached told her, "A little girl has been shot on the other side." Sara pulled out a rosary to calm herself.

To the Department of Justice, Sara's tambourine seemed borderline criminal. It also made her easy to identify. "The CCTV video of the Capitol Rotunda next shows the woman cross the room to an exit," reads the FBI's statement of facts. "Before exiting, however, the woman turns back to the room and raises her hands in the air. In her left hand, she holds a tambourine."[158]

When Sara finally emerged from the building thirty-four minutes after entering, red-faced from the mace, an independent videographer questioned her. "The breach happened," she said to him on camera. "Congress needs to come out, and President Trump needs to be certified. The crowd needs to move back so no one else gets hurt."[159] Sara admits to not being herself at the moment. Her ribs were bruised, and she likely suffered a concussion. "I was antagonized, brutalized, entrapped," she said.

Sara soon met up with her friend at a prearranged meeting spot. "Matt, we got to get the hell out of here," she told him. He had no idea what had happened. When Sara got to the car and started driving, a peace came over her. Every song she listened to seemed to have a tambourine in it. As shall be seen, that peace did not last long.

Victoria White had an even rougher go of it. Victoria was among the last people to leave the Ellipse. As she marched to the Capitol, she found herself amid a crowd of happy, singing people. Police made no effort to dissuade them from heading toward the Capitol despite the donnybrook well underway.

By the time Victoria arrived at the Capitol, the protestors had already swarmed the lower west terrace. More adventurous than was good for her, she joined them. There she saw a man pounding away at an exterior window with what appeared to be a crowbar. Victoria thought to herself, "Who brings something like that to a Trump rally?" The men nearby agreed. They were yelling, "Antifa," thinking him a plant.

Upset by his lawlessness, Victoria tried to pull the vandal down, yelling, "We don't do that. That's not us."

Then two men grabbed Victoria and pulled her off the man with the crowbar. "Get her out of here," said a guy with a bullhorn.

"I felt instantly they were going to kill me," said Victoria.[160] The *Epoch Times* interviewed her for a well-produced documentary, *The True Story of January 6*. At the time of the film's release, the "suspicious actor" breaking the window had still not been arrested.

Victoria's adventure was just beginning. Her account of what happened, substantiated by the video, differs from the DOJ's account as starkly as Johnny Depp's did from Amber Heard's. The DOJ does give Victoria credit for "arguing with rioters who were attempting to break the glass doors of an entrance."[161] The dispute, in fact, involved a window. In the DOJ account, Victoria then "pushed" her way to the tunnel entrance on the west terrace.

A high percentage of the selected video footage that entertained Democrats for the last three years was shot in and around this entrance. While protestors were freely walking into the Capitol through multiple other entrances, the police had withdrawn behind double-glassed doors well inside the tunnel. Not expecting to be stuck inside the tunnel, protestors surged in, some voluntarily, some not. If this wasn't a conscious trap on the cops' part, it was a lethal blunder.

At some point, the MPD, now in riot gear, decided to enter the fray and push the protestors out of the tunnel. This was made doubly difficult as protestors were still flooding in. As Victoria tells the story, she was "pushed into the tunnel" by the crowd and "sucked in" by the momentum.

The video leaves little dispute about what happened next. As documented in Victoria's lawsuit against two MPD officers, Jason Bagshaw, then a lieutenant, and Neil McAllister,

Victoria endured what was arguably the most severe police beating of a female ever captured on video.[162] This oddly gratuitous assault took place some ninety minutes after the last Congress member left the Capitol.

The five-minute sequence began with Bagshaw striking Victoria in the head with a baton five times in seven seconds. He then speared her with the baton twice. An officer standing on a ledge in the tunnel sprayed her in the face with mace despite Victoria's plea for him to stop. Visibly bleeding and unable to move, she caught seven more blows from Bagshaw while an unidentified officer pulled her back and forth by the hair. Bagshaw then maneuvered around the other officers to get a better shot at his victim, spearing and poking Victoria with the baton about the neck and head. The ledge officer sprayed her once again with mace, and another officer struck her twelve times in the face. Before he was through, Bagshaw punched Victoria in the face, landing five blows in five seconds, and took a few more baton swipes at her as she tried to flee. Use-of-force expert Stan Kephart thought the police actions in the tunnel dangerous and indefensible. Said Kephart, "They punished people, instead of dispersing or arresting them."[163]

In her documentary on Victoria White, journalist Lara Logan shows this sequence in graphic detail and documents the MPD regulations the officers violated.[164] When I asked Victoria why the officers might have singled out women for punishment, she answered, "They targeted the women to get the men riled up."

If that was the officers' motive, they seem to have succeeded with protestor Kyle Fitzsimons. His defense attorneys argued that he threw various objects at the officers to stop the beating. In making their case, the *prosecutors* confirmed Bagshaw as the primary offender. They conceded that he "threw five left-handed jab punches" at Victoria's face and that he "repeatedly struck or attempted to strike [her] in the head or upper body." That said, they argued that Bagshaw's actions did not prompt Fitzsimons to intervene on Victoria's behalf.[165] For his efforts, Fitzsimons was sentenced to eighty-seven months in prison. Bagshaw was promoted to the rank of commander.

"I remember saying to the officer," Victoria told Joe Hanneman of the *Epoch Times*, "'You took an oath to the Constitution, and you called me the B word,' and that's when I got one of the hardest blows that I can remember." In the melee, she lost her shoes, her coat, and her cell phone as she was "ping-ponged" between officers. The police took her into custody before releasing her into the cold of a Washington night, shoeless and coatless. Borrowing a phone, she called the one number she could remember, that of her sister back in Minnesota.

Once arrangements were made, Victoria walked in her stocking feet to Union Station to meet up with her friends. Still smelling of mace, she rode back to Minnesota frightened of what the future held but unbroken. "God allowed me to live for a reason," said Victoria, "and I believe it's to speak the truth and to tell people what happened that day and what's continuing to happen to American citizens."[166]

Excited by the atmosphere and Trump's speech, Yvonne St Cyr skipped along Constitution Avenue after the Trump rally, shooting video as she skipped. "I don't skip," Troy told her when prodded to keep up. Had Troy known what lay ahead, he would have done cartwheels to stay alongside Yvonne. He soon lost sight of her.

By the time Yvonne arrived at the Capitol, she found the protestors already at the doors on the west side of the building. Heading right to the front, she was among the first to enter the tunnel. "I wanted to be part of history. I wanted someday to tell my grandchildren I was there. I was there for you," she would say later.[167] As the tunnel filled up with protestors, Yvonne stood up on an air-conditioning unit on the side of the tunnel and recorded the action below. The police were surging forward, clearing out the protestors. Wary of stepping down on top of the police, she stayed in place until a police officer prodded her with a long pole. This was all captured on video. Forced down, she lost a shoe and her cell phone in the process.

What happened next was equal parts miraculous and unfortunate. Even if Yvonne had kept her phone and was able to get a signal, she would not have been able to call Troy from outside the building. It was simply too loud. Desperate to find him, she climbed through a nearby broken window, told an unknown man she had lost her phone, and asked if she could borrow his. He pulled a phone out of his pocket and asked, "Might this be yours?" It was. If the man wasn't a fed, he was a godsend. Yvonne prefers the latter interpretation: "I feel God put me in that room for a reason."

The unfortunate part is that her quest to call Troy put her inside the building for a few minutes. The DOJ took note. "After leaving the Tunnel," her sentencing document reads, "St Cyr climbed through a broken window, entering a Senator's hideaway room adjacent to the Tunnel. Once inside, St Cyr helped another rioter enter and made a livestreamed video of herself while occupying the room."[168]

Like many others, Troy and Yvonne lost cell phone coverage for most of the afternoon. This time they got through. As Yvonne was leaving the Capitol, the Capitol Police launched another inexplicable round of CS gas. "Why did they let it get that crazy," Yvonne wondered. "Were they setting us up?"

She was not alone in that assessment. Body cam footage captured an MPD officer saying, "They set us the fuck up. That's what they did. They set us up, they set up [Unit] Sixty-Four to fail."

A colleague responded, "Absolutely."[169]

The poor cell phone reception was not the only obstacle the president faced in calling off the protestors. For starters, they were not the zombies the media presumed them to be. For another, Trump was not about to yield to the obligatory lie that the election was "free and fair." Yes, Trump could have said more sooner, but when at 4:17 p.m., he said on a posted video, "You have to go home now. We have to have peace. We have to have law and order. We don't want anybody hurt," Twitter promptly applied a warning label, saying, "The claim of election fraud is disputed, and this tweet can't be replied to, Retweeted, or liked due to a risk of violence." Facebook blocked the post as well.[170]

It was almost dark when Yvonne and Troy managed to meet up at the West Front Fountain. By this time, the MPD had helped the USCP clear the Capitol of protestors. "I wasn't going to leave until I found her," said an increasingly anxious Troy. It was not the happiest of reunions. Each of the two was upset with the other for getting separated, although later Yvonne would think it providential that they had. Their children could not have endured the loss of both parents. The next morning, the couple did a Facebook live presentation from their Alexandria hotel. They had come to think of the Capitol incursion as a setup. Their message to the folks back in Idaho: we've got to get our country back somehow, some way.

At the rally, Rachel Powell had helped Kevin Lynn operate his camera. At rally's end, inspired by Trump's call to action, she and Kevin joined the march as well. Along the way, they got separated, and Rachel found herself alone amid the crowd on the Capitol's crowded West Front. It would prove to be a fateful separation. This mother of eight, and today the grandmother of six, got fully caught up in the moment.

At one point, Rachel can be seen on video in her telltale pink hat helping a row of men push a makeshift barrier manned by the police. From there, she found her way to the tunnel entrance. In her most dramatic act, Rachel helped some men smash a makeshift battering ram through a Capitol window. As she stood by the window, someone unknown passed her an ice axe to pull out the remaining shards. When asked how she got swept up in the mayhem, Rachel answered, "I am completely in pain. I was hit with a baton, grabbed and thrown, sprayed. My whole body was on fire."[171]

If the ice axe was not trouble enough, Rachel picked up a bullhorn and shouted what sounded like instructions to the rioters inside. Speaking of conspiracy theories, Forrest Rogers, the chief Sedition Hunter, reported Rachel to the FBI, thinking he had "identified a ringleader in a premeditated campaign to invade the Capitol." He hadn't.[172] As Powell explained, "I was by myself—I didn't rendezvous with a bunch of people…I didn't meet militias."

Powell knew she had screwed up, knew she got caught in a moment of unreason, but as remorseful as she was for "ruining my family's life," she had no regrets about the cause that brought her to Washington. "Our whole country and everything about our lives is determined by voting," she said. If she were "duped," she added, it was for walking into what very well may have been a setup.

In the first few weeks after her day at the Capitol, Rachel did an interview with celebrity journalist Ronan Farrow. Farrow's article on Rachel appeared in the *New Yorker* on February 1, 2021. In the course of her interview, Rachel told Farrow that when she was near the tunnel entrance, she heard a woman's dying breaths from beneath a pile of humanity and later saw her dead body. More than three weeks after the event, editors felt obliged to add this caveat—"The New Yorker was unable to confirm whether a woman died there."

A woman did die there. Her name was Rosanne Boyland. The *New Yorker* has a reputation for the thoroughness of its fact-checking. Its failure to confirm the manner of Rosanne's death suggests that the authorities were intent on keeping that information away from the media.

Rachel's memory did not deceive her. Rosanne's friend Justin Winchell confirmed as much. Likely worried about being arrested himself, Winchell has laid low these last few years. He did, however, do one interview the day after Rosanne died with a local Atlanta reporter named Zac Summers. According to Winchell, he and Rosanne waited until Trump had finished speaking before heading to the Capitol. "Everything was really, really positive," he said.

By the time the pair arrived at the Capitol, the West Front had already collapsed into chaos. He and Rosanne ascended to the lower terrace level among a crowd of protestors. "There were some people in the front that I don't think were really with us," Winchell told Summers. "Maybe—who knows?— they were radical Trump supporters. It just didn't feel like that. They had all the garb on, a little too much."[173] Pushed from all sides, Winchell lost touch with Rosanne but could still see her near the mouth of the infamous tunnel.

Ashli Babbitt arrived at the Capitol well before Rosanne did. At 2:00 p.m., a protestor behind her just happened to take a perfectly framed photo of Ashli as she approached the Capitol, her Trump 2020 flag worn cape-like over her shoulders, her uncapped hair flowing down her back. Some minutes later, with two undercover MPD officers discreetly trailing her, she arrived at the Capitol and ascended the steps to the west terrace, unaware that these were the last steps she would ever climb.

15

Shibboleths

"Then said they unto him, Say now Shibboleth: and he said Sibboleth: for he could
not frame to pronounce it right. Then they
took him, and slew him at the passages of
Jordan: and there fell at that time of the
Ephraimites forty and two thousand."

Judges 12:6, King James Bible

The word "shibboleth" in English has come to mean a word
or phrase that insiders know and use but that outsiders
do not. For the last few decades, Jacobins have been rolling
out new shibboleths like Apple rolls out iPhones. They rede-
fined gay marriage as "marriage equality," abortion rights as
"reproductive rights," and the sexual mutilation of children as
"gender affirming care."

In their most effective gambit, when temperatures started
to flatline two decades ago, their alchemists converted "global
warming" into "climate change." In so doing, they gave school

children a whole new range of climate horrors to spice up their nightmares. Creating anxiety was in the game plan.

The Jacobins stepped up their game in 2020. In the months before the election, the media routinely passed off violent riots as "mostly peaceful protests" and election integrity as "voter suppression." In the two months after the election, Club Jacobin launched a veritable shibboleth blitzkrieg, forcing the "big lie" and "free and fair election" down the throats of anyone desiring club membership.

On January 6, the master craftsmen at the shibboleth workshop outdid themselves. They introduced a new catchphrase and made it mandatory by day's end. In her indispensable book *January 6,* Julie Kelly does a thorough job explaining how quickly "insurrection" emerged as the word of the day throughout the media and Democratic Party ranks. Less than ninety minutes after the first bicycle rack fell, Rep. Ted Deutch tweeted, "This is a violent insurrection. An attempted coup by Trump supporters at his encouragement."[174]

At 4 p.m., Joe Biden gave the word his blessing. "It's not protest," he said. "It's insurrection."[175]

Insecure about club membership, certain Republicans rushed to the nearest mic to prove their bona fides. Said then US senator Mitt Romney, "What happened here today was an insurrection, incited by the President of the United States."[176] On that same January 6, before the OC gas had yet to settle at the Capitol, George Bush used the imprimatur of the "George W. Bush Presidential Center" to affirm his and wife Laura's membership.

"The violent assault on the Capitol—and disruption of a Constitutionally-mandated meeting of Congress—was undertaken by people whose passions have been inflamed by falsehoods and false hopes," said Bush, speaking for himself and Laura. Lest anyone be confused about where Bush stood, his remarks were headlined, "Statement by President George W. Bush on Insurrection at the Capitol."[177]

Bush and Romney might have checked the definition of the word before rushing to use it. Britannica defines "insurrection" as "an organized and usually violent act of revolt or rebellion against an established government or governing authority of a nation-state or other political entity by a group of its citizens or subjects."[178] The riot at the Capitol that day was anything but organized. If the protestors had a common mission, it was not to subvert the rule of law but to persuade Congress to honor it.

In the years ahead, Jacobins would have to ignore all evidence to maintain "insurrection" as the term of art. MAGA America understood what the media refused to, namely that if protestors had intended to "storm the Capitol"—another shibboleth—and stage an "insurrection," they would have come armed. They did not. As Micki Witthoeft wryly observed, "The gun-toting populous of the United States showed up that day without guns."

While still on Fox News, Tucker Carlson pointed out the obvious. "Just to be clear on terms, an insurrection is when people with guns try to overthrow the government," Carlson said in June 2022. "Not a single person in the crowd on January 6 was found to be carrying a firearm. Not one." Honoring their role in the war on truth, the "fact-checkers" rushed into the breach.

"Tucker Carlson Is Wrong," insisted PolitiFact in its headline. Its drones reviewed hundreds of case files and found "some" protestors who were "charged with having firearms on *Capitol grounds* [italics added] while others stashed them nearby." In other words, no was charged with carrying a gun in the Capitol, let alone shooting one.[179]

To maintain the illusion of an "armed insurrection," the media had to expand "armed" to include the "weapons" most often cited in the DOJ's charging documents, starting with "flagpole" and followed by chemical spray, baton, stick, pocketknife, and baseball bat. Even these charges are suspicious. Among the bat wielders was a young black man named Emanuel Jackson. Two weeks after January 6, the DOJ charged Jackson with "assault on a federal officer while armed with a deadly or dangerous weapon."

The video backs up the DOJ. On March 18, 2021, News4 in Washington showed a clip of Jackson, metal baseball bat in hand, flailing at police officers in the crowded tunnel. He repeated his attacks over a two-hour period. His were arguably the most violent acts committed by a protestor during the day.[180]

For all the obvious criminality, however, the media allowed Jackson to slip back into his netherworld. In a hearing on March 17, 2021, his attorney argued successfully for his release, citing Jackson's "severe intellectual disability." Homeless at the time, Jackson had been given a bat and a few talking points about globalism by some unknown person.[181] Unmentioned by any media is that this practice has a name. It's called "bird-dogging."

In 2016, Democrat operative Scott Foval told a Project Veritas undercover journalist how bird-dogging works. "I'm saying we have mentally ill people that we pay to do s---," said Foval, unaware he was being recorded. "Make no mistake. Over the last twenty years, I've paid off a few homeless guys to do some crazy stuff." In 2016, Foval and crew sent their recruits to Trump rallies to provoke brawls that the media would inevitably blame on Trump.[182] On January 6 and the days following, no one in the media wanted to know who gave the bat and the talking points to Jackson. He clearly did not fit their profile of a militant white supremacist.

To categorize Trump voters following the 2016 election, the Jacobins had resurrected "white supremacy" and added it to the expanding roster of shibboleths. In an October 2020 article, Michael Powell of the *New York Times* conceded that his publication "used the term fewer than 75 times in 2010, but nearly 700 times since the first of this year alone."[183] Throughout the summer of 2020, white supremacists were everywhere, infiltrating everything. Claimed one typical headline, this one from ABC News, "Man Who Helped Ignite George Floyd Riots Identified as White Supremacist: Police."[184]

Many in the media saw January 6 as a barely disguised Klan rally. Less than a week after the event, the prestigious Brookings Institute issued a report claiming "the Capitol insurgency was about making America great for white people." The photo accompanying the report showed a man carrying a Confederate flag inside the Capitol. Wrote report author Rashawn Ray, "The domestic terrorists showed America they fundamentally believe in maintaining and enacting white supremacy. Donald Trump, and Trumpism as an ideology, has opened a Pandora's box of hate into the American mainstream."

Although normative, Brookings' take on January 6 was ludicrous. In reviewing countless hours of video, I saw exactly one Confederate flag. I also saw one rainbow flag, but no one suggested the Capitol insurgency was about making America great for gay people. Of the ten women profiled, not a one even hinted at racism, let alone white supremacy, as a motivating force.

"We're labeled as terrorists, we're labeled as racists," lamented Victoria White. "I'm a mom of four mixed-race daughters. I love all people. Peoples' lies about us are causing myself and other January 6ers to endure unspeakable hell."[185] With COVID, at least there was a real threat, however exaggerated. Here, the threat of white supremacy was as fully manufactured as USCP officer Brian Sicknick's death by fire extinguisher. In both cases, the goal was to keep the American public anxious and compliant.

16

Imaginary Martyrs

Although the "Reichstag fire" metaphor is often abused, in the case of January 6, it hits pretty close to the mark. In February 1933, the German parliament building—the Reichstag—went up in flames. "The Nazi leadership and its coalition partners used the fire to claim that Communists were planning a violent uprising," the Holocaust Encyclopedia reports. "They claimed that emergency legislation was needed to prevent this. The resulting act, commonly known as the Reichstag Fire Decree, abolished a number of constitutional protections and paved the way for Nazi dictatorship."[186]

This is one of those rare occasions where a Hitler comparison makes sense. In fact, the response of the Biden administration to January 6 differs little from Hitler's response to the Reichstag fire. "On the basis of a wholly created myth about what happened that day," said Tucker Carlson accurately, "the Biden Pentagon conducted an unprecedented political purge of the entire U.S. military. The FBI and various intel agencies increased their control over the American media and most obviously, the DOJ has been allowed to prosecute and jail hundreds of nonviolent political protesters whose crime was having the wrong opinions."[187]

In both Hitler's Berlin and Biden's Washington, it was necessary to maintain the illusion of government as victim. To pull this off, the storytellers had to reaffirm the heroic role of the Capitol Police in the insurrection drama. They had, however, one major plot problem to overcome: the only person who fired a gun on January 6—in Micki Witthoeft's words—was "the son of a bitch who murdered my daughter." It wasn't enough to undermine Ashli Babbitt. The Jacobins had to create a martyr of their own. How they accomplished this was disgraceful even by their own abysmal standards.

Former NYPD officer Sara Carpenter opened a window on this unseemly plot. After leaving Washington late on the afternoon of January 6, Sara headed back to New York City. On the way home, she called an old friend from grade school who lived not far from I-95 in Maryland. When Sara mentioned she had been at the Capitol, her friend started screaming at Sara "like a rabid dog." She had never spoken to Sara like that before. "You killed somebody," the friend yelled, the "You" referring to the protestors. "You killed a Capitol Police officer with a fire extinguisher."

The woman's husband had once been a Capitol Police officer. Sara presumed he had inside information. She had no reason to doubt him or his wife. "It sent me reeling," said Sara. By the time she got back to New York City, her Maryland friend had posted news of Sara's presence at the Capitol on Facebook. The next day, said Sara, "I never felt so sick in my life."

The conspirators caught a break on January 7 when Capitol Police Officer Brian Sicknick died after suffering what would prove to be a pair of strokes. Someone in authority—the *New*

York Times would cite "two law enforcement officials"—made the conscious decision to wed Sicknick's death to the rumored death of an officer by fire extinguisher. On January 8, the *New York Times* told its readers that "pro-Trump rioters" were the ones who struck Sicknick with a fire extinguisher. The *Times* added this chillingly fraudulent detail: "With a bloody gash in his head, Mr. Sicknick was rushed to the hospital and placed on life support."

Glenn Greenwald, an independent journalist, made a screen shot of the *Times* story before it could be revised. "This horrifying story about a pro-Trump mob beating a police officer to death was repeated over and over, by multiple journalists on television, in print, and on social media," said Greenwald. He called this counterfeit murder "the single most-emphasized and known story of the event."[188]

When Sara heard on January 6 about an officer being killed, Sicknick was very much alive. Video released later would show him matter-of-factly performing his duties at the Capitol after the time of his supposed murder. To secure Sicknick's status as hero before the video surfaced or the medical examiner completed his report, the Jacobins got to work. Their operatives in the Democrat-controlled House of Representatives honored Sicknick with a public memorial service in the Rotunda of the Capitol. The previous American so honored was Supreme Court Justice Ruth Bader Ginsburg and, before her, civil rights hero John Lewis.

"The circumstances of his death do matter to the public," observed Naomi Wolf, "as without his death having been caused by the events of Jan 6, the breach of the capitol, serious though it was, cannot be described as a 'deadly insurrection.'" Sicknick bore no responsibility for this civic blasphemy—he was rumored to be a Trump supporter and served six years in the Air National Guard—but the record remains uncorrected. "He succumbed to his injuries on January 7, 2021," reads the official Capitol memorial.[189] From the Rotunda, Sicknick's ashes were moved to Arlington National Cemetery where they were buried with full military honors.

Not content with misrepresenting Sicknick's death, the Biden White House launched into a grotesque inflation of the day's body count. On the first anniversary of the protest, Attorney General Merrick Garland named five men "who demonstrated what true courage looks like" and "have since lost their lives." On the second anniversary, House Democratic Leader Hakeem Jeffries made the lie more specific, saying, "As a result of the events on January 6, the lives of five heroic officers were lost."[190] In the trials of the J6ers, judges or prosecutors would routinely repeat the saga of the five martyrs to provoke the jurors. In reality, of the five, one died of a stroke, and four committed suicide within two hundred days of January 6.

It was unfortunate that the men died, but it was opportunistic in the extreme to exalt the men as martyrs. The ample video footage shows that, with only a few exceptions, most of the officers faced less peril that day than did the thousands of urban police officers injured in the George Floyd riots by Molotov cocktails, bricks, guns, and frozen water bottles. "We will not only remember them," Garland concluded, "we will do everything we can to honor them."[191]

Despite her fourteen years of service and multiple deployments to military hot spots, Ashli got nothing. According to Micki, the Air Force denied Ashli a military funeral because of her participation in the "insurrection." Said Micki, "It's just an outrage. It's an outrage. Like so many other things."[192]

17

Casual Cruelty

COVID introduced America to what Dr. Simone Gold calls "an era of casual cruelty." The irrational fear generated by the media inspired many in their audiences to turn on friends and relatives who did not share the anxiety. Liberal women seemed most vulnerable to the panic. It was they who, in their fretfulness, became the nation's "Karens"—quick to lecture, to hector, and, if need be, to snitch. "Californians," said Gold of her fellow Golden Staters, "are not the same Americans they were five years ago."

As Christine Priola came to see, the damage was not limited to California. While following the news on the way back to Ohio, Christine sensed the worst. "I knew on the bus that my life was over," she said. "Everything I worked for in my life was going to be taken away." Christine was not being paranoid. Other than her faith and her family, everything would be taken away. On September 7, she resigned her position as an occupational therapist with the Cleveland Metropolitan School District (CMSD) before the district could fire her.

Christine took seriously the message on the sign she carried into the Senate chamber: "The Children Cry Out for Justice." In her resignation letter, she declared, "I do not agree with my union dues, which help fund people and groups that support the killing of unborn children." She also noted, "I will be switching paths to expose the global evil of human trafficking and pedophilia." Then, too, Christine had a more immediate reason to leave: "I will not be taking the corona virus 19 vaccine in order to return to in person learning."[193]

If COVID inspired random people to become what Dr. Gold called "citizen cops," January 6 inspired them to become wannabe Stasi. Ordinary Americans delighted in ratting out friends and co-workers. Christine was among those targeted. On January 8, having heard from "tipsters" within the school district, some twenty law enforcement officers came to the door of Christine's suburban home with warrant in hand.

This was impressive work. Within forty-eight hours, the FBI had been able to satisfy itself that the woman pictured on the CMSD ID card was the woman photographed in the Senate Chamber of the Capitol. On their January 8 visit, agents ransacked Christine's house, leaving her shattered and embarrassed. Fortunately, Christine's daughter had moved in with a friend just days before and would stick by her mother despite the threats and harassment. Still, she was initially as shocked as anyone else. "Mom," she said, "what have you done?"

Christine's twenty years of solid service made little impact on her employers. They promptly sent out a statement condemning her for her role in "the forcible takeover and willful destruction of our government."[194] The Cleveland Teachers Union was quick to abandon Christine as well. "We are aware of reports of a Cleveland educator who engaged in rioting at the Capitol. We take these allegations very seriously. If true, they [*sic*] must be held accountable."[195]

This was no time for nuance. That was reserved for lower order offenders like the teacher whose explicit sex tape found its way into the phones of some two hundred students. Said the union in a statement about the accused teacher, "Our collective bargaining agreement with the district provides for a process that protects our members, the district, and students when accusations are made involving members. We will work with our member and the district through this process."[196] There were no protections for Christine, no process.

The media were even more brutal. As one of the first patriots arrested after January 6, Christine made for good copy. The fact that she was concerned about child trafficking made for even better copy. In its headline, for instance, the UK *Daily Mail* described Christine as a "QAnon fanatic," one who, of course, "stormed [the] Capitol."[197] At the time, Christine scarcely knew what QAnon was.

The local media were relentless. On the evening her home was searched, January 8, WKYC 3 News was one of many local outlets to report breathlessly from the scene. This was a story, the news anchor told the audience, they had been "talking about all day." The reporter, outdoors but masked, acknowledged that Christine had not yet been charged, nor had the allegation been substantiated. That said, he treated the search of Christine's house as enthusiastically as he might have that of the Unabomber.[198]

Meanwhile, nervous conservative media moguls distanced themselves from January 6. "Feds Bust Ohio School Employee Seen Near Pence's Chair During Capitol Riot," read a headline story in Rupert Murdoch's *New York Post*. The accompanying article by Ben Feuerherd expressed not a drop of sympathy for Christine. Nor did he mention the conspiracy to kill the *Post*'s exposé about Hunter Biden's laptop.[199] Had that *Post* story not been suppressed, Christine would likely have been back in Cleveland on January 6 taking her Christmas tree down.

Almost as planned, the local, national, and international media agreed that a veteran educator with no criminal record deserved their attention. Her crime? Walking into the Capitol, wandering around for twenty minutes, and exiting without any prompting by the police. Christine broke nothing, touched no one. Her causes were just, her motives pure. "The thing that propelled us," said Christine of herself and her fellow protestors, "is that we were tired of not being heard." Yet for peacefully assembling and expressing her constitutionally protected beliefs, she instantly became a target of the media and a pariah in her own community.

Christine was pretty much alone in her world. "When you get so many people telling you how horrible you are," she confessed, "it takes a toll." A week after the search, the FBI came back to her house to arrest her. Despite the cold, they led her away coatless in handcuffs and transported her to the federal courthouse in Cleveland. Christine spent the day in a cell. It would not be her last day behind bars.

Sara Carpenter lived in a world even more hostile to her worldview than Christine. Rattled by the accusation of her friend in Maryland that she had abetted a homicide, Sara woke the next morning in terrible physical and emotional pain, so much so that she sought medical help. On January 15, when she had gotten her strength back, she and her eighteen-year-old son took the occasion of Martin Luther King Day to repair the front stoop of her Queens bungalow. While she was working, she heard someone behind her. "Hello, Ms.

Carpenter," the man said. She looked up to see three men and a woman staring down at her.

Sara had nothing to hide. To be on the safe side, she called her sister, a personal injury lawyer, to come monitor the interview. It went well enough. Sara told the three FBI agents and the one NYPD officer her story of being waved in by a cop who looked like a parking attendant. She recounted everything she had seen and shared the video she had taken. When her sister suggested that the scenario smelled of "entrapment," the officers seemed to agree. Sara even volunteered to help them discover who set the trap. At the end, the officers suggested she'd probably get a DAP, a desk appearance ticket like the ones handed out to the George Floyd rioters. Sara was okay with that. She could handle a $100 fine.

A hard knock on the door in early March undid the little peace Sara had managed to secure. Upon seeing the two large men behind the door, she felt the blood drain from her body. She had been around long enough to recognize guys who meant business. To discourage them from turning her house upside down, Sara cautioned, "Jesus Christ lives here." For the next several hours, people came and went, cars lined the street, a helicopter hovered overhead. Working through her sister, Sara arranged to turn herself in to the FBI.

The wheels of injustice turned slowly, and Sara had time to look for help. Looking did not mean finding. The local attorneys turned her down. The case was too toxic. She approached the priests in her parish, and they were as frightened as the attorneys. Said Sara, "They literally wouldn't even talk to me, wouldn't even pray with me." In her community, Sara became an outcast. Her friend from Maryland sent a Facebook message to a mutual friend in the parish. The word spread. Sara was sure that one of her "friends" had turned her in.

Months after January 6, the media were still pushing the lie that the Capitol protestors had killed a police officer. Murder was not a sin a good Catholic could countenance. "I didn't go into the Capitol thinking this was going to be the outcome," said Sara. "They twisted everything. We played right into their hands." And Sara's woes were just beginning.

A few days after January 6, a female agent came to Victoria White's home when Victoria was not there. She left a card. Victoria called her back. The agent assured her she was not in trouble. She just wanted to know if Victoria knew any people who tried to stop the certification process. Hoping to protect her daughters, Victoria volunteered to come to the FBI, but she did want the agents coming to her home. Her request was ignored. Three months later, the FBI and local police came in force at the crack of dawn. "They surrounded my block, weapons drawn," said Victoria, who was appalled by the gratuitousness of it all. "My daughters were freaking out." The agents handcuffed her outside her home and took her to the federal facility in Minneapolis for processing. "My name," said Victoria, "was forever tarnished."

Not all the J6 women suffered in the same way as did Sara and Christine and Victoria. Some came from large supportive families or lived among like-minded people. That emotional reinforcement made a major difference in the way the women weathered their respective ordeals.

On a blustery Idaho morning in March 2021, Yvonne St Cyr went to breakfast with her mother and sister. Upon returning home, she pulled into the driveway only to be greeted by a US Marshal in tactical gear. "Get out of the car," he told her. The Marshal was not alone, but he steered clear of the "shock and awe" tactics used to arrest other J6ers—reportedly at the request of the local FBI office. Yvonne was allowed to call husband Troy at his job before she was handcuffed and taken to the local sheriff's office for questioning.

Once processed, Yvonne cooperated fully. She did not believe she had done anything wrong and told her whole story unvarnished. She was kept overnight for arraignment and released the next day. Yvonne believes a former employee turned her in. Others shunned her, including members of her church. In a state like Idaho, however, for every friend she lost, she gained a new one. Perhaps most importantly, she had the unwavering support of her husband.

The FBI came for Rebecca Lavrenz on April 19, 2021. Rebecca does not think the choice of days a coincidence. April 19 is Patriots' Day, the day set aside to remember the citizens who resisted British world order in 1775 Massachusetts. Hearing a knock at the door of her semi-rural Colorado home, Rebecca opened it to find a man and a woman who had come to investigate.

"I'm sorry," said Rebecca, "I'm in the middle of baking a cake for my son's birthday." She asked if they could reschedule their visit. To her surprise, they agreed and returned later that month for a "consensual interview." Rebecca had nothing to hide. She told how she entered the Capitol through the open main door on the east side, spent ten minutes inside, and came out the same door she entered. She even provided the agents with a photo of herself at the Capitol.

A few months later, Rebecca heard back from the agents. They told her she had reason to be glad: she was only going to be charged with four misdemeanors. "Glad?" thought Rebecca. "I shouldn't be charged with anything." It was not until December 2022 that she learned of her impending arrest.

The El Paso County GOP did what most local GOP groups lacked the courage to do: show their support for a friend unjustly arrested. In this case, they gathered a group of patriots and drove to the federal courthouse in Denver where they prayed openly for Rebecca. "She is just a giving, praying grandmother who went to the Capitol and her only reason for going in that building—after being let in—was to pray," said GOP chair Vickie Tonkins of Rebecca. "She wanted to pray for the elected officials. She wanted to pray for our country. That's what she did. If that's a crime then they need to come lock me up."

Rebecca's son Michael, who stayed outside the Capitol with his son, was even more defiant. "This whole situation is wrong on so many levels," he posted on Facebook the morning of his mother's arrest. "We have the right as Americans to peacefully protest for whatever we believe in. There is absolutely no reason that she should be being arrested this morning. Our first amendment rights are being slowly taken away." As a parting shot, he added, "I'm extremely proud of her and I know she believes she did the right thing."[200]

With thirty or forty people praying outside the courthouse on the chilly morning of December 19, Rebecca surrendered. The authorities handcuffed the great-grandmother, fingerprinted her, took her mug shot, and put her in a cell awaiting the judge. "My heart was rejoicing," said Rebecca, "that I could stand up for my country." In the subsequent hearings and meetings with attorneys, Rebecca, her resolve stiffened by her faith and the support of her family, refused to do the one thing that the authorities counted on her to do: take a plea deal.

Plea deals were essential to keep the tumbrils rolling in DC. There were multiple thousands of citizens in and around the Capitol on January 6, and the Biden DOJ was hell-bent on arresting as many of them as possible. By itself, the FBI could not begin to keep up with the demand for heads, but the Bureau had help. Much the way the Castro regime relied on local "rapid response brigades" to sniff out the suspicious activities of their neighbors, the Biden regime came to rely on its own citizen snoops, the so-called "Sedition Hunters."

If Christine Priola and Sara Carpenter fell prey to local busybodies, many of the thousand-plus people arrested owed their bondage to the Sedition Hunters. On their website, they describe themselves as "a global community of open-source intelligence investigators (OSINT) working together to assist the U.S. FBI and Washington D.C. Capitol Police in finding people who allegedly committed crimes in the January 6 capitol riots." As an added bonus, they "are able to identify other crimes and pass that information along to law enforcement officers."[201]

The media loved the Sedition Hunters. A wonderfully revealing episode of NPR's *Morning Edition* captured the Jacobin mindset as of January 5, 2022, In the opening segment, reporter Rob Stein scolded the CDC for loosening its mask guidelines. Recall, this was *two* years after the introduction of COVID-19 to America's shores.

In the second segment, reporter Odette Yousef interviewed Forrest Rogers, the Sedition Hunters' most public face. That "a German American living in Switzerland" was hunting everyday Americans did not even strike Yousef as curious. In the segment, Rogers boasted about how he and his group combed through social media sites until they identified Rachel Powell, the Pennsylvania mother of eight. "They sent that information to the FBI," said an approving Yousef, "and Powell was arrested a few weeks later."[202]

In the liberal imagination, those who rooted out sedition—Joe McCarthy, J. Edgar Hoover, Richard Nixon—represented a greater threat to democracy than those who engaged in it. And by sedition we are not talking grandmas taking selfies in the Capitol Rotunda. We are talking genuine traitors—Alger Hiss, Harry Dexter White, Julius and Ethel Rosenberg—Soviet agents who conspired to share vital national security secrets with Stalin's Soviet Union.

That was then. In recent years, the Jacobins have been undermining old school liberalism. They cheer the industrial-scale round up of innocent victims. They applaud, and likely fund, internet narcs who gleefully ruin people's lives. And they flout core constitutional imperatives such as "due process of laws," "an impartial jury," "the right to a speedy and public trial," and "unreasonable searches and seizures."

As someone who endured more than his share of casual cruelty, the famed Russian dissident Aleksandr Solzhenitsyn understood how a seemingly decent person could behave so monstrously. The catalyst, in a word, was "ideology." Solzhenitsyn explained, "That is the social theory which helps to make his acts seem good instead of bad in his own and others' eyes, so that he won't hear reproaches and curses but will receive praise and honors."

Solzhenitsyn cited several ideologies whose belief systems, when applied, had lethal consequence. Among those listed were the "Jacobins (early and late)." As becomes more obvious by the day, the obsession of today's Jacobins with diversity, equity, and inclusion is proving as delusional and ultimately as destructive as the early Jacobins' obsession with what Solzhenitsyn described as "equality, brotherhood, and the happiness of future generations."[203]

DEI is expansive enough a concept to shelter just about all the "marginalized" tribes of the Jacobin empire, including Muslims. To explain their collective failures, Muslims have historically scapegoated Jews. So effective was the anti-Semitic propaganda in Gaza that on October 7, 2023, Hamas fighters devolved into butchers and rapists with no apparent qualms. So effective has been the anti-Trump propaganda here in America that educated people put J6ers on the same moral plane as Hamas.

Congressional drama queen Alexandria Ocasio-Cortez showed just how effective that propaganda has been in a hair-raising interview she did with CNN's Dana Bash. "White supremacy and patriarchy are very linked in a lot of ways," AOC told Bash. "There's a lot of sexualizing of that violence. And I didn't think that I was just going to be killed. I thought other things were going to happen to me as well." When Bash asked AOC if she thought she was going to be raped, AOC answered, "Yea, yeah. I thought I was."[204] The musings of Ocasio-Cortez raised no eyebrows in progressive circles. Her way of thinking, such as it is, permeates America's newsrooms. The steady stream of rubbish the media produce has clouded the minds and frozen the hearts of millions.

For many J6ers, the systematic cruelty began with that first knock on the front door. On the morning of January 8, a swarm of agents descended on the home of infamous "zip-tie guy" Eric Munchel. Since Eric was already at work, his brother answered the door, only to be clapped in handcuffs while still in his underwear. At the time, the FBI did not know that his mother, Lisa Eisenhart, was at the Capitol. It was she who would volunteer that information.

Eric was booked on January 9, Lisa on January 12, both at the federal courthouse in Nashville. "I was floored when

I read my charges," said Lisa. Having accused her of trying to overthrow the government, the feds deemed the fifty-seven-year-old nurse worthy of pre-trial detention. For the next eleven weeks, Lisa was shuttled among jails in Tennessee, Kentucky, and DC.

Like the other J6ers, Lisa was kept in maximum security. She spent those final six weeks in the notorious DC gulag—"hungry, tired, and lonely." For clothing, the jailers gave her the equivalent of hospital scrubs. For warmth, they gave her a single thin blanket in a unit so cold in the morning she could see her breath. Before showers, they chained her hand and foot. Unable to sleep at night or eat food always served cold, Lisa lost thirty-five pounds and a goodly chunk of hair.

When finally released to the limbo of home confinement, Lisa was denied access to the internet as well as any communication with Eric. Now jobless, she worried about her own finances and those of her son, but also about the effect her very public arrest would have on the people associated with her. Her work friends, save for her best friend who was black, "All thought I was a racist." Eric, of course, was tarred with the same brush even though the patriot group to which he belonged was largely black. "I felt like the whole entire world was against me," said Lisa.

On the morning of January 18, 2021, Dr. Simone Gold was at home in Los Angeles working with John Strand. They were on a conference call when Gold heard a pounding on the door and the "most blood curdling scream of my life, FBI, FBI, FBI." Disoriented by the violence, they froze for about thirty seconds until the FBI broke the door down with a battering ram.

Dr. Gold estimated about twenty agents with a dozen "huge guns" pointed right at her. "They arrested me," she told

Tucker Carlson. "They [yell], 'put your hands up, put your hands up, face the wall, face the wall,' they're screaming, 'face the wall'—handcuffed, shackled, take me downtown, orange suit, strip search, holding cell, fluorescent lights—it was terrible—no phone call, no Miranda rights."[205]

This gratuitously violent assault on the home of a prominent physician and attorney did not disturb the media, not at all. No, they were downright gleeful. They had something better than QAnon to pin on Gold—quackery. Dr. Gold, the media assured their audiences, "pushed Trump's favored COVID drug," "promoted false hydroxychloroquine claims," and was "anti-vaxx." Readers learned this much just from the headlines.

As the Gallup survey cited earlier made clear, corporate media fed their consumers a steady diet of junk news regarding COVID. This bad info scared many of them into hysteria. On March 4, 2022, the *New York Times* celebrated Dr. Gold's January 6 plea deal with a headline that accused her of spreading "pandemic misinformation." When posted on Facebook, this article drew more than a thousand comments, the great majority from liberal educated women. Two years into the COVID hysteria, these women remained as doggedly ignorant as on day one. Some samples:[206]

> "Apparently that 'first do no harm' thing didn't take. #quack"

> "Honestly she should lose her medical license for intentionally spreading so much misinformation."

> "Jail's too good for her. But I hope she serves more than a few months."

"With thousands of lives lost due to COVID, a felony charge would be more appropriate!"

"Hope she sees time behind bars."

"Given the number of people who have died from her COVID lies, she should be facing more serious charges."

"NYTIMES Stop referring to her as a doctor. She is not one of us."

This was not the first time fear of disease and death caused a mass psychosis. Frightened people often look for scapegoats. In the Middle Ages, during periods of plague, mobs were known to turn on Jews and accuse them of poisoning wells. During COVID mania, Dr. Gold endured her own personal pogrom. In this case, the stigma was not for being Jewish. It wasn't even for being a J6er. It was for being a COVID dissident. The fact that she would be proved right in her claims about COVID would only make the Jacobins hate her more.

18

Off Script

Justin Winchell had been texting back and forth throughout the day of January 6 with Rosanne Boyland's father, Bret. Bret and Rosanne had always been close. Sister Lonna described them as "fishing buddies." About six months before the election, Rosanne had started watching Fox News with her father, a gesture that alarmed her sisters but not Bret. In fact, during the campaign, he took Rosanne to a gun show where Donald Trump Jr. was speaking.[207]

The text exchanges between Bret and Justin were upbeat. "We are heading to the Capitol building with the masses of patriots. Hope you are having a great one. We are doing you proud," read one of Winchell's texts. Bret would respond with an overview of what he was seeing on TV.

When things started getting crazy, Bret texted Justin, "You guys probably should leave and go do some sightseeing, or something." At 4 p.m., always a father, Bret texted, "6 p.m. curfew, better get out shortly." He followed that text with, "Let us know what's happening." At 4:30 p.m., Winchell texted

Bret, "Please call me. I need to talk to you about Rosanne. She's been hurt."

Many of the protestors witnessed the death of Rosanne Boyland. They all tell the same story. Although some believe Rosanne was murdered by the police, the authorities have interviewed no witnesses, taken no crime scene photos, done no forensic testing.

The action took place in and around the Capitol's now notorious lower west terrace tunnel. About ten feet wide and fifteen feet long, the tunnel led, on the interior end, to two sets of glass double doors marked, "Members Entrance Only." The exterior end led to temporary stairs that descended to the recently erected inauguration stage. Protestors reached the tunnel by 2:40 p.m. They started to flood in after police, having gassed themselves, retreated behind the double glass doors. By this time, protestors had been wandering around inside the Capitol for half an hour or so, making little fuss, causing negligible damage. Colorado's Rebecca Lavrenz, for instance, left the Capitol at 2:43 p.m. after her stroll through the Rotunda.

That the police would engage in a life and death struggle at one entrance for two hours while many other entrances were wide open raises questions. Stranger still, at least if MSNBC's Ayman Mohyeldin is to be believed, a superior told the officers "to defend the entrance by any means necessary."[208] Incompetence might explain the uneven police response. So, too, might entrapment. A prolonged battle at such an easily accessible spot made for good visuals—never mind that almost all members of Congress, including its leadership, had left the building.

No one was closer to Rosanne at her moment of death than Philip Anderson. A Trump supporter, he showed up at the January 6 protest missing his two front teeth. In a well-documented incident three months prior, an Antifa supporter sucker punched Anderson during a free speech rally in San Francisco.[209] As an African American and a victim of Antifa violence, Anderson did little to support the Jacobin party line that white supremacists posed a unique threat to American democracy. Accordingly, the media pretended not to see him.

Jim Hoft of the Gateway Pundit caught up with Anderson in July 2021. Wrote Hoft, "This is an amazing eyewitness report that has been ignored by the fake news media because it does not fit their narrative."[210] Hoft was right. Called a liar by some at first, the video that later emerged fully supported Anderson's account, an account that never varied. Like many others, Anderson found himself at the tunnel entrance.

Justin Winchell and Rosanne were there as well, swept into the swarm without their willing it. A few people in the tightly packed crowd had come between Justin and Rosanne. "There were probably three or four guys in the back and people, I mean, actively just pushing people," Winchell would tell reporter Zac Summers. "Like, pushing people, pushing people, pushing people to get closer to the door, to go into the building."[211] Without intending, Anderson and Boyland entered the tunnel side by side. When the police made a concerted surge to drive back the protestors—what protestor Kim Sorgente called "a synchronized chemical attack, then a charge"—the protestors tumbled backwards.

The chemical irritant sprayed by the MPD displaced the oxygen in the tunnel, causing people to feel faint. Rosanne collapsed at the tunnel entrance. "After the police gassed us, everyone turned around to run away, but people, our bodies turned limp, we all fell down on top of each other," Anderson told OAN's Christina Bobb in December 2021. "And the police kept pushing more and more people on top of us. And they used mace, they used batons to beat us, their fists."[212] To *Epoch Times* reporter Joe Hanneman, the scene looked "like a waterfall going down the steps leading away from this entrance, people just tumbling out."[213]

Anderson found himself at the bottom of the pile. Next to him was Rosanne. "After we both fell down all these people fell on top of us, about 30 people. So we're both being crushed to death. She grabbed, she reaches out and grabs my hand. She was holding my hand for a little while and then she lets go," said Anderson. "And at that moment I'm thinking I'm about to die too. So I started yelling as loud as I can." Despite his shouts for help, the police continued to push more bodies on top of the pile. This Anderson still cannot understand or forgive. "I would be dead," he said, "if it weren't for Trump supporters who are sitting in prison right now."[214]

Winchell was desperate to save Rosanne. "Gimme your hand," he implored. Getting no response, he wailed, "She's dead. She's dead. Please, I need somebody. She's dead. Please, I need somebody."[215]

Hearing Winchell cry out Rosanne's name moved Sorgente, a California activist, to action. "I realized I had to do something," he told Joe Hoft. "So I started talking to the officers. I tried to reason with them. I told them, I said, 'Look, I don't want her to die,' and I begged them. I threw all my dignity out the window. I cried like a baby. I cried and pleaded with these officers I begged them for, like, two minutes. I kept saying, 'Please, I don't want her to die. You can save her. Please help her.'" Sorgente wanted the police to stop pushing, but the moment he turned his back, an officer clubbed him over the head.[216]

What happened next has not gotten nearly the attention it deserves. In their various reports on Rosanne's death, the major media scrupulously avoided discussing what policewoman Lila Morris did to Rosanne's body. Once the others were pulled off, Rosanne lay momentarily lifeless and exposed at the tunnel entrance. Keen on "equity," the MPD apparently thought it only fair to allow a small, slim female the opportunity to man the contested front of a police line. Morris, who had just reached the front, picked up what appears to be a tree branch, raised it up with both hands, and swung wildly. She struck Rosanne over the head at least three times before the branch snapped and flew out of her hands.

"She was already blue, and the Capitol Police hit her once in the face," Winchell said of Rosanne. "And some blood started coming out of her nose. I was like, 'I think she's dead. I think she's dead.' And I'm screaming this."

"I was horrified," said use-of-force expert Stan Kephart upon seeing the video. "We don't train officers to hit people in the head with a blunt object." Added Kephart, "It was definitely a crime."

To protect Rosanne from both the crowd and the police, a deeply spiritual Texan protestor named Luke Coffee stood over the dying woman holding a crutch horizontally above his head. For his efforts to save Rosanne, he was charged with a felony for striking Morris. Not until Coffee's January 2024 trial was Morris forced to testify about January 6.

Under oath, Morris admitted Coffee had never hit her, a major win for Coffee. She also conceded that a baton or, in this case a stick, was only to be used for defensive purposes, with a hand on either end as a way to push crowds back. "Are you ever trained to hold it like a bat and strike over somebody's head?" asked Coffee's attorney, Carol Stewart.

"No," said Morris. Stewart asked Morris what self-defense tactic justified the beating of an unconscious woman, but she promptly withdrew her question, likely not wanting to alienate the judge.[217]

Other protestors intervened to try to save Rosanne. As Winchell watched, Jake Lang and Ronald McAbee removed Rosanne from the tunnel entrance and began applying CPR. Failing to revive her after ten minutes, they and other protestors carried Rosanne back to the entrance in the hope that the police had the resources to revive her.

When Bret Boyland called after receiving Winchell's alarming late afternoon text, Winchell told him the details of the disaster he had just witnessed: the pileup, the desperate attempt to pull Rosanne out from under, the CPR. Several protestors, Winchell told Bret, "carried her up to the entryway there at the police line." Once the police and protestors pulled Rosanne into the tunnel, Winchell admitted to not knowing what happened next.

Until they knew for sure what did happen, Bret and his wife, Cheryl, kept this information to themselves. Cheryl turned her anxiety into action, calling every hospital and fire department in DC without success. Just before midnight, she got a call back from a police officer. "I believe we have your daughter," he said. At first, Cheryl thought Rosanne had been arrested. The officer's question—"Does she have a tattoo?"—shattered that illusion.

Rosanne's sister Lonna had an uneasy premonition all evening. When her phone rang at midnight, she knew what the message would be. Her mother confirmed her worst fears. Soon after midnight, Bret texted Winchell, "Got a call from a detective a while ago. Rosanne died. She was at one of the hospitals as a Jane Doe. She didn't have her ID, so they verified some of her tattoos with us. The medical examiner is supposed to call us in the morning." At this point, the Boylands had no reason to distrust the medical examiner. They would have plenty of reason soon enough.

With the release of Rosanne's name the next morning, the media swooped in. Swarms of reporters crowded the Boyland's front yard. Having a little TV experience, brother-in-law Justin Cave was designated to prepare a written statement and read it. Cave did what the family expected, reported MSNBC's Ayman Mohyeldin, until he "decided to go off script."

Mohyeldin would make himself a critical figure in this saga. As an MSNBC anchor, he had to like Cave's improvisation. "It's my own personal belief that the president's words incited a riot that killed four of his biggest fans last night," said Cave, "and I believe that we should invoke the 25th Amendment at this time." Mohyeldin knew Cave. Improbably enough, the Egyptian-born news anchor had gone to the same Kennesaw, Georgia, high school as Cave, and the two played soccer together.

Two days later, Cave reached out to his old soccer buddy through Facebook. "Ayman, I'm sure you've seen the news," Cave wrote. "I made a public statement about the death of my sister-in-law, Rosanne, from Kennesaw who died on Wednesday at the Capitol. My wife and I believe she was radicalized in a very short time inside of six months. Would you be willing to hear her story?"

The story Cave intended to tell featured Trump as the prince of lies and Rosanne as his innocent victim. Mohyeldin couldn't resist. Soon enough, however, he discovered that the plotline he hoped to follow was a red herring. The real story would lead him beyond the MSNBC pale and down a rabbit hole whose end he would never quite reach. Had Cave not gone "off script," Mohyeldin might never have followed the trail. Without his effort, little would have ever been known about Rosanne's tragic death.

19

Malpractice

As early as 4:30 p.m. on January 6, Bret Boyland knew from Justin Winchell the broad outlines of what had happened to his daughter. On January 7, Winchell shared the story with a mainstream TV station in Atlanta. "I lost a dear, dear friend, man, an amazing friend, whom I miss dearly," Winchell told Zac Summers. "She was killed by an incited event, and it wasn't incited by Trump supporters."[218]

On January 11, the *New York Times* first made mention of Rosanne. In its brief description, the *Times* reported that she "followed the baseless conspiracy theories of QAnon and latched onto Mr. Trump's false claims that he had won the election." The report noted, more or less accurately, that she appeared "to have been killed in a crush of fellow rioters." In acknowledging that there would be federal investigations into the deaths of Ashli Babbitt and Capitol Police Officer Brian Sicknick, the *Times* suggested, correctly as it turned out, that there would be none into the death of Rosanne.[219]

On January 15, the *New York Times* would do a more thorough report, repeating the fact that Rosanne appeared to have been killed in the crush but making no mention of her beating by Officer Lila Morris. In this and future articles, the *Times* would insist that her fellow protestors "trampled" Rosanne, a charge whose implication of cowardly behavior infuriated protestor Kim Sorgente.[220] No one trampled on Rosanne, he insisted. The protestors were shoved on top of her by the police.

Back in Kennesaw, the extended Boyland family was suffering not only from the heartbreak of losing a loved one but also from the opprobrium of having raised a terrorist. Antagonists were breaking into their vehicles, stealing their flags, and sending messages as cold as, "Here's some roses for your dead redneck daughter's casket." Attacked viciously from the left, the family made no friends on the right thanks to Justin Cave's impromptu smackdown of Trump.

On January 7, the District of Columbia Office of the Chief Medical Examiner (OCME), did an autopsy on Rosanne. Heading that office at the time was Dr. Roger Mitchell. When last heard from, Mitchell was threatening to ruin Dr. Andrew Baker's career unless he amended the autopsy report of George Floyd to include "neck compression," a necessary corruption if Derek Chauvin were to be accused of murder.

That was Mitchell's most flagrant abuse of power but not his only one. In daring to testify on Chauvin's behalf, the intrepid Dr. David Fowler provoked Mitchell's wrath. While the trial was still in progress, Mitchell enlisted four hundred physicians to sign an open letter to Maryland attorney general Brian Frosh. The signers demanded an "immediate investigation" into Fowler's practices during the seventeen years he spent as the State of Maryland's chief medical examiner. Weeks later, feeling the heat, Frosh launched a detailed review of more than one hundred autopsies during Fowler's tenure.[221]

On January 6, 2021, Mitchell was a major player in DC politics. He was serving in two DC government roles—interim deputy mayor for public safety and justice and chief medical examiner. He was soon to accept a new position as a professor and chair of pathology at nearby Howard University. Given his record as an activist, Mitchell likely called the political shots at the medical examiner's office as long as needed. Indeed, he coordinated the hit on Dr. Fowler more than three months after January 6. It was not until January 29 that DC mayor Muriel Bowser appointed Dominican native Dr. Francisco Diaz *acting* chief medical officer. "These are like the George Floyd coroners," said Ashli's mom, Micki Witthoeft, of the OCME. She was more right than she knew.

On April 6, 2021, Dr. Joanie Taylor of the OCME called Lonna Cave back in Kennesaw. Taylor wanted to give the Boyland family a heads-up on the impending release of the autopsy report. The cause of death, said Taylor, was "acute amphetamine intoxication."

On hearing Taylor's analysis, Lonna dropped to her knees and began crying. "That was exactly what Rosanne didn't want," she said. "That was why she was sober for so long." Lonna refused to accept Taylor's verdict: "I just thought that it was just—a load of shit, basically."

Amphetamine was the active ingredient in the Adderall that Rosanne had been taking by prescription for ten years to deal with her ADHD. Lonna and her family did not want Rosanne to be remembered as a drug addict. She begged Taylor to at least acknowledge that the drug was prescribed, but that was not part of the OCME's plan.

The fix was in from the beginning. On January 7, Lonna had received a call from DC Metro Police homicide detective Jonathan Shell. Shell had just left the autopsy. He passed along the news to Lonna that her sister had died of a fentanyl overdose. This made no sense. From Winchell's conversation with her father, she knew Rosanne had been caught in a crush of protestors. As time passed, with the media confirming Winchell's account, Lonna assumed the official autopsy report would set the record straight. It did not.

Although reluctant to see the larger picture, Mohyeldin was getting a glimpse into the workings of Jacobin justice. He tried reaching out to Detective Shell but got stonewalled. He and his team contacted the OCME several times, hoping to speak to Dr. Taylor or her new boss, Francisco Diaz, but "all our requests were denied." Lamented the MSNBC anchor, "The trampling, the riot, the video evidence, none of this was even mentioned in the official autopsy report."[222]

Mohyeldin interviewed Philip Anderson, the protestor caught in the crush right next to Rosanne. "When someone is killed," Anderson told Mohyeldin, "you can't lie about the cause of death. You can't hail someone as a hero when they kill someone. You can't do that." In Roger Mitchell's America, the real risk was not in lying but in telling the truth. His power plays cost four police officers their freedom, and the media played along.

In Hennepin County, the autopsy report on George Floyd was made public exactly one week after his death. The quick release of the altered report served a purpose. It allowed Minnesota attorney general Keith Ellison to charge Derek Chauvin with murder, a charge that met with little resistance given that Ellison was simultaneously suppressing the release of body cam footage that would have helped Chauvin's case.

In Washington, the medical examiner waited until the very last day of the standard ninety-day window for the release of Rosanne's autopsy report. Beyond the Boyland family, few noticed the report's surprise conclusion. It only appeared that Rosanne died "after being caught in a crush of rioters," reported the *New York Times* in May 2021. The OCME, the *Times* added, "did not find evidence of trampling and concluded that she had overdosed on amphetamines."[223] Once again, the editors honored the final, most essential command of the "Party": reject the evidence of your eyes and ears.

Mohyeldin and MSNBC had the autopsy and toxicology reports reviewed by two expert pathologists. The one, Dr. Priya Banerjee, did her best to avoid coming to any conclusion. The other, Dr. Adele Lewis, was stunned that the DC medical examiner overlooked the obvious. "As we say," said Lewis, "context is everything. So when you look at the videotapes and read the eye witness accounts of what happened, it's pretty clear that she probably was not a drug overdose death. She's being essentially trampled by several other people."

Lewis described the likely cause of death as "traumatic asphyxia due to being trampled or pinned under other people." The irony here is as deep as the deception: Mitchell discounted the drugs in Floyd's system and accused the Minneapolis cops of killing Floyd by asphyxia. A year later, Mitchell or his office cleared the DC cops of an "asphyxia" charge by blaming Rosanne's death on drugs. Floyd, of course, was the one whose blood tested positive for fentanyl and methamphetamines. Rosanne tested positive for neither.

Of note, too, the relevant body cam footage in Rosanne's death was strategically withheld just as it was for Floyd's. As Mohyeldin admitted, "We requested the officer in question's body camera footage, but we were denied." Bret Boyland, in fact, applied through the Freedom of Information Act for Morris's bodycam footage and was denied. In Floyd's case, the footage would have helped exonerate the cops. In

Rosanne's case, it would have incriminated them, Lila Morris in particular.

One other death has to be factored into this disturbing calculus, that of Brian Sicknick. On the day of his autopsy, January 8, the *New York Times* reported, "With a bloody gash in his head, Mr. Sicknick was rushed to the hospital and placed on life support." For more than one hundred days, the OCME withheld the autopsy results. There was no medical or legal reason to withhold them. Floyd's report, remember, was released in a week. The unstated motive, of course, was to preserve Sicknick's status as a martyr and the J6ers status as murderers as long as possible. To question either side of this equation was to risk a public shaming.

Always crafty, the OCME finally released Sicknick's autopsy report on April 19, 2021. Yes, April 19 was Patriot's Day, but more to the point, it was the day closing arguments were made in the Chauvin trial. This was no coincidence. The conspirators wanted as little attention paid to the results as possible. The OCME might never have released the results were it not for pressure from a Judicial Watch lawsuit. This suit also forced the medical examiner to reveal the true cause of Sicknick's death, specifically two strokes at the base of his brain stem caused by a clot. Sicknick died on *January 7*. There was no fire extinguisher. No bloody gash. No rush to the hospital.

In an interview with the *Washington Post*, new DC medical examiner Dr. Francisco Diaz called it a "natural death," meaning "a disease alone causes death." According to Diaz, Sicknick suffered no internal or external injuries, nor any allergic reaction to a chemical substance. To give the media a sound bite to salvage their narrative, he added, "All that transpired played a role in his condition."[224]

Drunk on their own disinformation, the media struggled with this unexpected dose of truth. The following day, April 20, CNN reporter Jen Christensen emailed the OCME, naively wondering "how someone could die of natural causes after a traumatic event." On that same day, Sarah Mimms of BuzzFeed emailed the OCME, "I'm really pressing on clarity here not only because of the importance of this case but also because USCP and the Justice Department initially said that Officer Sicknick died due to injuries he sustained at the Capitol."[225]

To preserve the illusion of Sicknick's matyrdom, the courts sentenced Julian Khater to nearly seven years in prison for using pepper spray on the officer. The US attorney overseeing the plea deal said of Khater, "He [was] incensed at having been personally sprayed by police chemical spray while standing on the front line of a riot, as if he had been an innocent victim."[226] Hundreds of protestors were sprayed that day as were scores of officers, most of the latter by friendly fire. Only Sicknick died. Like Chauvin, Khater was condemned to a lengthy prison sentence for "killing" a man who died of natural causes. As to Sicknick, having served his purpose for those hundred days, the House committee abandoned him. The report mentioned him once and then just to thank his family.

Rosanne Boyland was among the hundreds sprayed with chemicals. Reflecting on her death, a disillusioned Lonna Cave said to Mohyeldin, "I think that whatever happened happened. I don't know, you know, if it was some kind of chemical irritant, both sides were spraying it, so who knows." The Boylands had come to lose faith in the government. In September 2021, the DOJ released a previously unseen video that confirmed the family's worst suspicions.

"It doesn't show the police officers helping my sister whatsoever. The only people who are helping her are the guys sitting in jail right now," said Lonna. The video showed Rosanne's body lying inert at the entrance of the tunnel, her shirt partially lifted and her midriff exposed. Protestors surrounded her, yelling at the police. "These guys are all screaming," said Lonna Cave. "One guy's saying, 'You killed her. You killed her.'"

This one video made Lonna question who were the good guys and who the bad. She saw that the protestors had tried CPR on Rosanne and carried her body back to the tunnel entrance for help. "And the police are just standing there," said an angry Lonna. "There's blood coming out of her nose, her face is blue, and her body is blue. And then one police officer picks up her leg and starts to drag her." A protestor intervened, picked up her arms, and carried her past the police line. "And that's the last time she's seen," said Lonna.[227]

Increasingly frustrated both with the authorities and Mohyeldin, Lonna started talking to the Gateway Pundit, specifically reporter Cara Castronuova. "The Gateway Pundit is asking similar questions to what we've been asking: how did Rosanne actually die?" said Mohyeldin, but he clearly did not like the direction Castronuova was taking the investigation. On his podcast, he replayed an interview of Castronuova on Steve Bannon's show in which she said, "There's a 90 percent chance [Rosanne] was killed by police, there's video out there that shows her being beaten with a stick by a police woman named…." Here, Mohyeldin cut the tape lest his audience hear the name "Lila Morris."[228]

The people at the Gateway Pundit actually wanted to know how Boyland died. They wanted to see the video, interview the witnesses, talk to the police. Mohyeldin hoped to stay on script. To lend credence to the autopsy report, he sought out Trump-hating friends of Rosanne's who speculated she was still using drugs.

To discredit the Gateway Pundit, he turned to NBC's resident "expert on disinformation and the dark web," Ben Collins. Collins insisted right-wingers had been "work-shopping narratives" until they settled on police violence and self-defense. To discredit the J6ers' few supporters in Congress, Mohyeldin turned to NBC's congressional correspondent Leigh Ann Caldwell. Caldwell assured him their inquiries served no larger purpose than "to sow distrust in the deep state."

To show the bad faith of friendly congressmen, Mohyeldin replayed an exchange between Rep. Louis Gohmert (R-Texas) and Attorney General Merrick Garland at an October 2021 hearing on Capitol Hill. "Was a determination ever made as to who repeatedly struck Rosanne Boyland in the head with a rod before she died?" Gohmert asked.

Replied Garland, "Again, I think this was a matter that was investigated by the U.S. Attorney's office." Except, of course, Boyland's death was never investigated by the US Attorney's office. Gohmert was not the one sowing distrust. That was Merrick Garland.[229]

In the concluding chapter of his five-part podcast, Mohyeldin met with Lonna Cave for the final time. "Things," he admitted, "are a little tense." Although he could not bring himself to say as much, the Boylands no longer trusted his motives. They hoped to learn more about Rosanne's fate. He wanted to learn more about QAnon. The podcast series ended inconclusively with him guilt-tripping Rosanne's sisters for not saving Rosanne from "dangerous conspiracy theories designed to entrap vulnerable people like her." Two years after the series ended, the Boylands know little more about Rosanne's death than they did when the series wrapped up.

For Lila Morris, the rewards came quick. She was one of three police officers honored at the Super Bowl a month later "in recognition of their heroism." Morris remained an unquestioned hero until September 2021 when that damning video surfaced of her striking Rosanne. Disturbed by what he saw, J6 video expert Gary McBride filed a police brutality complaint with the DC Metropolitan Police Department. McBride believes Rosanne was still alive when Morris struck her. "When she takes that second hit to the head, watch her left arm, her left arm straightens up and lifts off the ground," he told the *Epoch Times*.[230]

Morris need not have worried. Two months after Mc-Bride filed his complaint, he was informed via email, "The use of force within this investigation was determined to be objectively reasonable." Morris would remain on the force and would face no criminal charges.[231] The men who tried to save Rosanne with CPR did not fare as well. As of this writing, Jake Lang of Newburgh, New York, has spent more than three years in the DC gulag awaiting a trial now scheduled for September 2024. And Ronald McAbee, a deputy sheriff from Tennessee, was convicted of five felonies and awaits sentencing. Luke Coffee, who shielded Rosanne with a crutch, spent twenty months in home detention before his bench trial in January 2024.

If the Boyland family had any hope of clearing Rosanne's name, that hope lay with the House Select Committee. Before finishing its work, the committee would interview more than a thousand witnesses and obtain more than a million documents. The eight-hundred-page final report, released in December 2022, goes into great detail about the two-hour battle for the lower west terrace tunnel, a battle that resulted in one fatality. Curiously, however, the report ignores all the eyewitnesses to that fatality—Winchell, Anderson, Coffee, McAbee, Lang, Sorgente, even Lila Morris. As to the much loved and deeply missed Rosanne Boyland, she doesn't even make the footnotes.

20

Show Time

In January 1793, the deputies of the French National Convention voted on the guilt or innocence of their king, Louis XVI. The deliberation went slowly what with all the charges and the frequent croissant breaks, but the outcome was never in doubt. The deputies voted 683 to 0 to convict. As a progressive, Robespierre had recently advocated for the abolition of the death penalty, but given the politics of the moment, he felt the need to add a wrinkle to that advocacy. "The sentiment that led me to call for the abolition of the death penalty," he argued with pure Jacobin logic, "is the same that today forces me to demand that it be applied to the tyrant of my country." Four days after the verdict was returned, Louis was executed.

The equally godless Soviet Union allowed itself a similar moral flexibility, especially in the years from 1936 to 1938. In that roughly two-year period, Josef Stalin and his henchmen staged a series of "show trials" designed to eliminate the "Right Opposition" and to intimidate those who had, literally, dodged the bullets. In *The Gulag Archipelago*, Solzhenitsyn quotes a Soviet leader on the adaptive ethics of the Cheka, the state police: "Soviet power is proud of the decree of the Cheka abolishing the death penalty," said the apparatchik. But, he added, this "still does not force us to conclude that the question of the abolition of the capital punishment has been decided once and for all."[232]

Obviously not. An estimated seven hundred thousand people were executed in the two-year period of the Great Purge. Although the outcome of these trials was predetermined, they gave Stalin's "useful idiots" in the West cover enough to continue their support of the Soviet Union.

As it stands now, Trump and the January 6 protestors have no better shot at justice in the DC courts circa 2024 than the Trotskyites did in Moscow circa 1938.

Not content with humiliating Trump and the J6ers behind closed doors or on daytime TV, the House Select Committee recruited veteran TV executive James Goldston. His job, wrote the *New York Times* approvingly, was "to produce the hearings as if they were a docudrama or a must-watch mini-series."[233] In 2020, Goldston served as president of ABC News. Under his guidance, on an almost nightly basis that spring and summer, his producers used their editing tricks to convert violent riots into largely peaceful protests. Using those same tricks for the House Select Committee, his producers managed to turn a largely peaceful protest into an insurrection.

For his efforts, Goldston, a British native, got the best reviews of his career. "They did it. They pulled it off," said his hometown *Guardian*. "Anyone who feared that the January 6 committee's season finale would turn into an anti-climax— more Game of Thrones than M*A*S*H—need not have worried. There were shocks, horrors and even laughs."[234]

Those paying attention, especially those concerned with the trafficking of children, had reason to distrust Goldston even before he put the "show" in show trial. In 2019, Goldston made news, at least on the right, for spiking a 2015 interview ABC's Amy Robach had done with Virginia Roberts Giuffre, a Jeffrey Epstein victim. In 2019, an ABC insider leaked a hot mic moment in which Robach complained about the burial of this story.

In the 2015 interview, Giuffre claimed that at seventeen she had been forced to have sex with Prince Andrew. She also claimed to have seen Bill Clinton on Epstein's island.[235] Had ABC aired the interview, Epstein's predatory ways may well have ended four years and countless victims sooner. Fortunately for Epstein, Goldston was a friend of both the Clintons and the royal family. The Jacobins take care of their own.

The Goldston miniseries further inflamed would-be jurors, not that they needed inflaming. For the J6ers, from day one, proceedings in the DC courts had been all show and no justice. "IMPOSSIBLE to get a fair trial in Washington, D.C., which is over 95% anti-Trump, & for which I have called for a Federal TAKEOVER in order to bring our Capital back to Greatness," Trump posted on Truth Social in August 2023.

Trump was not exaggerating. In 2016, Hillary Clinton may not have won the states of Wisconsin or Michigan, but she crushed Trump in the District of Columbia. In fact, Hillary was the first presidential candidate ever to win more than 95 percent of the district's two-party votes. Trump received just 4 percent. In 2020, incumbent president Trump upped his total but only to 5 percent. Of the fifty states, by contrast, none gave Trump less than 30 percent of the vote.

Historically, "liberals" would have been quick to recognize the injustice of submitting Trump and the J6ers to the

DC courts. For nearly a century, the Left has memorialized the injustice visited on the famed Scottsboro Boys, the nine young black men accused of rape in 1931 Alabama. The attorneys representing the nine argued that they were denied an impartial jury. The case became a liberal *cause celebre* and was twice litigated before the US Supreme Court. In the years since, movies have been made, songs written, and shows staged about the nine. What seems clear is that, whether innocent or not, the Scottsboro Boys were denied their constitutional rights in Jim Crow Alabama.

Liberals, to the degree they exist, should have been defending the rights of the J6ers the way they did the Scottsboro Boys. To say the least, they have not. On the first anniversary of January 6, for instance, all fifty-one ACLU chapters signed on to the kind of letter the ACLU chapter of ancient Rome might have written about the Vandals or the Visigoths. "On January 6 of last year, the residents of D.C. were traumatized as an insurrectionist mob roamed our streets, harassed our neighbors, and violently broke into the Capitol Building, killing at least five people—all in an attempt to overthrow the counting of American citizens' votes." The only thing the ACLU got right in this letter was the date.

The liberal Constitutional Accountability Center (CAC) was equally mendacious, just subtler. Yes, Washington was "a predominantly Democratic and Black city." But to question the city's ability to muster an "impartial jury," the CAC hinted, was racist.[236] Race aside, the CAC ignored the fact that the city's white jurors were at least as hostile to the MAGA movement as were the black ones.

Hoping to be a voice for her late daughter, Micki Witthoeft attended many of the J6 trials. Said Micki of the jurors,

"They look like a slice of D.C. that are waiting to tell their grandchildren that this was the J6er I fried."

Said John Strand of his jurors, "They know who I am and what I represent to them. And it's clear they hate me."[237]

Having watched the *voir dire* for the trial of his wife, Yvonne, Troy St Cyr causally observed, "I'm 100 percent positive jurors are handpicked."

By August 2023, when the CAC weighed in, the discussion of impartiality was no longer theoretical. DC juries had convicted 100 percent of those J6ers who pled their innocence, every single one of whom was denied a change of venue. The judges seemed no fairer. Only one defendant secured an acquittal at a bench trial. Although acknowledging roadblocks ahead, *Politico* noted in a January 2024 headline, "DOJ Has a Near-Perfect Record in Jan. 6 Cases."[238] Anecdotal evidence suggests that many of the J6ers' appointed attorneys held them in as much contempt as the prosecutors and judges did.

Faced with such impossible odds, most of the accused accepted plea deals, but some did not. In her shocking March 2023 *mea culpa* to the men and women of MAGA, one-time liberal icon Naomi Wolf helped clarify why these defendants saw themselves as innocent.

"In the media furore around Jan 6," wrote Wolf, "it was erased from memory that the White House itself and the Capitol too have always been open to US citizens and foreign visitors. The interior of the Capitol is open to the public. These are public buildings." As mentioned earlier, those attending the Trump rally did not even see any "restricted" signs. They saw no reason not to protest inside the Capitol.

"Look at all the people going in. It's our house. We're going in," said Lisa Eisenhart as she and her son Eric queued up to enter the building. "This is our house and we're the people," she repeated.

Once inside, the protestors could have ransacked the building. They did not. One exchange shot in the Senate chamber helps explain why there was so little gratuitous vandalism. A sole police officer found himself negotiating with about a dozen men. "Any chance I can get you guys to leave the Senate wing?" asked the officer.

"We will," responded a man sitting on the floor nursing a wound to his face from an illegally discharged plastic bullet. "I been making sure they ain't disrespecting the place."

Said the officer, "This is like the sacredest place."[239] The man nodded in agreement.

Like the others, Yvonne St Cyr was offered a plea deal, but she did not believe she had committed a crime, let alone the two felony counts with which she had been charged: obstructing and interfering with law enforcement during a civil disorder. Like many others, Yvonne got sucked into the mess at the front of the tunnel roughly at the same time as Rosanne Boyland did. According to the DOJ, "St Cyr entered the Tunnel twice and eventually climbed onto a ledge overlooking the crowd of rioters, which she filmed with her phone and shouted at the crowd, 'We need fresh people' and 'Push, push, push.'"[240]

This former Marine drill sergeant remained unrepentant. She thought it "impure" to compromise with an out-of-control Justice Department and continued to post live on Facebook even after her conviction. By this time, local public opinion had begun to swing in Yvonne's favor. As Troy St Cyr noted, "People are absolutely more supportive now."

What helped cause this shift in sentiment, both locally and nationally, was the airing of previously unseen Capitol video footage by Tucker Carlson in early March 2023. Carlson did not have to show much: an officer peacefully escorting QAnon shaman Jacob Chansley around the Capitol, Officer Brian Sicknick performing his duties hours after his murder, protestors walking respectfully through the building, honoring rope lines. It was this imagery that moved Wolf to write a "formal letter of apology. From me. To conservatives and those who 'put America first' everywhere."

Wolf's words penetrated few newsrooms. Six months after Carlson's revelations, the report on Yvonne's sentencing by the NBC affiliate in Boise showed that, even in solid red states, local stations remained captive to their Jacobin overlords. Fresh out of a local J-school, reporter Andrew Baertlein managed a sneer worthy of an MSNBC veteran. Upon hearing Yvonne insist the protest was largely peaceful, Baertlein scoffed, "Peaceful. Marching in lockstep, with the like-minded mass, directed through the former president."[241] As Baertlein spoke, viewers saw frightening images from January 6. In wrapping up, he and the news anchor expressed disappointment that Yvonne blew off the idea of "rehabilitation."

In Washington, Yvonne put the court on notice with the opening line of her allocution, a forceful "I do not comply." The allocution is the defendant's one opportunity to be heard before sentencing. Traditionally, judges refrain from interfering. Judge John Bates defied tradition. Bored by her message, he ordered Yvonne to wrap up her seven-page statement in one minute. In truth, it didn't much matter what Yvonne might have said. The courts weren't listening. Bates sentenced St Cyr to thirty months in prison and thirty-six months of supervised release.

The courts sent Yvonne to Federal Correctional Institution Waseca in Minnesota, a purposely inconvenient twenty-two-hour drive from Boise. On the plus side, the prison is a repurposed college and has a dormitory feel. When last I spoke with Yvonne—fifteen minutes max—she sounded surprisingly upbeat and seriously unrepentant.

In a CNN interview, Rachel Powell expressed "nothing but contempt for the court and the legal system." It is not hard to see why. Although she agreed to a plea deal, prosecutors repeatedly asked the judge for "upward departures" from the standard sentencing guidelines. In doing so, they showed again and again how thoroughly the legal system was rigged against the J6ers.

Out of spite, the prosecutors insisted on a "two-level enhancement" of Rachel's proposed sentence, citing her "pattern of intentionally destroying and concealing material evidence." Specifically, Rachel removed "incriminating videos and photographs of herself from January 6." She also "purposely hid her iPhone from law enforcement on the date of her arrest."[242] In 2016, however, as Rachel surely knew, even CNN was running headlines such as, "FBI: Clinton Staff Destroyed Devices with Hammers."[243] In addition to the hammers, Clinton and her attorneys famously used a computer software known as "BleachBit" to erase emails so completely even God would be hard-pressed to read them. There was, of course, no punishment for Hillary Clinton.

Rachel's sentencing documents also reveal how the courts used their allies in the media against their shared enemies. To build its case, prosecutors cited Rachel's attendance at pro-Trump rallies in December 2020. "Multiple newspapers reported the violence in Washington, D.C., during these election protests," said the prosecutors. To confirm their point, they cited a *Washington Post* headline, "Violence Erupts in Washington D.C. after Trump Supporters Rally."[244]

Left unsaid in the sentencing document is that the violence was initiated by the so-called "counterprotestors." Trump supporters were the ones being stabbed, beaten, and assaulted with firecrackers and bottles. Those who came to Washington on January 6 expected more of the same, which is why some carried defensive weapons like pepper spray or the ice ax handed to Rachel a moment before she used it to pull glass shards out of a window.

What they didn't carry were guns. "Truth," Rachel posted on August 9, 2021. "I used to carry all the time, but as an 'insurrectionist' went to the Capitol unarmed. I'm guilty of being in a protest that got out of control where police instigated and then murdered a woman in front of me. Oh, & they stole an election." The woman Rachel referred to was Rosanne Boyland. The prosecutors cited this post to show Rachel's lack of remorse.

Rachel did help break a window. She pushed against police barricades and encouraged others to surge forward against police lines. Prosecutors asked for eight years, one year, a cynic might suggest, for each of her eight children. A soft-hearted judge gave her fifty-seven months, forty-two more months than attorney Urooj Rahman received for fire-bombing a police car.

"I'm with family right now," Rachel texted me on January 7, 2024. "It would be better to write me because I have one day left which I will spend with family. I might be able to email you as well." Rachel left the next day for FCI Hazelton in Bruceton Mills, West Virginia.

That same evening, Anderson Cooper showed a recent interview Rachel did with a CNN reporter at her home in rural Pennsylvania. She had been confined there for nearly three years. "I don't have remorse for attending protests," she said calmly. "I don't have remorse for speaking out and saying I believe the election was stolen. I do have remorse for breaking a window and destroying my whole family's life."

Cooper concluded the segment with a homily so deep in mindless sanctimony it belongs in a time capsule. "It's amazing to me, although it shouldn't be," said Cooper, "that you know she spent three years locked up in her home and could have done some research, and she continues to believe things which are demonstrably false and just lies. I mean, it's pathetic."[245]

A US attorney offered Rebecca Lavrenz a plea deal for her crimes. The great-grandmother from Colorado Springs had walked into an open Capitol to pray and did just that, leaving ten minutes after she arrived. Members of Congress had already evacuated the building by the time she entered.

Rebecca refused to plead guilty. Surprised by her forthrightness, her defense attorney at the time told her, "To be honest, you are a breath of fresh air." In the months and years ahead, Rebecca used the platform her arrest afforded her to spread the good word. Rebecca's avowed mission is "to know God and make Him and His ways known, with a vision of restoring our nation back to God's original intent and that of our founding colonists."[246] Despite her legal travails, Rebecca refused to despair. "I treat this as an opportunity to be victorious," she told me, "I will never be treated as a victim."

After three years in limbo, Rebecca went to trial in late March 2024 before Magistrate Judge Zia M. Faruqui at the United States District Court for the District of Columbia. She was charged with the same four misdemeanors as were many, perhaps most, of the 1,300 or so protestors arrested on January 6: entering and remaining in a restricted building; disorderly and disruptive conduct in a restricted building or grounds; disorderly conduct in a capitol building; parading, demonstrating, or picketing in a capitol.

Eight of the fourteen jurors, including two alternates, were white. Eight were female. As one of Rebecca's hard-boiled attorneys told me, "The government strikes anyone who seems normal." The common denominator among them seemed to be boredom. When the prosecutors elicited from a squat, female Capitol Police officer that she feared for her life, the jurors looked nonplussed. Living in a city whose media are geared to please the 95 percent of its audience that voted against Donald Trump, they had heard it all before.

Rebecca must have disappointed them. Human nature being what it is, they were likely hoping for some fire-breathing Proud Boy or Oath Keeper, a trophy perp whose conviction they could dine out on until Armageddon. Instead, they got a prayerful, well-turned-out great-grandma who did nothing worse than enter the "People's House" through a door that had opened from within.

On Day 6, a Monday, Rebecca took the witness stand in her own defense, wearing, says daughter Laura, "her beautiful yellow dress and blue high heels." She remained on the stand throughout the morning and into the afternoon. "This past week you've seen videos of what I look like on the outside," she told the jury, "but now, I hope you get to see my heart." Under questioning from her attorney, Rebecca described how she accepted Jesus into her life as a teenager, met her future husband in high school, married him when he came back from Vietnam, and gave birth to four children. As she explained, she now has seven grandchildren and one great-grandchild.

The two young prosecutors—both thin, white, and be-spectacled—evoked Hannah Arendt's immortal phrase, "the banality of evil." Arendt made that comment in reference to Nazi executioner-in-chief Adolf Eichmann. To be sure, the prosecutors had not ascended to that level of evil, but in their untroubled eagerness to send a prayerful great-grandmother to prison they seemed capable. When badgered, Rebecca reiterated her firmly held belief, "It was my First Amendment Right to be seen and heard. I wanted my presence to be known."

Late Monday afternoon, Day 6, the jury received its instructions and began deliberating. At the end of the day, they still had not reached a verdict. This was encouraging. The jury took less than four hours to convict Guy Reffitt, the first J6 defendant to seek a trial by jury. Although Reffitt did not go into the Capitol, he was sentenced to more than seven years in prison for helping to "ignite the crowd." His adolescent son turned him in. His wife, Nicole, attends the nightly vigil at Freedom Corner. She still wonders why the much more visible "igniter" of crowds, Ray Epps, received no jail time at all.

On Wednesday, Day 8, the jury remained in deliberation for the entire day. "This means someone on that jury is obviously fighting for me," Rebecca posted at day's end, "and to me that means God is making tremendous power available through the fervent, heartfelt, continued prayers of you, His saints." It seems likely that the other jurors finally wore that "someone" down. Toward the end of the fourth day of deliberation, they delivered their verdict: guilty on all four counts.

Rebecca received the news stoically. She thought the jurors might at least acquit her on the "disorderly and disruptive conduct" charge. That said, even before she left the courthouse that afternoon, Rebecca reasoned that the conviction was part of God's plan. She did not have to wait long for confirmation. People were fighting for her.

Former President Trump took to Truth Social claiming that Rebecca had been "been unfairly targeted by Crooked Joe Biden's DOJ" and now faced up to one year in prison for "praying for our Failing Nation on January 6th!" When "End Wokeness" tweeted news of her conviction—viewed by more than a million people—Elon Musk responded, "Not right." Utah Senator Mike Lee meanwhile called for Rebecca to be pardoned. Rebecca's sacrifice, she understood, was not in vain. People were beginning to wake up. Rebecca's sentencing is scheduled for August 2024. Attention will be paid.

21

Reality Check

Weeks before Anderson Cooper opined about things that are demonstrably false, CNN ran a story headlined, "See the Surveillance Video Trump Allies Are Using to Sow Doubts about Voting."[247] The video captured illegal ballot harvesting on behalf of incumbent Joe Ganim during a Democratic mayoral primary in Bridgeport, Connecticut's largest city. A whistleblower handed over the video to the challenger, John Gomes. As a Democrat and a racial minority, Gomes could not easily be ignored. So blatant was the fraud that a judge nullified the election. This did not trouble Connecticut governor Ned Lamont. He and the state's Democratic Party endorsed Ganim, who won on the fourth go-around.

This "wild" story being too big for CNN to bury, the producers found a way to turn it against Trump. Asked anchor Kristin Fisher, "How are Trump and other right-wing figures trying to capitalize off this scandal?"

Reporter Marshall Cohen smirked, "They have had a bonanza with it in the right-wing media." Cohen dismissed Trump's claims about widespread voter fraud as "completely wrong." He consulted with the "experts," and they assured him that voter fraud is extremely rare. Case closed.

Not so fast. Two weeks after the "pathetic" Rachel Powell headed to prison, a victim of Trump's lies about voter fraud, the *New York Times* dug a little deeper into the Bridgeport scandal. Knowing its readers were not keen on learning about such mischief, the editors put their minds at ease with the semantic pretzel of a headline, "Election Fraud Is Rare. Except, Maybe, in Bridgeport, Conn."

Here, too, "experts" were recruited to assure readers "election fraud is rare." Bridgeport was an exception but, admittedly, the 2023 election was not a one-off. "Ballot manipulation has undermined elections for years," reported Amelia Nierenberg. "Residents of the city's low-income housing complexes described people sweeping through their apartment buildings, often pressuring them to apply for absentee ballots they were not legally entitled to."

Nierenberg explained the phenomenon to her disbelieving audience as though it had never happened before. "Sometimes, residents say, campaigners fill out the applications or return the ballots for them—all of which is illegal."[248] OMG! This was the kind of granny farming Project Veritas unearthed in Minneapolis in 2020, and that the *Times* so grossly misreported that Project Veritas felt compelled to sue for libel.

Of course, it's not just Bridgeport. As I am editing this book, I received a neighborhood post from a friend in San Francisco: "Mailbox theft potentially tied to elections…. Our building's mailboxes on 28th street were broken into two nights ago. I ran into our mailman this morning and he said tons of mailboxes were broken into that night, including most of our block (between Church & Dolores). The mailman said the thieves are after ballots." There are many ways to steal an election.

The Dinesh D'Souza film *2000 Mules* used geo-tracking data to make the case that schemes similar to Bridgeport's were routine in Democratic strongholds. Specifically, D'Souza accused the Democrats of throwing the 2020 election to Biden through the use of illegal vote trafficking in the major cities of critical swing states.

The much-anticipated film premiered in packed theaters across America on Monday, May 2, 2022. On that same May 2, 2022, *Politico* reported on the leaked initial draft of the Supreme Court opinion striking down *Roe v. Wade*. The leak was unprecedented. In fact, as *Politico* reported, "No draft decision in the modern history of the court has been disclosed publicly while a case was still pending."[249] This story gave the media all the excuse they needed to ignore *2000 Mules* and all the time its "fact-checkers" needed to "debunk" and "discredit" the film's claims. The leaker, of course, was never identified. The Jacobins take care of their own.

The *Dobbs* decision overturning *Roe* was formally announced in late June 2022. In July, Ohio resident Christine Priola pleaded guilty to obstructing an official proceeding. In October 2022, during her sentencing hearing, Christine got the sense that *Dobbs* did not sit well with Judge Tanya Chutkan. "Is this about abortion?" Chutkan snapped in the middle of her allocution.

Christine was not being argumentative. She began her allocution by apologizing for going into the Capitol. She was merely responding to Chutkan's question of why she backed Trump. Christine mentioned his support of the pro-life position and his efforts to stop child trafficking. This was not something Chutkan wanted to hear. "She was totally biased," said Christine. "How she is presiding over Trump's case I have no idea."

Christine's lawyer, Charles Langmack, pleaded for mercy. He argued that Christine had done no harm in the Capitol, had no negative interactions with law enforcement, had cooperated with the authorities, and had zero chance of reoffending. Having lost her home and her job with Cleveland schools, Christine, now fifty, was living in her mother's basement. To make herself useful, she helped elderly relatives with their chores. Christine had suffered enough, her attorney pleaded. Chutkan thought otherwise. "There is no mob without members of the mob," said the judge and sentenced her to fifteen months in prison.

A month later, a relative drove Christine to the federal prison in Hazelton, West Virginia, the same prison to which Rachel Powell would be dispatched a year later. Christine expected to be assigned to a camp for nonviolent offenders. Hazelton wasn't that. It was the state's highest security prison for women, the kind where cell doors lock shut at night.

When Christine arrived in late November 2022, prison officials put her in the SHU, the secure housing unit often called "the hole." The sensory deprivation—no exercise, no TV, one book a week—would have been bad enough, but for five of her fourteen days, Christine had to share the tiny cell and its open toilet with a man, a sexual predator who claimed to be a woman. "I was very uncomfortable," said Christine. "I was not okay with this." To prison officials, what Christine was okay with was of no consequence.

Life in the general population was a different kind of hell. "You have to appear a certain way just to survive," Christine elaborated. What she saw at Hazelton was the chaos one sees on the perversely popular prison reality shows—fighting, backstabbing, open homosexuality. Participating in none of the above made Christina stand out: "They knew I was out of place, and they knew what I was in for."

Fortunately, Christine was not there long. Thanks to the First Step Act signed into law by President Trump and her own good behavior, Christine left prison after seven-plus months. A month at a halfway house followed, and a month of home confinement followed that. In September 2023, Christine reentered society without a career, without a home, a pariah among those who chose to know no more about January 6 than what they saw on CNN. "We were willing to give our lives that day," Christine told me. "We had to do something. If something doesn't change, our country is gone."

The charges read to Victoria White at her sentencing hearing in November 2023 seemed more severe than those leveled at Christine Priola. White allegedly raised her fist and cheered as "rioters" pushed a flagpole into an entryway. She helped hoist up a "rioter" who kicked MPD officers from above. "Officers pushed White back with their riot shields and fended her off with a baton," prosecutors insisted. "White then grabbed one of the shields and blocked the baton with her hand." Finally, she was apprehended by the police and "escorted out of the Capitol building."[250]

As the videos actually show, Victoria grabbed one officer's plastic shield to stay upright lest she get trampled and reached out to another officer to stop from getting sprayed with mace. Tossed about like a rag doll, she could go neither forward, nor back, and was beaten mercilessly.

For her felony charge, Judge Bates sentenced Victoria to ten days in prison—to be served on successive weekends— and three months of home confinement. If there were a reason Victoria served less time than Christine Priola or Dr. Simone

Gold, it was because she had something that the others did not—leverage. By the time she was sentenced, the graphic video of her being brutally beaten in the tunnel had surfaced. Prosecutors had withheld this footage. Victoria received it from a friendly journalist.

Victoria had originally planned to take her case to trial, but as Julie Kelly explained, a trial was the very last thing the DOJ wanted. The video that surfaced was damning enough. If there was additional footage of Victoria being dragged shoeless through the Capitol, booked by the MPD, and released without a cell phone into the freezing darkness of a January night, the authorities preferred to keep that from the public.

"This tiny woman posed no threat to anyone," said Kelly. That lack of threat may have inspired at least one MPD officer to thrash her like a "human pinata." Not given to hyperbole, Kelly described the police action on January 6 as "the worst incident of police brutality since the civil rights era." If that brutality had an enduring image, it was the bloodied head of Victoria White.[251] As I write, Victoria is still confined to her home. "I think God allowed me to live for a reason," she told Liz Collin of Alpha News. "To speak to the truth and tell people what happened that day and what's continuing to happen to American citizens."[252]

Sara Carpenter has turned to the Psalms as she awaits whatever God has in store for her. Barring divine intervention, that is likely to be twenty-four months in a federal prison, the sentence she received in December 2023. Upon her conviction in March 2023, the *New York Times* ran a subhead that captured both the triviality of Sara's offenses and the petty vindictiveness of the *Times'* editors: "Sara Carpenter yelled at, pushed against and slapped the arms of police officers, all while wielding a tambourine, prosecutors said."[253]

Had the five-foot-four Sara been wielding, say, a tomahawk, one could understand the pearl-clutching, but a tambourine?

As Sara tells it, once she contested the charges against her, she was not given the choice of a bench trial. "If this was a jury of my peers, I would accept that," said Sara. "But it's clear these were not my peers." Throughout her trial, Sara had to deal with the condescension of her attorney, who hoped to portray her as a mindless female led astray by alpha dog Trump. Said Sara of Trump, "He was finally saying what I knew all along." As a nine-year veteran of the NYPD, she had seen a lot. On Election Day 2020, she saw the mischief in her own neighborhood, as scores of "illegals" lined up at her local polling station.

What made Sara Carpenter and those like her so dangerous was that they dared to see what the media refused to. When they showed up in Washington on January 6 in the hundreds of thousands, they stuck a massive thumb in the eyes of the media. Unable to ignore this story, the media had to rewrite it, even if it meant turning tiny tambourine-wielding women into domestic terrorists.

In January 2024, Lisa Eisenhart and her son Eric Munchel requested release from their impending imprisonment while they waited to learn the fate of their appeal. They are two of the three hundred or so January 6 defendants charged with obstructing an official proceeding. Their fate hinges on the outcome of *United States v. Fisher*, a case argued before a skeptical Supreme Court on April 16, 2024.

Pending a decision in that case, Lisa was granted release. Eric was not. As of this writing, Eric, thirty-three and a newlywed, is serving a four-year sentence at Yazoo City Correctional Institution in southern Mississippi, a six-hour drive from Nashville. The injustice of his sentence tears at Lisa—"I talked way more crap than my son did."

While she waits, Eisenhart has turned to the Psalms for guidance, particularly Psalm 31: "For I hear the slander of many; there is terror on every side; they conspire against me and plot to take my life. But I trust in you, O LORD; I say, 'You are my God.'"[254] Strengthened by prayer, Lisa tries not to fear the judgment of the state. "No punishment can be worse than taking my career from me," she told me, "or putting my son in prison."

Dr. Simone Gold showed up at the Capitol on January 6 as a respected physician/attorney and founder of America's Frontline Doctors, but she, too, left as a domestic terrorist. For a year after her arrest in January 2021, Gold negotiated her future through a series of Zoom meetings with US Attorneys in Washington. During that year, the authorities subjected Dr. Gold to what she calls "extrajudicial punishment."

"The anger against me is so aggressive," she believes, "because they think I betrayed my social class." Given her role as a head of a national organization, these gratuitous abuses derailed her career. Despite a perfect FICO score of 850, Dr. Gold was unable to open a bank account. She was first put on a no-fly list and then later on an SSSS (secondary security screening selection) list whose time-consuming humiliations made commercial flying all but impossible. Many prominent conservatives, James O'Keefe among them, have been subjected to this ritual abuse as well as just about all J6ers.

As much as it pained her to accept a plea deal, Dr. Gold did not feel she had much of a choice. Prosecutors were threatening a twenty-year sentence. In the year after her arrest, DC juries had shown open hostility to J6 defendants. She and John Strand were indicted on many of the same counts as were the other protestors: civil disorder, parading, impeding, disrupting, and disturbing "the orderly conduct of a session of Congress."[255] Many, if not most, of the protestors similarly charged received three years of probation and a fine. What the prosecutors had in store for Gold and particularly for Strand was shocking.

The judge at Dr. Gold's sentencing hearing, Christopher Cooper, accused her of showing no remorse for the real victims, namely the five police officers who allegedly died as a result of their being at the Capitol on January 6. To include among the "victims" one officer who died of natural causes and four who later committed suicide served only to stoke Cooper's already inflamed sense of self-righteousness.

An Obama appointee, Cooper sentenced Dr. Gold to sixty days at the Miami Federal Detention Center, a maximum-security prison. This was an unusually severe punishment for a single misdemeanor, even by January 6 standards. It was also the first time in Cooper's career he had leveled such a sentence for a nonviolent misdemeanor. The fact that Dr. Gold had rejected Cooper's advances while both were law students at Stanford may have affected the sentence. "He was filled with rage towards me," said Dr. Gold. She believes Cooper should have recused himself.

At her June 2022 sentencing, prosecutors made the case for prison time by lying about an incident that involved both her and Strand. Assistant US Attorney April Ayers-Perez argued that the pair watched as a police officer on the Capitol steps was "pulled to the ground." Although Gold was a medical doctor, "She does not stop. She does not help."[256] The officer's name was Joshua Pollitt.

His experience would receive even greater play in the trial of John Strand.

Dr. Gold describes John as a "righteous Christian," a term that has special meaning for Jews. By accepting a plea deal, Strand felt he would be bearing false witness against himself. "I am not guilty of anything," said Strand. "I needed to stand up for truth and give truthful witness." He opted for a jury trial.

At his trial, prosecutors accused Strand not merely of ignoring Officer Pollitt but of assaulting him. They had to know this wasn't true. As the video footage showed, Pollitt fainted. The FBI reported three days after the incident, "Joshua Pollitt stated that he blacked out. When he regained consciousness, he was no longer in the door foyer area and still had possession of his baton." A later FBI memo affirmed, "He falls down," and concluded, "There was not enough to charge assault."[257]

Pollitt collapsed into the crowd. The protestors promptly lifted him to his feet and steadied him until he regained his bearings. He did not bother to seek medical help. As the video clearly shows, Dr. Gold could not have gotten to him even if she knew what was going on. The incident was over almost as soon as it began, in a matter of seconds. The crowd was surging toward the doors, and she could not resist it. "The only safe option," said Strand, "was to move forward."

The prosecutors also accused Strand of shaking his fist menacingly at the door before it opened. The fist that the prosecutors showed in a dramatic still was white and ungloved. Strand wore black gloves when at the Capitol and never took them off. The prosecutors were not through with their deceptions. They showed the jury a still shot of a seemingly angry Strand raising his black-gloved hand in a fist as the police walked down the Capitol steps.

Strand felt a "sickening shock" on seeing this. He knew how false the image was. Standing on the steps after exiting the building, he watched a line of police officers walk by and "enthusiastically clapped and cheered for them in appreciation." Prosecutors pulled the split-second still with his raised hand from that video of him applauding the police and argued to the jury that he was expressing his anger. "It was shameful," said Strand, "that I had to prove my innocence when the evidence of it was so clearly seen in the government's own video." After more than a full day of deliberation, the jury convicted Strand on all counts. Cooper sentenced him to thirty-two months in prison—an excessive length even compared to Cooper's other J6 sentences.[258]

The media were gleeful. "Ex-Beverly Hills Underwear Model Gets 2 Years, 8 Months for Role in Capitol Riot," screamed the headline of the *Los Angeles Times*.[259] Despite Strand's varied career as a model, actor, musician, and security specialist, *Mother Jones* mockingly reduced Strand to the "insurrectionist underwear model." Its hopeful subhead read, "John Strand could face 25 years in prison."[260] The real Mother Jones must have been turning in her grave. In 1913, she was unjustly sentenced to twenty years in a state penitentiary for her role in a coal miner's strike. A century later, the Left had forgotten its own icons.

When Dr. Gold was sentenced a year earlier, the media defined her first and foremost as an "anti-vaccine doctor," which she never was. Her children are fully vaccinated, and so was she. She complied with all vaccination requirements of an emergency physician—right up until the COVID shot. Dr. Gold simply made the argument that the information the government was feeding the public about COVID was a "complete fraud." This was the "only so-called 'vaccine' in the world that has proven not to be able to stop transmission or infection." CNN described Dr. Gold as someone "known for spreading debunked claims about Covid-19."[261] To this day, Dr. Gold defies her critics to find anything that she said about COVID that has proved to be untrue.

To find prominent people on the left who have made spectacularly false claims is not hard at all. Dr. Gold cited the example of Supreme Court Justice Sonia Sotomayor. At a January 2022 hearing on the legality of vaccine mandates, Sotomayor insisted, "We have over 100,000 children, which we've never had before, in serious condition, and many on ventilators." As even the CNN fact-checker had to admit, the "wise Latina" jurist overstated the numbers by a factor of at least twenty.[262]

Said Dr. Gold, "How are we allowing people to judge other people when they don't know basic facts?" As an attorney, Dr. Gold was troubled by the disparity in her sentence and John Strand's. Each faced the same charges. Strand should not have been punished for exercising his Sixth Amendment right to a jury trial, but he was. Cooper presided over his trial as well, which may explain the thirty additional months. Young, stylish, and handsome, Strand was many things Cooper was not.

To clear Strand's name and hers, Gold and Strand prepared a fourteen-minute video of sufficient power to shame even a Liz Cheney.[263] The video followed the pair through their brief and innocuous sojourn at the Capitol. The prosecutors had access to all this video evidence at the time of Gold's plea deal. Gold did not. Their withholding of that evidence and lying about its contents induced Gold to accept a plea deal and caused her problems down the road with professional licensing authorities.

In early September 2022, Dr. Gold was released from prison after having served forty-eight days, eight of them in solitary confinement. Feisty as ever and uncontrite, she still had many battles ahead. The New York Bar leveled disciplinary charges against her. On her application to the Florida medical board for a physician license, the FBI correctly cited the misdemeanor to which she had pled guilty—18 US Code 1752—but mysteriously changed the words of the actual offense from disrupting "the orderly conduct of Government business" to "treason." And the Medical Board of California (MBC) came after her license.

In December 2021, the MBC accused Gold of "misinformation—giving public speeches on Covid-19-related lockdowns, vaccinations and the use of Ivermectin and hydroxychloroquine as potential treatments." This charge served as pretext to accuse Gold of "unprofessional conduct" for her J6 political speech and her presence at the Capitol. Gold refused to accept the legitimacy of MBC meddling in criminal cases given that no state medical board has that authority. In November 2023, Gold went to trial to maintain her medical license.[264]

Instead of putting forth any evidence of "misinformation," the MBC spent three days relitigating Gold's J6 presence at the Capitol—this despite Judge Cooper's having stated from the bench that J6 had nothing to do with Gold being a doctor. At risk was the right of any California physician to speak freely on matters medical or political. Fortunately for the future of free speech, Gold prevailed. "One important lesson I've learned over the last few years," said the undaunted Dr. Gold in January 2024: "When they try to discredit you by labeling you a conspiracy theorist, it's probably because they're hiding a conspiracy."[265]

22

No Exit

At one point, as they wandered through the Capitol looking for an exit, Dr. Gold and John Strand found themselves engulfed in a crowd that surged forward mindlessly, and they along with it. The crowd reached an impasse at a set of double doors with glass panels and glass transoms on either side at the end of a small, narrow corridor. The pair held themselves off to the side, at the top of a set of stairs, to avoid the crush.

In minutes, police appeared and informed the protestors that this was not an exit. If they wanted to get out, as Gold and Strand did, they would have to retrace their steps. The protestors complied, leaving the corridor that led to the east entrance of the Speaker's Lobby empty, at least for a while. Gold and Strand had no idea that moments later that hallway would be the scene of one of the most dramatic encounters in the Capitol's history.

It was a little after noon in California when Micki Witthoeft's daughter-in-law called her at work with the news about Ashli. "I truly lived a blissful experience," Micki told me, choking back the tears, "until my whole fucking world blew up."

Ashli's husband, Aaron, got a call from an acquaintance. He could hear the tremble in the man's voice. Aaron turned on the television. "The very first image I saw," he said, "was Ashli laying on the ground with blood coming out." He collapsed on seeing her. "At that point my life really just changed forever."[266]

After recovering from their initial shock, Micki Witthoeft and her son-in-law, Aaron Babbitt, took up Ashli's cause. Micki, who to this day will not look at videos of the shooting, vowed "to be a voice for the voice that was stolen from my daughter." Now spending most of her time in Washington, Micki has dedicated her life to getting justice for Ashli and for the J6ers held in the DC Central Detention Facility, some for more than three years without trial. Each evening, the no-nonsense Micki and other protestors stand vigil at Freedom Corner, an isolated spot between the "gulag" and the Congressional Cemetery. In the beginning, they would sing the National Anthem along with the prisoners. The authorities tried to kill this exchange by moving the prisoners to an inaccessible side of the building. Now they sing via telephone. "We may be late to the game," said Micki, "but we are the right messengers for prison reform."

Although initially as reluctant as Micki to view the crime scene, Aaron steeled himself: "I had to make that jump into basically watching and looking at every picture that no husband should ever have to look at." Aaron's resolve led to a wrongful death lawsuit filed in January 2024 by Judicial Watch.[267] Working off the data in that suit, *Epoch Times* senior reporter Joe Hanneman was able to put together a precise timeline of Ashli's final movements.

Ashli Babbitt entered the Capitol alone on the Senate side of the Capitol through a broken window at 2:23 p.m. Once in, she encountered a female police officer who directed her towards the House side. As Ashli walked, recording her fellow protestors with her iPhone along the way, she would have seen what Gold and Strand did, crowds wandering peacefully through the many rooms and corridors of this vast building. Uniformed police officers looked on, seemingly as clueless and confused as the protestors. John Strand described the scene as "eerily calm and surreal." There were no commands being given, no arrests being made, no police being attacked or abused.

At 2:25 p.m., Ashli climbed over a velvet rope to honor the walking lane designated for visitors. Still alone, Ashli made her way to the hallway leading up to the main door of the House Chamber. A crowd had already gathered there. Not one to follow the crowd, literally or figuratively, she continued to explore the Capitol. At 2:36, Ashli, now accompanied by citizen journalist Tayler Hansen, walked down the long, narrow corridor leading to the Speaker's Lobby, the space Gold and Strand had vacated moments before. Hansen recorded her as she walked. Guarding the lobby doors were three USCP officers—Sgt. Timothy Lively, Officer Kyle Yetter, and Officer Christopher Lanciano. Hansen offered the officers some water, while Ashli joked with them.

Within a minute or two, the trailing crowd of roughly thirty people quickly filled up the hallway in front of the lobby doors. In that crowd was Zachary Alam, thirty, from Centreville, VA. In October 2023, former CBS reporter Sharyl Attkisson did a feature on Alam and two other potential provocateurs for her show *Full Measure*. Attkisson explained. "I didn't see key provocateurs removed from the crowd. In fact, the key provocateurs in this case seem to be sort of tolerated, if not encouraged, by some of the police officers on the front line."[268]

Free to roam despite his erratic behavior, Alam moved to the front of the crowd, reached between the officers, and began punching the glass panels while yelling, "Fuck the blue." This was not a MAGA thing to say or do. In fact, as Attkisson pointed out, Alam had no social media history tying him to Trump or the MAGA movement. He had been arrested a half-dozen times in the previous four years and later told relatives, while still on the lam, that he didn't want to go back to prison.[269]

Appalled by Alam's behavior, Ashli's police training kicked in. "Call fucking backup!" she shouted at the feckless officers as they stood in place with their backs to the doors, doing nothing. "She was basically yelling at these officers telling them to do their jobs," said Hansen. Hansen meanwhile yelled at Alam, "Chill out! Chill the fuck out, bro!" For more than a minute after the first window was cracked, protestors argued with the officers but did not touch them or threaten them. Nor did they smash any more windows. At one point, Alam stood with his back to the officers keeping the crowd at bay. Clearly frustrated, Ashli wandered away from the doors.

In a press release clearing Lt. Byrd of any wrongdoing, the DOJ observed, "Eventually, the three USCP officers positioned outside the doors were forced to evacuate."[270] The video does not bear this out at all. The officers were not in any imminent danger. They appear to have noticed a USCP emergency response team mount the stairs to the lobby and abandoned their post before the response team could reach them.

As soon as the officers pulled away, rioter Chad Jones joined Alam in smashing the windows of the unguarded doors. House Sergeant at Arms employee Jason Gandolph, a licensed police officer, stood behind Ashli and did nothing to stop Jones or Alam. Now with a helmet he grabbed from another protestor, Alam broke out all the glass from the transom on far the right side. "Ashli was actively trying to disarm these people," Hansen observed, "trying to calm them down through this entire kind of confrontation with these police officers."[271]

By this time, several of the protestors on the left side of the hallway had noticed a weapon leveled parallel to the doors. A few yelled, "gun, gun" or "there's a gun, there's a gun." Self-styled video journalist John Earle Sullivan happened to be in that narrow corridor as well. Through the lens of his camera, he saw the extended arm, gun in hand, and joined the chorus of those shouting "gun."

On the right side of the clamorous lobby, Ashli either did not hear the warning or feared that the gunman was on her side of the lobby doors. After yelling for Alam to stop, Ashli took matters into her own hands, literally. A southpaw, she yanked at Alam's backpack with her right hand. As he spun around, she slugged him square in the face with her left fist. His glasses flew off on impact. Fleeing the madness, Ashli hopped with some assistance into the window frame now fully free of glass. Only a person as small as she could have managed that feat.

Hansen was finally able to post this frame-by-frame breakdown of the punch in January 2022. Hell-bent on denying Ashli martyr status, the *Washington Post*'s Philip Bump recoiled at Hanson's interpretation. "Even if this were true," Bump tweeted indignantly, "I'll just add that all of this is gross and dishonest and probably not worth elevating at all, even to identify as garbage."[272]

USCP lieutenant Michael Byrd, the incident commander for the House on January 6, had all the time he needed to assess the scene. He knew that the doors were heavily barricaded and that other armed officers hovered nearby in the Speaker's Lobby. "Members and staffers were just feet away when Babbitt attempted to climb through a shattered glass," the House report writers insisted. That again was false.

No members of Congress remained in the lobby, and the handful that remained on the House floor were Republicans, four from Texas, one from Oklahoma. They stood guard at the main door one hundred feet away and tried to calm the crowd through the broken window.[273] Three dozen House Democrats meanwhile hovered in the balcony, "socially distancing." Panicked by their own propaganda, they feared the worst. "Just remember, we're on the right side of history," Rep. Val Demings told a colleague. "If we all die today, another group will come in and certify those ballots."[274]

The House report did not mention Byrd by name, let alone question the shooting. To the degree that the report mentioned Ashli it was to build the specious case that Trump was indifferent to her death. How Byrd came to be there, as incident commander, had a lot to do with the racial politics of DC. Some years back, Byrd fired shots into his own moving vehicle. Some teenagers had stolen it and were fleeing the scene. Not the best of shots, Byrd sent a few stray bullets into the sides of nearby homes. An official investigation ruled that his use of force was unjustified. In another city, the officer gets canned. Not in Washington. Not Byrd.

In 2019, Byrd made the news when he left his Glock 22 in the Capitol Visitor's Center. As many as twenty thousand people pass through the center on a given day. More troubling still, the Glock does not have a traditional safety. A child could have found it and fired it. According to *Roll Call*, Byrd told fellow officers, "I will be treated differently." He was. After the Monday night incident, he was back on the job Tuesday.[275]

The IRS seems to have treated Byrd differently as well. As licensed private investigator Susan Daniels has reported, Byrd owes the IRS $56,365.71 in taxes dating back to 2019. In December 2023, Daniels called Prince George's County Courts, MD, and confirmed that the money had not yet been paid.[276]

Just seven seconds after she slugged Alam, said Hansen, "Michael Leroy Byrd ended up issuing the kill shot with no verbal warning." Said Thomas Baranyi, a young protestor who had been right behind Ashli when she fell, "[The protest] was a joke to them until we got inside, and then all of a sudden the guns came out."[277]

According to Aaron Babbit's suit, "The bullet pierced Ashli in her left anterior shoulder, perforated her left brachial plexus, trachea, upper lobe of the right lung and second anterior rib, and landed in her right anterior shoulder." Once shot, Ashli instantly fell backward onto the marble floor. She was still alive after the fall. According to Baranyi, Ashli "started to say she's fine, it's cool, and then she started like moving weird and blood was coming out of her mouth and neck and nose."

When California physician Austin Harris tried to treat Ashli, the police pulled him off and cleared the other protestors trying to help. According to Hansen, that is all they did. "The cops just continued to stand there," he told filmmaker Nick Searcy. "They didn't help her. She clearly needed her throat cleared from the blood. They didn't do anything. They just let her bleed out. And that was it."[278]

The FBI would later arrest Harris on the same cocked-up charges they did most other protestors. A half-hour after the shooting, Ashli was pronounced dead at Washington Hospital Center. As with Hansen, no official ever talked to him or asked to see his video despite Hansen's repeated attempts to reach out. "I begged and I begged these people on the committee," said Hansen, but no one wanted to know what he saw.

As Ashli lay dying, Byrd wasted no time trying to establish his alibi. Within one minute of shooting Ashli, Byrd made an astonishing radio call:

> 405B. We got shots fired in the lobby. We got shots shots fired in the lobby of the House Chamber. Shots are being fired at us and we're sh, uhh, prepared to fire back at them. We have guns drawn. Please don't leave that end. Don't leave that end.

Like the Democrats huddling in the balcony, Byrd had fallen prey to the media scare stories about the MAGA hordes. Less than a minute later, Byrd made a follow-up call: "405B. We got an injured person. I believe that person was shot." Believe? Indifferent to the possibility that the shooting had been recorded, Byrd reflexively created his own reality. With a history of being "treated differently," he was confident his version would prevail.

Sullivan made either option difficult. Sniffing a payday for his footage, he had his agent contact CNN on January 6 and enter into a one-week agreement for use of the critical forty-four seconds. CNN paid him $35,000. The network, however, would quickly come to regret this vestigial act of journalism.

After Sullivan appeared with Anderson Cooper, Trump supporters like Rudy Giuliani pointed out that Sullivan was a black activist in the BLM mode. A video from his Instagram account, long since deleted, showed him at a Salt Lake City rally in the summer of 2020 telling the crowd, "We gotta fucking rip Trump right outta that office…. No, no—we ain't' about waitin' until the next election, we're about to go get that motherfucker!"[279] At the Capitol, however, Sullivan played patriot and egged on the crowd. He recorded himself saying, "There are so many people. Let's go. This shit is ours! Fuck yeah," and, "Let's burn this shit down."[280]

Sullivan showed up at the Capitol carrying a knife and wearing a ballistics vest and gas mask. He seemed the prototype of the agent provocateur. The Jacobins could not let this imagery stand. Twitter deleted Giuliani's tweets. Instagram removed Sullivan's videos. CNN scrubbed the Anderson Cooper interview. The FBI silenced Sullivan by arresting him just a week after his appearance on CNN. And the DOJ threw the book at him. He was convicted in November 2023 on all charges, including five felonies. In his defense, he said he was just trying to blend in. He almost did. Had he not come forward with the Ashli Babbitt footage, he may have passed unnoticed like other still unidentified "suspicious actors."

Whatever Sullivan's motives, his video made life difficult for Byrd and his patrons. To preserve the narrative of heroic Capitol police resisting an insurrectionist mob, Byrd had to be protected. This would not be easy. As the Babbitt suit makes clear, Byrd violated just about every USCP directive on the use of deadly force.

Masked and out of uniform, Byrd did not identify himself as a police officer, did not give Ashli verbal orders to stop, nor give her a chance to comply. He did not "diligently assess" the situation before firing. He never considered any other defensive tactics or compliance techniques. He disregarded the presence of seven other police officers in his line of fire. And as incident commander for the House, he appeared to have no comprehension of who was in the Speaker's Lobby or the House Chamber or what was going on around him. Most critically, Ashli did not pose "an imminent danger of death or serious injury." When Byrd fired, he did not even know she was a female.

"I was bound to the same use of force continuum as the police are in D.C.," said Aaron Babbitt of his time working security at a nuclear facility. "I knew it was a bad shoot."[281]

Use-of-force expert Kephart was even more definitive. "Ashli Babbitt was murdered," said Kephart. "She was shot and killed under the color of authority by an officer who violated not only the law but his oath." Kephart considered the shooting "an arrestable offense."

To Byrd's good fortune, Sullivan's video only showed the masked Byrd briefly. This gave his patrons time to hide the still unidentified Byrd from public view until they came up with a public relations strategy. For six months, the USCP put Byrd and a pet up in a "distinguished visitor suite" at the "Presidential Inn" on the grounds of Joint Base Andrews.[282]

For nearly nine months after the shooting, the media showed no interest in Byrd's identity. Not until August 28, 2021, did the Capitol Police publicly identify Byrd by name. James Goldston could not have orchestrated Byrd's coming out any better than did NBC. Welcoming Byrd with an exclusive interview was Lester Holt, perhaps the most empathetic black newsman in the business. Byrd was well coached. For those who knew nothing of the facts—NBC's core audience—he came across as bipartisan, patriotic, and sensitive to a fault. Those who knew the facts witnessed a master class in dissembling.[283]

Holt began by asking Byrd why the Capitol Police withheld his name as long as it did.

Byrd responded, "Threats."

To further insulate Byrd, Holt followed his initial question with the inevitable, "Racist threats?"

Long before internet sleuths even deduced Byrd's identity, the NBC audience was led to believe Trump supporters were making racist threats. "I do hate that son of a bitch," said Ashli's mom, Micki, "not because he's black, but because he killed my child."

As Holt repeated twice, the USCP, the MPD, the FBI, and the DOJ had all cleared Byrd of any wrongdoing. This was true. According to the DOJ, the fact that "an officer acted out of fear, mistake, panic, misperception, negligence, or even poor judgment" did not make him criminally culpable. That officer would have had to act "with a bad purpose to disregard the law."[284] By this standard, Lila Morris was surely guilty and Byrd at least as guilty as, say, Derek Chauvin or Kim Potter, the Minnesota officer imprisoned for the accidental 2021 shooting of Daunte Wright.

The DOJ publicly cleared Byrd in April 2021—without mentioning his name. What no one could clear him of, especially after his one-time appearance on NBC, was lying. Byrd lied about things big and small, even things he didn't have to lie about. Most grandiose was his claim, "I know that day I saved countless lives." Among those he claimed to have saved were members of Congress who were "disabled" or very nearly so. "Some of those individuals were in the lobby with me," said Byrd. In fact, there were no members of Congress in the lobby, let alone disabled ones.

Not until the twenty-three-minute mark of the interview did either Holt or Byrd mention Ashli by name. Holt asked what Byrd made of the fact that "some have elevated Ashli Babbitt to the status of the martyr."

Replied Byrd, who surely had the questions provided to him in advance, "I have no reaction to that." Holt then set up Byrd for the interview's takeaway message, "I just want the truth to be told." Apparently, Byrd told *his* truth well enough to please his Jacobin masters. To show their indifference to *the* truth, they had Byrd promoted to captain two years after the interview.

Unlike Byrd, Ashli never got the chance to explain her actions.

Why exactly she mounted the windowpane no one will ever know. Best guess is that, given her size, she wanted to avoid being crushed against the doors by a crowd surging mindlessly into that compressed space. The men surrounding her were as much as a foot taller and a hundred pounds heavier. Many of the women profiled—Sara Carpenter, Rosanne Boyland, Victoria White, Yvonne St Cyr, Dr. Simone Gold—struggled to maintain their balance, even their wits, when engulfed in such a crowd. In that crowd, too, was at least one chronic law breaker, Zachary Alam, and at least one black anti-police activist, John Sullivan. Said Micki of her daughter, "She suddenly realized that she was surrounded by people without her intentions."

It is possible, too, that Ashli just wanted members of Congress to hear her out. This is what Thomas Baranyi, Ashli's blood still on his hands, told a reporter that afternoon. "We wanted to tell them," he said, "that we need some kind of investigation into [election fraud]."[285] Worst case is that Ashli hoped to do what the Kavanaugh protesters actually did, namely, disrupt an official proceeding. If so, she was too late. The vote count had already been postponed, and the members of Congress evacuated. Whatever her end game, both Micki and Ashli's husband, Aaron, believe that it was very much like Ashli, the oldest of five siblings, to take the lead.

The one interpretation that makes no sense of these last few minutes of Ashli's life is that she hoped to further an insurrection. Her brief interlude inside the Capitol refutes any such notion. Ashli Babbitt was a respecter of sacred spaces, a champion of the Constitution, and, above all, a patriot. For the Jacobins, her very virtues are what made her so dangerous.

23

John Doe #3

At 2:00 p.m., Ashli Babbitt approached the Capitol, having completed the forty-five-minute walk from the Ellipse where President Trump had been speaking. She and the others who had attended the rally arrived an hour behind schedule. The conspirators had expected them about 1 p.m.

I use the word "conspirators" here advisedly. If these sundry people shared a goal—humiliating Trump and ending MAGA as a movement—they did not necessarily share the same game plan. The law enforcement agencies had legitimate reasons to have undercover operatives in the crowd. Most, one hopes, performed appropriately. Some obviously did not. There were also clearly rogue actors in the crowd. Some, like videographer John Earle Sullivan and window-smasher Zachary Alam, did not have benefactors. They went to prison. Others, like Ray Epps and the bat-wielding Emanuel Jackson, apparently did have friends in high places. They did not go to prison.

"I don't think that this is a perfect puzzle where all the pieces go together," FBI whistleblower Steven Friend told

Sharyl Attkisson. "I do think, though, that there were some just blatant behaviors that day that were not normal, they were very unnatural, that necessitate a full, transparent, and open investigation."[286]

What makes it difficult to delineate the conspiracy with more precision is the failure of the media and government at all levels to investigate. In fact, the various members of Club Jacobin have used their enormous powers to bury the truth whenever it proved inconvenient. The *samizdat*, fortunately, has continued to dig it up.

On January 6, as he has a habit of doing, Donald Trump threw the conspirators a curve. On January 5, Trump posted on Facebook, "I will be speaking at the SAVE AMERICA RALLY tomorrow on the Ellipse at 11AM Eastern. Arrive early—doors open at 7AM Eastern. BIG CROWDS!"[287] Trump started his speech an hour late. Had he started on time, audience members would have arrived at the Capitol just about 1 p.m. when they would have been most useful.

For the conspirators, 1 p.m. on January 6 appears to have been the witching hour. This was the time scheduled for Vice President Mike Pence to begin the certification process in the House Chamber. Minutes before 1 p.m., Pence tweeted his decision not to intervene in the counting of electoral votes.

At about 12:40 p.m., Karlin Younger, a Commerce Department employee, spotted what appeared to be a six-inch pipe bomb as she walked down an alley near the RNC headquarters in Washington. The timer appeared to be set for the bomb to explode in twenty minutes, at 1 p.m. At 12:50 p.m., USCP officers responded to the scene. It seems likely the USCP activated a parallel search at the DNC headquarters.

Minutes after 1 p.m., an undercover USCP officer spotted an apparent bomb sitting conspicuously in a bush next to a park bench outside the DNC. We know this because Rep. Thomas Massie shared the surveillance video with Darren Beattie of Revolver News and Steve Baker of The Blaze. At 1:05, video shows the USCP officer informing officers in a Metropolitan PD vehicle of his discovery. He shared that same information with the Secret Service agents sitting in a car next to the MPD's. The Secret Service was there to protect vice president-elect Kamala Harris.[288]

The conspirators, it appears, had not counted on Harris being at the DNC just as they had not counted on the delay in Trump's speech. They went ahead with their plans nonetheless. For the previous half hour or so, Ray Epps had been shepherding his crew down Pennsylvania Avenue. "We are going to the Capitol," he shouted. "That's where our problems are." On the west side of the Capitol, Epps and those he influenced breached the outer gates at 12:53 p.m.[289] None of those involved in this breach could have heard Trump's speech. Had Trump started his speech on time, Epps would have had thousands more potential troops behind him.

This account of events, I should note, is a work in progress. By the time this book is released, we will know much more about the convergence of events at 1 p.m. This new information will come from the right side of the blogosphere, the *samizdat*. The Jacobins will, of course, do their best to limit the spread of new evidence. Through sheer clumsiness, however, they have already shown their hand. Their efforts to conceal Harris's presence at the DNC, protect Epps, and memory-hole the pipe bomber mark January 6 in no small part as an inside job.

Politico did not break the story of Harris's whereabouts until January 6, *2022*. Within minutes of the bomb's discovery, *Politico* reported, the Secret Service whisked Harris off to some undisclosed location but not the Capitol—"Harris had said little about her movements during the siege." As others in the media had been doing for the past year, *Politico* attributed the bomb to Trump supporters, claiming "that the riots could have been far more destructive than they already were, with the incoming vice president's life directly endangered." For its part, the FBI continued to insist that the bombs were "viable" and "could have been detonated, resulting in serious injury or death."[290]

The Biden White House suppressed news of Harris's presence at the DNC for a year. Despite her penchant for contrived drama, Harris somehow resisted the urge to present herself as the near victim of a white supremacist terror plot. Biden resisted the urge as well. There was obviously something about this little drama they did not like. The suppression of that information had real-world consequences. Prosecutors had been telling J6 judges and juries that Harris was among those under threat from the mob at the Capitol. Not until November 2021 did they amend their filings to correct this error. Said *Politico*, "It's unclear why DOJ included the erroneous information in the first place and continued to do so for months."[291]

The management of the Ray Epps saga is equally curious. By January 8, Epps ranked high on the FBI's "most wanted" list. Not only did he encourage the initial breach and a secondary breach, but he also provided hands-on help to those pushing a large metal Trump sign into a line of police officers. By July 2021, the evidence notwithstanding, he was off the list altogether. Perversely, the more evidence that surfaced against Epps, the more the media embraced him. For its part, the House Select Committee treated Epps as though he were an endangered species.

Not until September 23, 2023, did Epps plead guilty to a single misdemeanor charge and only then because his preferential treatment embarrassed the keepers of the narrative. On January 9, 2024, NBC News headlined his plight, "Ray Epps, a Jan. 6 Defendant 'Scapegoated' by Far-Right Media, Sentenced to Probation."[292] Effective propaganda requires a fine touch. The NBC article was written with a sledgehammer.

Comically naive, the NBC reporters quoted the Epps judge as saying, "More than 700 people have been sentenced in this courthouse for their role in January 6th. Not one is a member of Antifa or a FBI agent." Here, the savvy reader smacks his forehead and says, "Duh!" Of course, no Antifa or FBI agents were prosecuted. That's just the point. It took three years' worth of incriminating videos to force an arrest of the day's most conspicuous provocateur. For his crimes, Epps got a year's probation. Of the eight living women profiled in this book, six have already been imprisoned, two more are likely to go, and not a one of them bragged, as Epps did, "I was in the front with a few others, I also orchestrated it."[293]

The FBI took the pipe bomber even more seriously than they took Epps. On September 8, 2021, the Bureau released an elaborate map and new supporting video to trace the alleged bomber's movements on the night of January 5, 2021. The release documented the FBI's Herculean effort to find the bomber and renewed the call for tips. "We know it is hard to report information about a friend or family member," said Steven M. D'Antuono, assistant director in charge of the FBI's Washington Field Office, "but these pipe bombs were viable devices that could have detonated, causing innocent bystanders to be seriously injured or killed."[294]

The mayor of Madison, Wisconsin, Satya Rhodes-Conway, took the bomb plot as seriously as the FBI. On February 1, 2021, Rhodes-Conway issued a mayoral proclamation honoring hometown hero Karlin Younger for her "quick work and calm head" in reporting the RNC bomb.

In a swing state like Wisconsin, Rhodes-Conway saw the added value of advancing the party line: "January 6th will live in infamy as a day in which an armed mob overran the U.S. Capitol and Ms. Younger's swift action prevented further injuries and deaths on that terrible day."[295] In the People's Republic of Madison, citizens took it for granted that the would-be bomber was an extension of that "armed" mob. So did most Americans. In one of life's little ironies—or not—Younger has subsequently gone to work for the Pendulum Corporation, an information forensic company with the unsettling motto, "Deep technology to combat harmful narratives."

As to the motive behind the bombs, the House Select Committee offered an opinion: "Responding to these incidents required a commitment of significant USCP resources for mitigation and to evacuate nearby buildings, preventing their deployment to the Capitol to help secure the building." Although credible on its surface, informed citizens have no reason to take seriously any official statement about the bombs. As late as January 2024, the FBI was spreading the same disinformation it spread three years prior: the bombs were planted during the evening of January 5; they were "viable;" and they "could have seriously injured or killed innocent bystanders."[296]

The *samizdat* has shredded all these claims. Harris had Secret Service protection while at the DNC. Through friends in Congress, Revolver News secured video of a Secret Service sweep done of the DNC's exterior with a bomb-sniffing dog shortly before Harris's arrival and hours after the bombs were allegedly planted. The dog turned up nothing. Then, too, the bombs were equipped with a common kitchen timer of an hour's duration. If the bombs had been planted the night before, the timer would have been useless.[297]

Despite the FBI promise of a $500,000 reward, the DC pipe bomber has vanished into the ether as miraculously as did John Doe #2. To refresh the reader's memory, on April 19, 1995, a truck bomb destroyed the Murrah Federal Building in Oklahoma City, killing 168 people. A week later, John Hersley, the primary FBI case agent in the investigation, testified to multiple "eyewitness accounts of a yellow Mercury with [Timothy] McVeigh and another man inside speeding away from a parking lot near the federal building."[298] Several other witnesses had seen McVeigh's accomplice in the hours leading up to the blast.

The FBI created a composite drawing of this man, described as "full-faced and stocky, with dark hair and an olive complexion," and labeled him "John Doe #2." As the *Washington Post* reported, "hundreds of investigators" joined in the nationwide manhunt for McVeigh's elusive co-conspirator. They need not have wasted their time.

Sensing an opportunity, Bill Clinton advisor Dick Morris immediately sent the president a memo: "Permanent possible gain: sets up Extremist Issue vs. Republicans." The Clinton White House had in McVeigh a poster boy for Newt Gingrich's "Republican Revolution." If John Doe #2 proved to be a Muslim co-conspirator or a confidential FBI source, he would have spoiled the picture. Clinton followed Morris's advice and saved his flailing presidency.[299] With Clinton's poll numbers rising, the White House and the media lost interest in finding John Doe #2. Inevitably, so did the FBI. To this day, he has never been identified.

A quarter century later, in 2020, the FBI relied on "confidential informants" to report on a plot to kidnap Michigan's Democratic governor, Gretchen Whitmer. As likely happened in Oklahoma City, these operatives, a dozen in total, exceeded their brief. "Working in secret, they did more than just passively observe and report on the actions of the suspects," the liberal Buzzfeed News reported in July 2021. "Instead, they had a hand in nearly every aspect of the alleged plot, starting with its inception. The extent of their involvement raises questions as to whether there would have even been a conspiracy without them."[300]

Playing her role in the "deep rig," Whitmer revealed this nefarious plot just four weeks before the 2020 election. Just as Clinton did in Oklahoma City, then candidate Joe Biden seized the opportunity to score political points, however specious. "There is a through line from President Trump's dog whistles and tolerance of hate, vengeance, and lawlessness to plots such as this one," said Biden on the day the FBI announced the arrests. "He is giving oxygen to the bigotry and hate we see on the march in our country." Biden took the occasion to repeat his lies about Trump's Charlottesville comments, the "through line" of his own campaign.[301] Biden's silence about the terrorist bomb plot on January 6 tells us who the conspirators are *not*.

What happened in the wake of Oklahoma City happened again after January 6: the media lost interest in finding the most wanted man in America. The pipe bomber—for continuity's sake, John Doe #3—has all but faded from memory. Those pulling the strings likely sensed that finding the bomber would undo the story they had so successfully spun. Better to let him disappear into the night. Like the ill-fated Brian Sicknick, he had served his purpose.

The management of the Harris story suggests orchestration at the highest level. This was no rogue plot. Those in the know stood to gain by having the certification process shut down and Trump blamed for the disruption. That group did not include President Donald Trump. He remained hopeful to the end. Even if Pence rejected the proposal to allow each state a ten-day election audit before certification, that day's scheduled airing of fraud allegations would have revealed why so many people believed the election was stolen.

Trump supporters knew none of this background as they marched happily to the Capitol. The trap had been set when Samsel and Epps breached the first protected police barrier. Within minutes of that first breach, USCP chief Steven Sund called the House sergeant at arms, Paul Irving, demanding help from the National Guard. Irving told Sund he had to run the request up the chain to Pelosi.

With some notable exceptions, the USCP and MPD were as much pawns as the protestors. When thrown into the breach, a few of the MPD officers openly expressed their disgust at being set up to fail. Their numbers thinned by the reported bombs, the police faced a growing crowd with limited resources and no reliable backup.

If clever, the conspirators likely counted on law enforcement's amateurish and often violent overreaction to the incoming masses. Some among the police seemed to understand the good intentions of the MAGA crowd. Others, like Michael Byrd and Lila Morris, saw a horde of killer white supremacists. If the police behaved badly, the conspirators weren't worried. This wasn't Chicago 1968. There would be no talk of a "police riot" as there had been at that year's Democratic National Convention. The media, they knew, would denounce the "insurrectionists" as they "stormed" the Capitol without prompting.

At 2:09 p.m., an inexplicable seventy-one minutes and thirty-two phone calls after Sund's initial call, the Capitol Police Board approved the use of the National Guard. Although President Trump had pre-authorized the deployment of ten thousand troops—unusual behavior for an insurrectionist—the Pentagon hesitated.

According to Sund, Gen. Walter Piatt told him, "I don't like the optics of the National Guard on Capitol Hill." In his April 2024 testimony to the House Subcommittee on Oversight, National Guard Captain Timothy Nick confirmed Sund's memory. As aide de camp to Major General William Walker, the commanding General of DC National Guard, Nick recorded the events of the day meticulously.

"The DC National Guard was ready to help and assist Capitol Police, but we were not allowed to do our job due to paralyzed decision making," Nick testified. He denounced the Department of Defense Inspector General's multidisciplinary review as a whitewash "riddled with inaccuracies, misstatements, and perhaps false flags."

Nick quoted the generals as saying, "It would be in their best military advice to recommend to the Secretary of the Army, Ryan McCarthy, to deny the request from Command General William Walker."[302] Only after the first shot was fired did the Pentagon get the National Guard into gear, but by then it was too late for Ashli Babbitt and too late for Rosanne Boyland as well.

Standing to benefit from the disrupted proceeding were House Speaker Nancy Pelosi and, more passively, Senate Majority Leader Mitch McConnell. Twelve hours of serious fraud allegations, presented by members of Congress, would have shown the "big lie" to be the big lie that it was. If the disruption had a downside for Pelosi and McConnell, it was that they were the ones responsible for the security of the Capitol. Not since the War of 1812 had leadership so clearly failed in its duty.

The question remains whether the failure was by design. "People don't really want to get to the bottom of this," Sund told Tucker Carlson in 2023. "This didn't have to happen."[303] The details of a larger conspiracy may never be sorted out, but as with so many seeming conspiracies—the Epstein jailers come to mind—incompetence masks many a sin.

The conspirators may not have needed to include USCP assistant chief for intelligence Yogananda Pittman in the plot. Knowing her history, they might have just counted on her to screw things up. She was the rare intelligence chief, after all, who would admit, "I am not an intelligence analyst, and that takes specific training and usually years of training."[304]

That said, it was Pittman who led Sund to believe that the January 6 rally would be a reprise of the November and December MAGA rallies. It wasn't. Rather than discipline the head of intelligence, Pelosi promptly fired Sund and promoted Pittman to acting USCP chief, another clumsy move. To get a sense of the contempt in which Pittman's colleagues held her, a staggering 92 percent of them voted no confidence in her leadership.[305] Forced to leave the USCP after an embarrassing intelligence failure and a resounding vote of no confidence, Pittman secured a cozy gig as chief of the University of California Berkeley's police department. Her application surely had Pelosi's fingerprints all over it, probably Gov. Gavin Newsom's as well.

For all the screwups, by 2:40 p.m., Jacobin insiders had to be popping their champagne corks. The plot had worked well enough. The crowds behaved badly, the TV crews captured the misbehavior, and the talking heads feigned outrage. And the best was yet to come. At 2:43 p.m. a signal flare was launched high over the Capitol. At that moment, Ray Epps and others began pushing a huge metal Trump sign into the police line, promising more mayhem still. There would be no election challenge, no talk of a stolen election, no future for Donald Trump. And then at 2:44 p.m. Michael Byrd went and bollixed everything up.

A minute or so after the shooting, a red warning flare popped, and an eight-person team—four in front, four in back—quickly extracted Epps from the scene. He was alleged to be alone. He wasn't. The video evidence is inarguable. "Every military guy I know, every three-letter guy I know that was at January sixth, we all saw the same things happening," J6 video expert Gary McBride told filmmaker Nick Searcy. "We all knew that this was an operation."[306] Say what you will about Michael Byrd, he wasn't part of the plan.

24

ASHLI

lthough "not a perfect person," Micki Witthoeft said of her daughter Ashli, "she was an amazing woman." To be sure, feminists will never claim Ashli as one of their own. That's too bad. Ashli was the "strong woman" leftist women aspire to be but are too fond of their safe spaces to ever become. The traits of such a woman, one typical feminist site reported, include "being self confident, productive, optimistic, a go-getter, a fear-tackler, caring, unafraid to stand up for what one believes in, proud, unbothered by what others say or think, and true to one's self."[307]

That was Ashli to the letter. "Babbitt was a leader rather than a follower and liked being her own boss," her airman friend told the FBI.[308] "She loved life," said husband Aaron. "She woke up every day wanting to take on the world. Never had a task she didn't want to conquer. The harder it was, the more she wanted to fight for it." Ashli never expected to die in the fight, and, to be fair, the Jacobins had no interest in seeing her die.

Without intending, they created a martyr, and more than a martyr, an archetype of the American patriot. As each day passes, and more and more people learn the story of Ashli's life and the facts surrounding her death, the rebellion against Jacobin rule will grow. Naomi Wolf bears witness to a wakening still in its early stages.

"The gatekeepers who lie to the public about the most consequential events of our time," Wolf wrote, "and who thus damage our nation, distort our history, and deprive half of our citizenry of their right to speak, champion and choose, without being tarred as would-be violent traitors—deserve our disgust." This one-time liberal icon wasn't through. "I am sorry I believed so much nonsense," she concluded her *mea culpa*. "Though it is no doubt too little, too late—Conservatives, Republicans, MAGA: I am so sorry."

In time, the plot to steal the nation's glory will unravel. America's Jacobins, like their French forbears, will be remembered only for their excesses, their sins against justice, and their savage indifference to the truth.

The memory of Ashli Babbit will live on in a different light. In the years to come, God willing, hers will be the face of the Great American Awakening, an awakening commemorated every year on the anniversary of the day the nation's patriots risked their lives, their fortunes, and their sacred honor to rouse their fellow citizens to action, the Feast of the Epiphany, January 6, 2021.

Endnotes

1   "The French Revolution and the Organization of Justice," Government of Canada, updated August 26, 2022, https://www.justice.gc.ca/eng/rp-pr/csj-sjc/ilp-pji/rev5/index.html#:~:text=These%20rights%20are%20liberty%2C%20property%2C%20security%20and%20resistance%20to%20oppression.

2   "Declaration of Independence: A Transcription," America's Founding Documents, National Archives, https://www.archives.gov/founding-docs/declaration-transcript.

3   "Them vs. U.S.," Committee to Unleash Prosperity, January 2024, https://committeetounleashprosperity.com/wp-content/uploads/2024/01/Them-vs-Us_CTUP-Rasmussen-Study-FINAL.pdf.

4   Victor Davis Hanson, "The Real Story of January 6 Part 2: The Long Road Home," *Epoch Times*, January 6, 2024, https://www.theepochtimes.com/epochtv/therealstoryofjan6part2-5548012.

5   Nicole Bietette, "Madonna to Crowd at Women's March: 'I've Thought a Lot about Blowing Up the White House,'" *Daily News*, January 21, 2017, https://www.nydailynews.com/2017/01/21/see-it-madonna-to-crowd-at-womens-march-ive-thought-a-lot-about-blowing-up-the-white-house-warning-graphic-language/.

6   "Ashli Babbitt: The US Veteran Shot Dead Breaking into the Capitol," January 8, 2021, https://www.bbc.com/news/world-us-canada-55581206.

7   Teri Figueroa, "San Diego Woman Killed in Capitol Siege Was Iraq War Veteran," *San Diego Union-Tribune*, January 7, 2021, https://www.sandiegouniontribune.com/news/public-safety/story/2021-01-07/san-diego-woman-killed-in-capitol-siege-was-iraq-war-veteran.

8   Rebecca Lavrenz Legal Defense Fund, https://www.givesendgo.com/rebeccalavrenz.

9   Unless specified otherwise, all information about Rosanne Boyland and her family comes from an MSNBC five-part podcast titled *American Radical*, https://www.msnbc.com/msnbc-podcast/american-radical.

10   Evan Mealins, "Capitol Riot: Nashville's 'Zip-Tie Guy' Guilty on All Charges," *Tennessean*, April 18, 2023, https://www.tennessean.com/story/news/2023/04/18/jan-6-capitol-riot-nashvilles-zip-tie-guy-guilty-on-all-charges/70126910007/.

11   Tucker Carlson Today (@TuckerToday), "Our full interview with @drsimonegold is streaming exclusively on @foxnation," Twitter (now X), November 9, 2022, https://twitter.com/TuckerToday/status/1590524644662153217?lang=en.

12   Anderson Cooper 360° (@AC360), "Tonight Rachel Powell is spending her first night in prison for her role in the January 6 attack. CNN's Donie O'Sullivan spoke to the mom of eight and grandmom," X, January 9, 2024, https://twitter.com/AC360/status/1744919579158077490.

13   News2Share, "January 6 defendant Yvonne St Cyr speaks out at DC Jail after being sentenced to 30 months," YouTube, September 14, 2023, https://www.youtube.com/watch?v=bi8WX5l9Yk0.

14   Ellen Barry, Nicholas Bogel-Burroughs, and Dave Philipps, "Woman Killed in Capitol Embraced Trump and QAnon," *New York Times*, January 7, 2021, https://www.nytimes.com/2021/01/08/us/who-was-ashli-babbitt.html.

15   Ibid.

16   Mike Smith, dir., *Out of Shadows* (2020), https://rumble.com/v4duwck-out-of-shadows-documentary-foc-show.html.

17   Noah Goldberg, "Keith Raniere, Leader of NXIVM Sex Cult, Sentenced to 120 Years," *New York Daily News*, October 27, 2020, https://www.nydailynews.com/2020/10/27/keith-raniere-leader-of-nxivm-sex-cult-sentenced-to-120-years-in-prison/.

18   "iMeet The First Lady," iCarly Wiki, https://icarly.fandom.com/wiki/IMeet_The_First_Lady.

19   HBO, *Real Time with Bill Maher*, April 19, 2024, https://www.youtube.com/watch?v=9xFq3WvMxHg.

20   Gabby Orr, "Trump Poses with QAnon, Pizzagate Conspiracy Theorist at Mar-a-Lago," CNN, December 7, 2022, https://www.cnn.com/2022/12/07/politics/trump-qanon-conspiracy-theorist-mar-a-lago/index.html.

21 Megan McCluskey, "How *Sound of Freedom* Became the Surprise Box Office Hit of the Summer," *Time*, August 29, 2023, https://time.com/6304595/sound-of-freedom-controversy-success/.

22 Rob Kuznia and Curt Devine, "The Believer," CNN, https://edition.cnn.com/interactive/2021/06/us/capitol-riot-paths-to-insurrection/yvonne-st-cyr.html.

23 Sam Baker, "Female QAnon Fanatic Who Stormed Capitol and Took Selfies by Pence's Chair Is a School Therapist Who Quit So She Could 'Expose Global Evil of Human Trafficking and Pedophilia,'" *Daily Mail*, January 18, 2021, https://www.dailymail.co.uk/news/article-9159337/Female-QAnon-fanatic-stormed-capitol-ex-school-therapist.html.

24 Kelly Rissman, "Trump Calls for 'Immediate' Death Penalty for Child Traffickers after Watching Qanon-Linked Movie," *Independent*, July 21, 2023, https://www.the-independent.com/news/world/americas/us-politics/donald-trump-child-trafficking-sound-of-freedom-b2379820.html.

25 John Harris and Peter Baker, "White House Memo Asserts a Scandal Theory," *Washington Post*, January 10, 1997, https://www.washingtonpost.com/wp-srv/politics/special/pjones/stories/pj011097.htm.

26 Ibid.

27 The Rubin Report, "I Can't Overstate How Dire This Is," YouTube, December 10, 2023, https://www.youtube.com/watch?v=yKWM-76weXBc.

28 James Bennet, "When the New York Times Lost Its Way," *Economist*, December 14, 2023, https://www.economist.com/1843/2023/12/14/when-the-new-york-times-lost-its-way?utm_source=newsletter&utm_medium=email&utm_campaign=newsletter_axiosam&stream=top.

29 Ibid.

30 FBI Investigation of Ashli Elizabeth Babbitt, April 15, 2021, page 54, https://vault.fbi.gov/ashli-babbitt/ashli-babbitt-part-01/view.

31 Warren Fiske, "Donald Trump Says 'All Mexicans Are Rapists,'" Politifact, August 8, 2016, https://www.politifact.com/fact-checks/2016/aug/08/tim-kaine/tim-kaine-falsely-says-trump-said-all-mexicans-are/.

32 Jacqueline Tempera, "Joe Biden Officially Announces 2020 Presidential Run: 'We Are in the Battle for the Soul of This Na-

tion,'" MassLive, April 25, 2019, https://www.masslive.com/politics/2019/04/joe-biden-officially-announces-2020-presidential-run-we-are-in-the-battle-for-the-soul-of-this-nation.html.

33 Katie Reilly, "Read Hillary Clinton's 'Basket of Deplorables' Remarks about Donald Trump Supporters," *Time*, September 10, 2016, https://time.com/4486502/hillary-clinton-basket-of-deplorables-transcript/.

34 Erin Doherty, "Biden: Jan. 6 Capitol Riot 'Was about White Supremacy,'" Axios, October 21, 2021, https://www.axios.com/2021/10/21/biden-jan-6-capitol-riot-white-supremacy.

35 Seyward Darby, "The Far Right Told Us What It Had Planned. We Didn't Listen," *New York Times*, January 7, 2021, https://www.nytimes.com/2021/01/07/opinion/white-supremacists-capitol-riot.html.

36 Vera Bergengruen, "'Our First Martyr.' How Ashli Babbitt Is Being Turned Into a Far-Right Recruiting Tool," *Time*, January 10, 2021, https://time.com/5928249/ashli-babbitt-capitol-extremism/.

37 Ruth Marcus, "Donald Trump's Remarkably Gross Comments about Women," *Washington Post*, October 7, 2016, https://www.washingtonpost.com/blogs/post-partisan/wp/2016/10/07/donald-trumps-remarkably-gross-comments-about-women/.

38 Jonathan Karl, "The Day That Changed Politics, 4 Years Ago Today," ABC News, October 7, 2020, https://abcnews.go.com/Politics/day-changed-politics-years-ago-today/story?id=73478987.

39 Capt. Renee Lee, "DC Air National Guard Airmen Depart for Deployment," DVIDS, February 15, 2014, https://www.dvidshub.net/news/120981/dc-air-national-guard-airmen-depart-deployment.

40 Barry et al., "Woman."

41 Ibid.

42 Sudhin Thanawala, Stefanie Dazio, and Jeff Martin, "Family: Trump Supporter Who Died Followed QAnon Conspiracy," Associated Press, January 8, 2021, https://apnews.com/article/election-2020-joe-biden-donald-trump-police-elections-7051411972c58cfbbf079876ce527ab4.

43 News2Share, "January 6 Defendant Yvonne St Cyr Speaks Out at DC Jail after Being Sentenced to 30 Months," YouTube, September 14, 2023, https://www.youtube.com/watch?v=bi8WX5l9Yk0.

44 Kuznia and Devine, "Believer."

45 Ronan Farrow, "A Pennsylvania Mother's Path to Insurrection," *New Yorker*, February 1, 2021, https://www.newyorker.com/news/news-desk/a-pennsylvania-mothers-path-to-insurrection-capitol-riot.

46 Eduardo Medina, "'Zip Tie Guy' and His Mother Get Prison Terms in Jan. 6 Riot," *New York Times*, September 8, 2023, https://www.nytimes.com/2023/09/08/us/mother-son-guilty-jan-6-zip-ties.html.

47 Olivia Waxman, "'Hate Never Disappears. It Just Takes a Break for a While.' Why the U.S. Capitol Attack Makes Holocaust Remembrance Day More Important Than Ever," *Yahoo! News*, January 25, 2021, https://news.yahoo.com/hate-never-disappears-just-takes-170424981.html.

48 "The Jan. 6 Rioter Who Wore a 'Camp Auschwitz' Sweatshirt Gets 75 Days in Jail," Associated Press, September 16, 2022, https://www.npr.org/2022/09/16/1123424585/jan-6-rioter-camp-auschwitz-sweatshirt-sentenced-jail.

49 Larry and Andy Wachowski, *The Matrix*, https://www.dailyscript.com/scripts/the_matrix.pdf.

50 Walter Isaacson, *Elon Musk* (New York: Simon & Schuster, 2023).

51 *Tucker Carlson Today*, "Covid Insurrectionist," November 10, 2022, https://tv.apple.com/us/episode/tucker-carlson-today/umc.cmc.39pvyoukndlz72rk9oo7q743y.

52 R. Kelly Garrett and Robert M. Bond, "Conservatives' Susceptibility to Political Misperceptions," *Science Advances*, June 2, 2021, https://www.ncbi.nlm.nih.gov/pmc/articles/PMC8172130/.

53 Figueroa, "San Diego Woman."

54 Samuel Braslow (@SamBraslow), "Today, a group of anti-maskers protested at Ralph's and the Century City shopping mall. Lots of angry confrontations with customers and a few physical altercations [video].," Twitter (now X), January 3, 2021, via Internet Archive, https://web.archive.org/web/20210107032355/https://twitter.com/Ashli_Babbitt.

55 Rebecca Lavrenz Legal Defense Fund, https://www.givesendgo.com/rebeccalavrenz.

56 Kuznia and Devine, "Believer."

57 Farrow, "Mother's Path."

58   Joel Stein, "How a Squad of MAGA Warriors Flush with Cash Turned on Each Other," *Financial Times*, July 19, 2023, https://www.ft.com/content/7d0a7dfb-c0a3-4b55-b1ac-3e6cbf1f84b8.

59   Grace-Marie Turner, "600 Physicians Say Lockdowns Are a 'Mass Casualty Incident,'" *Forbes*, May 22, 2020, https://www.forbes.com/sites/gracemarieturner/2020/05/22/600-physicians-say-lockdowns-are-a-mass-casualty-incident/?sh=3704e7ce50fa.

60   Office of Governor Gavin Newsom, "State Issues Limited Stay at Home Order to Slow Spread of COVID-19," November 19, 2020, https://www.gov.ca.gov/2020/11/19/state-issues-limited-stay-at-home-order-to-slow-spread-of-covid-19/.

61   Carlson, "Covid Insurrectionist."

62   Office of Governor Gavin Newsom, "Governor Newsom Names Scientific Safety Review Workgroup to Advise State on COVID-19 Vaccines," October 19, 2020, https://www.gov.ca.gov/2020/10/19/governor-newsom-names-scientific-safety-review-workgroup-to-advise-state-on-covid-19-vaccines/.

63   Woody Allen, *Bananas*, https://www.scripts.com/script/bananas_3530.

64   "School Responses in California to the Coronavirus (COVID-19) Pandemic," Ballotpedia, https://ballotpedia.org/School_responses_in_California_to_the_coronavirus_(COVID-19)_pandemic.

65   Benjamin W. Cottingham et al., "What Does It Take to Accelerate the Learning of Every Child?" PACE, December 2023, https://edpolicyinca.org/publications/what-does-it-take-accelerate-learning-every-child#:~:text=Summary,remaining%20well%20below%20prepandemic%20levels.

66   Angelo Fichera, "COVID Treatments Weren't Suppressed to OK Vaccines' Emergency Use," Associated Press, December 30, 2022, https://apnews.com/article/fact-check-covid-vaccines-emergency-use-873264912929.

67   Carlson, "Covid Insurrectionist."

68   Barry et al., "Woman."

69   Molly Ball, "The Secret History of the Shadow Campaign That Saved the 2020 Election," *Time*, February 4, 2021, https://time.com/5936036/secret-2020-election-campaign/. All future refer-

ences to Molly Ball or the Ball Dossier can be traced to this article.

70	Charles Dickens, *A Tale of Two Cities*, Nook edition, 216.

71	Houston Keene, "Minnesota Bail Fund Promoted by Kamala Harris Freed Convict Now Charged with Murder," Fox News, August 30, 2022, https://www.foxnews.com/politics/minnesota-bail-fund-promoted-kamala-harris-freed-convict-now-charged-murder.

72	Chandelis Duster, "Waters Calls for Protesters to 'Get More Confrontational' If No Guilty Verdict Is Reached in Derek Chauvin Trial," CNN, April 19, 2021, https://www.cnn.com/2021/04/19/politics/maxine-waters-derek-chauvin-trial/index.html.

73	Bloomberg Quicktake, "Pelosi Thanks George Floyd for 'Sacrificing Your Life for Justice' after Verdict," YouTube, April 21, 2021, https://www.youtube.com/watch?v=lb-8cOjkFO4.

74	Jack Cashill, "How George Floyd Actually Died," *American Spectator,* November 12, 2023, https://spectator.org/how-george-floyd-actually-died/.

75	Amy Forliti and Steve Karnowski, "Medical Examiner: Floyd's Heart Stopped While Restrained," Associated Press, June 1, 2020, https://apnews.com/article/george-floyd-minneapolis-heart-disease-mn-state-wire-homicide-d41cdf6cefbb3e5603a28e6d-c07f9589.

76	Dean Meminger, "Police Unions Say They Have No Regrets in Endorsing President Trump," Spectrum News, November 24, 2020, https://ny1.com/nyc/all-boroughs/news/2020/11/24/police-unions-say-they-have-no-regrets-in-endorsing-president-trump.

77	Bayliss Wagner, "Fact Check: Claim about Biden Quote on MLK Assassination, George Floyd Death Is Missing Context," *USA Today*, January 20, 2022, https://www.usatoday.com/story/news/factcheck/2022/01/20/fact-check-biden-quote-mlk-george-floyd-taken-out-context/6577210001/.

78	Veera Korhonen, "Number of Arrests for All Offenses in the United States from 1990 to 2022," Statista, October 20, 2023, https://www.statista.com/statistics/191261/number-of-arrests-for-all-offenses-in-the-us-since-1990/#:~:text=There%20were%20over%207.36%20million,arrests%20was%20over%2014.1%20million.

79 Vandana Rambaran, "At Least 60 Secret Service Members Injured during George Floyd Protests in DC," Fox News, May 31, 2020, https://www.foxnews.com/us/more-than-60-secret-service-officers-injured-during-violent-george-floyd-protests-in-washington-d-c.

80 Shawn McCreesh, "Protests Near White House Spiral Out of Control Again," *New York Times*, May 31, 2020, https://www.nytimes.com/2020/05/31/us/politics/washington-dc-george-floyd-protests.html?action=click&module=RelatedLinks&pgtype=Article.

81 Katie Rogers, "Protesters Dispersed with Tear Gas So Trump Could Pose at Church," *New York Times*, June 1, 2020, https://www.nytimes.com/2020/06/01/us/politics/trump-st-johns-church-bible.html.

82 Rebecca Shabad, "'What Is This, a Banana Republic?': Pelosi Unloads on Trump over Tear-Gassing of Protesters Outside White House," NBC News, June 3, 2020, https://www.nbcnews.com/politics/congress/what-banana-republic-pelosi-unloads-trump-over-gassing-protesters-outside-n1223346.

83 W. James Antle III, "Trump Photo Op at Church Wasn't Why Lafayette Square Was Cleared. Where Are the Mea Culpas?," NBC News, June 11, 2021, https://www.nbcnews.com/think/opinion/trump-photo-op-church-wasn-t-why-lafayette-square-was-ncna1270502.

84 Alanna Durkin Richer et al., "Records Rebut Claims of Unequal Treatment of Jan. 6 Rioters," Associated Press, August 30, 2021, https://apnews.com/article/records-rebut-claims-jan-6-rioters-55adf4d46aff57b91af2fdd3345dace8.

85 "Over 300 People Facing Federal Charges for Crimes Committed During Nationwide Demonstrations," Department of Justice, September 24, 2020, https://www.justice.gov/opa/pr/over-300-people-facing-federal-charges-crimes-committed-during-nationwide-demonstrations.

86 Tom Cotton, "Send In the Troops," *New York Times*, June 3, 2020, https://www.nytimes.com/2020/06/03/opinion/tom-cotton-protests-military.html.

87 Tom Perkins, "Most Charges against George Floyd Protesters Dropped, Analysis Shows," *Guardian*, April 17, 2021, https://

www.theguardian.com/us-news/2021/apr/17/george-floyd-pro-testers-charges-citations-analysis.

88 "Remarks by President Biden on the Verdict in the Derek Chauvin Trial for the Death of George Floyd," White House, April 20, 2021, https://www.whitehouse.gov/briefing-room/speeches-remarks/2021/04/20/remarks-by-president-biden-on-the-verdict-in-the-derek-chauvin-trial-for-the-death-of-george-floyd/#:~:-text=We%20have%20a%20chance%20to,George%20Floyd%20and%20his%20family.

89 Bob Price, "WATCH: D.C. Cops Direct Trump-Supporters into Gauntlet of Protesters, Do Nothing When They Are Assaulted," Breitbart News, November 15, 2020, https://www.breitbart.com/law-and-order/2020/11/15/watch-d-c-cops-direct-trump-supporters-into-gauntlet-of-protesters-do-nothing-when-they-are-assaulted/.

90 Deb Riechmann and Dino Hazell, "Sen. Paul Complains about 'Angry Mob' Encounter after RNC," Associated Press, August 28, 2020, https://apnews.com/article/election-2020-ky-state-wire-shootings-politics-police-reform-115c91d3b85f5c5ba9ed995482af6dc3.

91 Hurubie Meko and Rebecca Davis O'Brien, "During George Floyd Protests, 2 Lawyers' Futures Went Up in Flames," *New York Times*, January 26, 2023, https://www.nytimes.com/2023/01/26/nyregion/lawyers-sentenced-molotov-police-car.html.

92 Ben Feuerherd, "'Go Burn Down 1PP': Molotov-Cocktail Lawyers Eyed Police Headquarters, Prosecutors Say," *New York Post*, October 20, 2021, https://nypost.com/2021/10/20/molotov-cocktail-lawyers-eyed-police-headquarters-prosecutors/.

93 Eduardo Medina, "'Zip Tie Guy' and His Mother Get Prison Terms in Jan. 6 Riot," *New York Times*, September 8, 2023, https://www.nytimes.com/2023/09/08/us/mother-son-guilty-jan-6-zip-ties.html.

94 David Gotfredson, "Local Man Fired Ashli Babbitt after Political Rant over the Telephone," CBS 8, July 8, 2021, https://www.cbs8.com/article/news/local/local-man-fired-ashli-babbitt-after-political-rant-over-the-telephone/509-cdb867b5-4d7d-450c-be48-d9e-8698be6ae.

95 Alisha Haridasani Gupta, "For Far-Right Movements, Ashli Babbitt Is Now a 'Rallying Cry,'" *New York Times*, January 8, 2021,

https://www.nytimes.com/2021/01/08/us/ashli-babbitt-capitol-president-trump.html.

96 Adam Goldman and Michael S. Schmidt, "Rod Rosenstein Suggested Secretly Recording Trump and Discussed 25th Amendment," *New York Times*, September 21, 2018, https://www.nytimes.com/2018/09/21/us/politics/rod-rosenstein-wear-wire-25th-amendment.html.

97 Asha Rangappa, "The Mueller Investigation Is Bigger Than Rod Rosenstein," *New York Times*, October 9, 2018, https://www.nytimes.com/2018/10/09/opinion/rod-rosenstein-trump-robert-mueller-russia.html?searchResultPosition=9.

98 Adam Entous, Devlin Barrett, and Rosalind S. Helderman, "Clinton Campaign, DNC Helped Pay for Work on Dossier about Russia and Trump," *Washington Post*, October 24, 2017, https://www.seattletimes.com/nation-world/clinton-campaign-dnc-helped-pay-for-work-on-dossier-about-russia-and-trump/.

99 Maggie Haberman (@maggieNYT), Twitter (now X), October 24, 2017, https://twitter.com/maggieNYT/status/922962880206647297.

100 Mollie Hemingway, *Rigged: How the Media, Big Tech, and the Democrats Seized Our Elections* (Washington, DC: Regnery, 2022), Kindle edition, ix.

101 "Building Confidence in U.S. Elections, Report of the Commission on General Election Reform," September 2005, https://www.eac.gov/sites/default/files/eac_assets/1/6/Exhibit%20M.PDF.

102 Adam Liptak, "Error and Fraud at Issue as Absentee Voting Rises," *New York Times*, October 6, 2012, https://www.nytimes.com/2012/10/07/us/politics/as-more-vote-by-mail-faulty-ballots-could-impact-elections.html.

103 L. V. Anderson, "White Women Sold Out the Sisterhood and the World by Voting for Trump," *Slate*, November 9, 2016, https://slate.com/human-interest/2016/11/white-women-sold-out-the-sisterhood-and-the-world-by-voting-for-trump.html.

104 "'That's What's the Matter.' Boss Tweed. 'As Long as I Count the Votes, What Are You Going to Do about It? Say?," Massachusetts Historical Society, https://www.masshist.org/database/viewer.php?item_id=5900&pid=41.

105 James O'Keefe, *American Muckraker: Rethinking Journalism for the 21st Century* (Nashville: Post Hill Press, 2022), 191–206.

106 Maggie Astor, "Project Veritas Video Was a 'Coordinated Disinformation Campaign,' Researchers Say," *New York Times*, September 29, 2020, https://www.nytimes.com/2020/09/29/us/politics/project-veritas-ilhan-omar.html.

107 Camille Caldera, "Fact Check: No Proof of Alleged Voter Fraud Scheme or Connection to Rep. Ilhan Omar," *USA Today*, October 16, 2020, https://www.usatoday.com/story/news/fact-check/2020/10/16/fact-check-project-veritas-no-proof-voter-fraud-scheme-link-ilhan-omar/3584614001/.

108 O'Keefe, *American*, 103.

109 Mariah Timms, "Mother of Nashville Man Accused of Carrying Zip Ties during Capitol Riot Says Pair Had No 'Nefarious' Intent," *Tennessean*, January 12, 2021, https://www.tennessean.com/story/news/crime/2021/01/12/nashville-eric-munchel-mom-says-pair-had-no-nefarious-intent-u-s-capitol/6639134002/.

110 Joe Concha, "Poll: Dems More Likely to Unfriend People Due to Political Posts," *Hill*, December 19, 2016, https://thehill.com/homenews/311047-poll-dems-more-likely-to-unfriend-people-due-to-political-posts/.

111 Carlson, "Covid Insurrectionist."

112 Stein, "Squad."

113 Joseph Clark, "Twitter Files: Ex-FBI Lawyer Tried to Label Trump 'Don't Be Afraid of Covid' Post as Misinformation," *Washington Times*, December 26, 2022, https://www.washingtontimes.com/news/2022/dec/26/james-baker-tried-have-donald-trump-post-covid-rec/.

114 "Protecting Speech from Government Interference and Social Media Bias," Committee on Oversight and Accountability, House of Representatives, February 8, 2023, https://www.govinfo.gov/content/pkg/CHRG-118hhrg50898/html/CHRG-118hhrg50898.htm.

115 Farrow, "Mother's Path."

116 Jared Gans, "Zuckerberg Tells Rogan Facebook Suppressed Hunter Biden Laptop Story after FBI Warning," *Hill*, August 26, 2022, https://thehill.com/policy/technology/3616579-zuckerberg-tells-rogan-that-facebook-suppressed-hunter-biden-lap-

top-story-after-fbi-warning-defends-agency-as-legitimate-institution/.

117　Alexis Benveniste, "Mark Zuckerberg and Priscilla Chan Are Donating $300 Million to Voting Efforts," CNN, September 1, 2020, https://www.cnn.com/2020/09/01/business/zuckerberg-300-million-voting/index.html.

118　"Testimony Reveals FBI Employees Who Warned Social Media Companies about Hack and Leak Operation Knew Hunter Biden Laptop Wasn't Russian Disinformation," House Judiciary Committee press release, July 20, 2023, https://judiciary.house.gov/media/press-releases/testimony-reveals-fbi-employees-who-warned-social-media-companies-about-hack.

119　"Protecting Speech from Government Interference and Social Media Bias," Committee on Oversight and Accountability, House of Representatives, February 8, 2023, https://www.govinfo.gov/content/pkg/CHRG-118hhrg50898/html/CHRG-118hhrg50898.htm.

120　"The Hunter Biden Statement: How Senior Intelligence Community
Officials and the Biden Campaign Worked to Mislead American Voters," Interim Joint Staff Report of the Committee on the Judiciary, Select Subcommittee on the Weaponization of the Federal Government, and Permanent Select Committee on Intelligence, May 10, 2023, https://judiciary.house.gov/sites/evo-subsites/judiciary.house.gov/files/evo-media-document/2023-05-10_the_hunter_biden_statement_how_senior_intelligence_community_officials_and_the_biden_campaign_worked_to_mislead_american_voters-sm.pdf.

121　Natasha Bertrand, "Hunter Biden Story Is Russian Disinfo, Dozens of Former Intel Officials Say," *Politico*, October 19, 2020, https://www.politico.com/news/2020/10/19/hunter-biden-story-russian-disinfo-430276.

122　Tim Murtaugh, "Media's Suppression of Hunter Biden's Laptop Was Election Interference," *Washington Times*, March 24, 2022, https://www.washingtontimes.com/news/2022/mar/24/medias-suppression-of-hunter-laptop-was-election-i/.

123　Hemingway, *Rigged*, 27.

124　Patrick Byrne, The *Deep Rig: How Election Fraud Cost Donald J. Trump the White House, By a Man Who Did Not Vote for Him (or What to Send Friends Who Ask, "Why Do You Doubt the Integrity of Election 2020?")* (Deep Capture, LLC, 2021), Kindle edition, 27.

125 Ilya Shapiro, "Ballot Counting Is Delayed in These Six States with Legal Battles on the Horizon," *Federalist*, November 4, 2020, https://thefederalist.com/2020/11/04/ballot-counting-is-delayed-in-these-six-states-with-legal-battles-on-the-horizon/.

126 "NALC Endorses Biden-Harris," NALC, August 13, 2020, https://www.nalc.org/news/nalc-updates/nalc-endorses-biden-harris.

127 Ibid.

128 Byrne, *The Deep Rig*, 37.

129 Julie Kelly, *January 6: How Democrats Used the Capitol Protest to Launch a War on Terror against the Political Right* (Nashville: Bombardier Books, 2022), Kindle edition, 4.

130 "It's Official: The Election Was Secure," The Brennan Center for Justice, December 11, 2020, https://www.brennancenter.org/our-work/research-reports/its-official-election-was-secure.

131 Melissa Block, "Can the Forces Unleashed by Trump's Big Election Lie Be Undone?" NPR, January 16, 2021, https://www.npr.org/2021/01/16/957291939/can-the-forces-unleashed-by-trumps-big-election-lie-be-undone.

132 Ibid.

133 Farrow, "Mother's Path."

134 "Hillary Clinton Supporters Caught Crying," CNBC, November 8, 2016, https://www.cnbc.com/video/2016/11/08/hillary-clinton-supporters-caught-crying.html.

135 Casey Newton, "Breitbart Posted a Leaked Video of Google's First All-Hands Meeting after the 2016 Election," *The Verge*, September 12, 2018, https://www.theverge.com/2018/9/12/17852502/breitbart-google-all-hands-meeting-the-2016-election-leaked-video-alphabet.

136 "The Real Story of January 6," *Epoch Times*, July 23, 2022, https://www.theepochtimes.com/epochtv/the-real-story-of-jan-6-documentary-4596670.

137 News2Share, "January 6 Defendant Yvonne St Cyr Speaks Out at DC Jail after Being Sentenced to 30 Months," YouTube, September 14, 2023, https://www.youtube.com/watch?v=bi8WX5l9Yk0.

138 "The Real Story of January 6," *Epoch Times*.

139   Federal Bureau of Investigation, "Domestic Terrorism Symbols Guide."

140   Matthew Boyle, "President Trump to Address the 'Stop the Steal' Protestors on White House Lawn on January 6," Breitbart, January 3, 2021, https://www.breitbart.com/politics/2021/01/03/president-trump-to-address-stop-the-steal-protesters-on-white-house-lawn-on-january-6/.

141   Brian Naylor, "Read Trump's Jan. 6 Speech, A Key Part of Impeachment Trial," NPR, February 10, 2021, https://www.npr.org/2021/02/10/966396848/read-trumps-jan-6-speech-a-key-part-of-impeachment-trial.

142   "Final Report," Select Committee to Investigate the January 6th Attack on the Capitol, December 22, 2022, https://www.govinfo.gov/content/pkg/GPO-J6-REPORT/pdf/GPO-J6-REPORT.pdf.

143   "Read Pence's Full Letter Saying He Can't Claim 'Unilateral Authority' to Reject Electoral Votes," PBS, January 6, 2021, https://www.pbs.org/newshour/politics/read-pences-full-letter-saying-he-cant-claim-unilateral-authority-to-reject-electoral-votes.

144   A. J. Fischer, "J6: A True Timeline," Open.Ink, https://open.ink/collections/j6.

145   Ibid.

146   "The Real Story of January 6," *Epoch Times*.

147   KUSI News, "Videos Taken by Journalist Tayler Hansen Prove Ashli Babbitt Was Not Violent Inside US Capitol," YouTube, January 25, 2022, https://www.youtube.com/watch?v=hSt2LJWo-kI0.

148   Nick Searcy (producer), *The War on Truth* (advance copy, not released at time of writing), 2024.

149   "The Real Story of January 6," *Epoch Times*.

150   *The Tucker Carlson Encounter*, "Steven Sund," August 10, 2023, https://tuckercarlson.com/the-tucker-carlson-encounter-steven-sund/.

151   Ryan J. Reilly, "Zip Tie Guy Capitol Attack Video," YouTube, October 12, 2021, https://www.youtube.com/watch?v=u2MY-602iXOs.

152   United States of America v. Eric Gavelek Munchel and Lisa Marie Eisenhart, https://ecf.dcd.uscourts.gov/cgi-bin/show_public_doc?2021cr0118-24.

153 Laura Pullman, "Trump's Militias Say They Are Armed and Ready to Defend Their Freedoms," *Times* (UK), Jan. 10, 2021, https://www.thetimes.co.uk/article/trumps-militias-say-theyare-armed-and-ready-to-defend-their-freedoms-8ht5m0j70.

154 "Senate Votes to Confirm Kavanaugh as Hundreds Protest at Capitol," PBS News Hour, October 6, 2018, https://www.pbs.org/newshour/show/senate-votes-to-confirm-kavanaugh-as-hundreds-protest-at-capitol.

155 Jason Breslow, "The Resistance at the Kavanaugh Hearings: More Than 200 Arrests," NPR, September 8, 2018, https://www.npr.org/2018/09/08/645497667/the-resistance-at-the-kavanaugh-hearings-more-than-200-arrests.

156 Rebecca Lavrenz, "Statement of Facts," September 19, 2022, https://extremism.gwu.edu/sites/g/files/zaxdzs5746/files/Rebecca%20Lavernz%20Statement%20of%20Facts.pdf.

157 Trendsout, "Sara Carpenter Seemingly Possessed," YouTube, March 16, 2023, https://www.youtube.com/watch?v=U45iMsl-JA4g.

158 Sara Carpenter, "FBI Statement of Facts," March 18, 2021, https://www.justice.gov/usao-dc/case-multi-defendant/file/1393356/download .

159 FreedomNews TV, "Ex-NYPD Spokesperson Charged in Capitol Riots," YouTube, March 23, 2021, https://www.youtube.com/watch?v=JwLD32zUJnQ.

160 "The Real Story of January 6," *Epoch Times*.

161 "Minnesota Woman Sentenced on Felony Charge for Actions During Jan. 6 Capitol Breach," United States Attorney's Office, November 20, 2023, https://www.justice.gov/usao-dc/pr/minnesota-woman-sentenced-felony-charge-actions-during-jan-6-capitol-breach.

162 *Victoria Charity White v. Jason Bagshaw and Neil McAllister*, United States District Court for the District of Columbia, filed March 27 2024.

163 Ibid.

164 "The Rest of the Story with Lara Logan Episode 10 'Victoria White,'" March 15, 2024, https://subsplash.com/hisgloryme/programs/mi/+xbxw83q?autoplay=true.

165 *United States of America v. Kyle Fitzsimons*, United States District Court for the District of Columbia, https://www.docu-

mentcloud.org/documents/22273591-government-brief-identifying-bagshaw.

166   Alpha News, "'I Should Be Dead': Minnesota J6 Defendant Responds to New Bodycam Video," Liz Collin Reports, YouTube, March 21, 2023, https://www.youtube.com/watch?v=zxskx8Xtuig.

167   News2Share, "January 6 Defendant Yvonne St Cyr Speaks Out at DC Jail after Being Sentenced to 30 Months," YouTube, September 14, 2023, https://www.youtube.com/watch?v=bi8WX5l9Yk0.

168   "Idaho Woman Sentenced on Felony and Misdemeanor Charges for Actions During Jan. 6 Capitol Breach," United States Attorney's Office, September 13, 2023, https://www.justice.gov/usao-dc/pr/idaho-woman-sentenced-felony-and-misdemeanor-charges-actions-during-jan-6-capitol-breach.

169   "The Real Story of January 6," *Epoch Times*.

170   Brian Naylor, "Trump Downplays Insurrection but Tells Supporters to 'Go Home,'" NPR, January 6, 2021, https://www.npr.org/sections/congress-electoral-college-tally-live-updates/2021/01/06/954098712/in-video-trump-sympathizes-with-protesters-but-tells-them-to-go-home.

171   "Reporter Asks Mom Going to Prison for Jan. 6 If She Blames Trump. Hear Her Response," CNN, January 9, 2024, https://www.cnn.com/videos/politics/2024/01/09/convicted-january-6-rioter-prison-sentence-bu-orig.cnn.

172   Farrow, "Mother's Path."

173   *America Radical*, Part 2, MSNBC.

174   Ted Deutch (@RepTedDeutch), Twitter (now X), January 6, 2021, https://twitter.com/RepTedDeutch/status/1346919622369533953?ref_src=twsrc%5Etfw%7Ctwcamp%5Etweetembed%7Ctwterm%5E1346919622369533953%7Ctwgr%5Ee910f72455e2bccec4da1c8a186cacc1aa024224%7Ctwcon%5Es1_&ref_url=https%3A%2F%2Fthreadreaderapp.com%2Fthread%2F1743643824394477980.

175   Kelly, *January 6*, 44.

176   Caroline Kelly and Nicky Robertson, "Romney: 'What Happened Here Today Was an Insurrection, Incited by the President,'" CNN, January 6, 2021, https://www.cnn.com/2021/01/06/politics/romney-trump-insurrection-capitol/index.html.

177 "Statement by President George W. Bush on Insurrection at the Capitol," George W. Bush Presidential Center, January 6, 2021, https://www.bushcenter.org/newsroom/statement-by-president-george-w-bush-on-insurrection-at-the-capitol.

178 Brian Duignan, "Insurrection," Britannica, https://www.britannica.com/topic/insurrection-politics.

179 Samantha Putterman, "Tucker Carlson Is Wrong. Firearms, Other Weapons at Capitol on Jan. 6," *Austin American-Statesman*, June 15, 2022, https://www.statesman.com/story/news/politics/politifact/2022/06/15/fact-check-were-firearms-other-weapons-capitol-jan-6/7621149001/.

180 Scott MacFarlane and Rick Yarborough, "News4 Obtains Video of Alleged Baseball Bat Attack at US Capitol Insurrection," News4, March 18, 2021, https://www.nbcwashington.com/news/local/news4-obtains-video-of-alleged-baseball-bat-attack-at-us-capitol-insurrection/2611519/.

181 Matthew Russell Lee, "In DC Insurrection Case Emanuel Jackson Is Freed after Hit Cop with Bat but Low IQ," Inner City Press, March 2, 2021, https://www.innercitypress.com/ddc-26jacksonicp030221.html.

182 James O'Keefe, *American Pravda, My Fight for Truth in the Era of Fake News* (New York: St. Martin's Publishing Group, 2018), 173.

183 Michael Powell, "'White Supremacy' Once Meant David Duke and the Klan. Now It Refers to Much More," *New York Times*, October 17, 2020, https://www.nytimes.com/2020/10/17/us/white-supremacy.html.

184 Karma Allen, "Man Who Helped Ignite George Floyd Riots Identified as White Supremacist: Police," ABC News, July 29, 2020, https://abcnews.go.com/US/man-helped-ignite-george-floyd-riots-identified-white/story?id=72051536.

185 "The Real Story of January 6," *Epoch Times*.

186 "The Reichstag Fire," Holocaust Encyclopedia, https://encyclopedia.ushmm.org/content/en/article/the-reichstag-fire#:~:text=Commonly%20known%20as%20the%20Reichstag%20Fire%20Decree%2C%20the%20resulting%20act,the%20way%20for%20Nazi%20dictatorship.

187 Tucker Carlson, "Lies about January 6 Have Enabled Unscrupulous People to Make a Mockery of Our Bill of Rights," Fox News,

January 6, 2023, https://www.foxnews.com/opinion/tucker-carl-son-lies-january-6-enabled-unscrupulous-people-mockery-bill-of-rights.

188   Glenn Greenwald, "The False and Exaggerated Claims Still Being Spread about the Capitol Riot," February 16, 2022, https://docs.house.gov/meetings/GO/GO00/20210615/112771/HHRG-117-GO00-20210615-SD006.pdf.

189   "Lying in State or in Honor," Architect of the Capitol, https://www.aoc.gov/what-we-do/programs-ceremonies/lying-in-state-honor.

190   "House Minority Leader Jeffries Marks January 6 Anniversary," C-SPAN, January 6, 2023, https://www.c-span.org/video/?525199-1/house-minority-leader-jeffries-marks-january-6-anniversary.

191   Nicole Sganga, "Garland Says 'The Actions We Have Taken Thus Far' on January 6 Rioters 'Will Not Be Our Last," CBS News, January 6, 2022, https://www.cbsnews.com/news/merrick-garland-january-6-capitol-riot-arrests-charges/.

192   Brian Trusdell, "Ashli Babbitt's Mother to Newsmax: My Daughter Was Murdered," Newsmax, October 14, 2021, https://www.newsmax.com/newsmax-tv/ashli-babbitt-mother-jan-6/2021/10/14/id/1040581/.

193   Camryn Justice, Ian Cross, and Joe Pagonakis, "Federal Agents at Home of CMSD Staffer Who Resigned Thursday," ABC News 5 Cleveland, January 8, 2021, https://www.news5cleveland.com/news/local-news/oh-lake/federal-agents-at-home-of-cmsd-staffer-who-resigned-thursday.

194   Farnoush Amiri, "School Therapist Resigns after Alleged Involvement in Riots," Associated Press, January 8, 2021, https://apnews.com/article/donald-trump-media-coronavirus-pandemic-cleveland-ohio-cdae5f05bd3a43e3b9b5da98b258e999.

195   Peggy Gallek, "Cleveland Schools Employee Resigns after Law Enforcement Investigates Possible Involvement in DC Riots," Fox 8, January 8, 2021, https://fox8.com/news/i-team/cleveland-teacher-resigns-after-law-enforcement-investigates-possible-involvement-in-dc-riots/#:~:text=The%20Cleveland%20Teachers%20Union%20released,said%20union%20president%20Shari%20Obrenski.

196 Ben Axelrod and Carmen Blackwell, "Police Investigating Sex Video of Teacher Sent to Students," WKYC, February 22, 2022, https://www.wkyc.com/article/news/local/cleveland/cleveland-police-investigating-sex-video-ginn-academy-teacher/95-86fe4244-2521-4785-8074-3c67c9422ac1.

197 Sam Baker, "Female QAnon Fanatic Who Stormed Capitol and Took Selfies by Pence's Chair Is a School Therapist Who Quit So She Could 'Expose Global Evil of Human Trafficking and Pedophilia,'" *Daily Mail*, January 18, 2021, https://www.dailymail.co.uk/news/article-9159337/Female-QAnon-fanatic-stormed-capitol-ex-school-therapist.html.

198 "FBI Searches Home of Former Cleveland Schools Employee after Her Alleged Involvement in Riots at the US Capitol," WKYC, January 8, 2021, https://www.wkyc.com/article/news/education/cmsd-staffer-resigns-citing-q-anon-type-beliefs/95-21a37574-f8a8-4072-943d-c8a5b08bbca5.

199 Ben Feuerherd, "Feds Bust Ohio School Employee Seen Near Pence's Chair During Capitol Riot," *New York Post*, January 14, 2021, https://nypost.com/2021/01/14/ohio-school-employee-busted-by-feds-for-raiding-us-capitol.

200 Heidi Beedle, "Springs Woman Arrested for Jan. 6 Involvement," *Colorado Springs Indy*, December 21, 2022, https://www.csindy.com/news/springs-woman-arrested-for-jan-6-involvement/article_925a27dc-8108-11ed-ae3f-37a37dfc6b45.html.

201 Sedition Hunters, https://seditionhunters.org/.

202 *Morning Edition*, "News Brief: Isolation Guidelines, Sedition Hunters, Theranos Whistleblower," NPR, January 5, 2022, https://www.npr.org/2022/01/05/1070471221/morning-news-brief.

203 Aleksandr Solzhenitsyn, *The Gulag Archipelago* Volume 1 (New York: HarperPerennial, 2004), Kindle edition, 174.

204 Gregory Krieg, "'I Didn't Think That I Was Just Going to Be Killed': Ocasio-Cortez on Her Fears on January 6," CNN, August 9, 2021, https://www.cnn.com/2021/08/09/politics/alexandria-ocasio-cortez-january-6-cnntv/index.html.

205 Carlson, "Covid Insurrectionist."

206 *New York Times*,, "A Doctor Prominent in Fomenting Opposition to Covid Vaccines Pleads Guilty to Capitol Riot Charges," Facebook, March 4, 2022, https://www.facebook.com/nytimes/

posts/dr-simone-gold-the-founder-of-a-group-known-for-spreading-covid-misinformation-a/10152885107974999/.

207   All references in this chapter to Justin Winchell or the Boyland family come from MSNBC's *American Radical*, https://www.msnbc.com/msnbc-podcast/american-radical.

208   American Radical, Episode 1.

209   Jim Hoft, "Black Trump Supporter Viciously Beaten at San Francisco Free Speech Rally—Sucker-Punched—Teeth Knocked Out," Gateway Pundit, October 17, 2020,,https://www.thegatewaypundit.com/2020/10/video-black-trump-supporter-viciously-beaten-san-francisco-free-speech-rally-sucker-punched-teeth-knocked/.

210   Jim Hoft, "Riveting OAN Interview: Jan. 6 Witness Philip Anderson Who Was Knocked Unconscious Next to Rosanne Boyland When She Died Says Police Caused a Stampede and Killed Her," Gateway Pundit, December 10, 2021, https://www.thegatewaypundit.com/2021/12/riveting-oan-interview-jan-6-witness-philip-anderson-knocked-unconscious-next-rosanne-boyland-died-says-police-caused-stampede-killed/.

211   American Radical, Episode 2.

212   Hoft, "Riveting OAN Interview."

213   "The Real Story of January 6," *Epoch Times*.

214   Hoft, "Riveting OAN Interview."

215   American Radical, Episode 1.

216   JoeHoft, "Kim Sorgente Cries for Boyland," Rumble, https://rumble.com/v3odfj1-kim-sorgente-cries-for-rosanne-boyland.html.

217   Cara Castronuova, "Violent Jan 6 Police Officer Lila Morris Who Beat a Dying Rosanne Boyland 4 Times with Her Stick Takes the Stand," Gateway Pundit, January 23, 2024, https://www.thegatewaypundit.com/2024/01/violent-jan-6-police-officer-lila-morris-who/?utm_source=rss&utm_medium=rss&utm_campaign=violent-jan-6-police-officer-lila-morris-who.

218   American Radical, Episode 2.

219   Jack Healy, "These Are the 5 People Who Died in the Capitol Riot," *New York Times*, January 11, 2021, https://www.nytimes.com/2021/01/11/us/who-died-in-capitol-building-attack.html?searchResultPosition=3.

220 Evan Hill, Arielle Ray, and Dahlia Kozlowsky, "Videos Show How Rioter Was Trampled in Stampede at Capitol," *New York Times*, January 15, 2021, https://www.nytimes.com/2021/01/15/us/rosanne-boyland-capitol-riot-death.html.

221 Jack Moore, "Md. to Review 100 In-Custody Deaths as Audit into Former Medical Examiner Continues," Maryland Matters, October 19, 2022, https://www.marylandmatters.org/2022/10/19/md-to-review-100-in-custody-deaths-as-audit-into-former-medical-examiner-continues/#:~:text=Frosh%20launched%20the%20audit%20last,law%20enforcement%20bias%20in%20his.

222 American Radical, Episode 4.

223 Nicholas Bogel-Burroughs and Evan Hill, "Death of QAnon Follower at Capitol Leaves a Wake of Pain," *New York Times*, May 30, 2021, https://www.nytimes.com/2021/05/30/us/capitol-riot-boyland-qanon.html.

224 Peter Hermann and Spencer Hsu, "Capitol Police Officer Brian Sicknick, Who Engaged Rioters, Suffered Two Strokes and Died of Natural Causes, Officials Say," *Washington Post*, April 19, 2021, https://www.washingtonpost.com/local/public-safety/brian-sicknick-death-strokes/2021/04/19/36d2d310-617e-11eb-afbe-9a11a127d146_story.html.

225 "Judicial Watch Obtains Additional Documents on Death Investigation of Capitol Police Officer Sicknick—Show Media Pressured Medical Examiner on Natural Causes Conclusion,"Judicial Watch, August 11, 2021, https://www.judicialwatch.org/jw-sicknick-documents/.

226 Martin Pengelly, "Capitol Rioter Who Assaulted Brian Sicknick Gets Near-Seven Year Sentence," *Guardian*, January 27, 2023, https://www.theguardian.com/us-news/2023/jan/27/capitol-rioter-assaulted-officer-brian-sicknick-sentence.

227 American Radical, Episode 5.

228 Ibid.

229 Ibid.

230 Joe Hanneman, "Police Beating of Unconscious Trump Supporter Was 'Objectively Reasonable,' Department Rules," *Epoch Times*, February 15, 2022, https://www.theepochtimes.com/us/police-beating-of-unconscious-rosanne-boyland-was-objectively-reasonable-department-rules-4267104.

231 Ibid.

232 Solzhenitsyn, *Gulag*, 324.

233 Annie Karni, "The Committee Hired a TV Executive to Produce the Hearings for Maximum Impact," *New York Times*, June 9, 2022, https://www.nytimes.com/2022/06/09/us/the-committee-hired-a-tv-executive-to-produce-the-hearings-for-maximum-impact.html.

234 David Smith, "Hearing Delivers Gripping 'Finale' Full of Damning Details about Trump," *Guardian*, July 22, 2022, https://www.theguardian.com/us-news/2022/jul/22/january-6-panel-gripping-finale-trump-us-capitol-riot.

235 Brian Flood, "ABC News Buried Prince Andrew's Ties to Jeffrey Epstein after 'Fawning Grotesquely' over Royal Family: Insider," Fox News, November 6, 2019, https://www.foxnews.com/media/abc-news-jeffrey-epstein-prince-andrew-amy-robach.

236 "The GOP's New Trump Standard: You Can Only Prosecute Him in Red Areas," Constitutional Accountability Center, August 3, 2023, https://www.theusconstitution.org/news/the-gops-new-trump-standard-you-can-only-prosecute-him-in-red-areas/.

237 "The Real Story of January 6, Part 2: The Long Road Home," *Epoch Times*, July 23, 2022, https://www.theepochtimes.com/epochtv/the-real-story-of-jan-6-documentary-4596670.

238 Kyle Cheney and Josh Gerstein, "DOJ Has a Near-Perfect Record in Jan. 6 Cases. But It's Starting to Stumble," *Politico*, January 18, 2024, https://www.politico.com/news/2024/01/18/doj-jan-6-insurrection-cases-setbacks-00136524.

239 The New Yorker, "A Reporter's Footage from Inside the Capitol Siege," YouTube, January, 17, 2021, https://www.youtube.com/watch?v=270F8s5TEKY.

240 "Idaho Woman Sentenced on Felony and Misdemeanor Charges for Actions During Jan. 6 Capitol Breach," US Attorney's Office, District of Columbia, September 13, 2023, https://www.justice.gov/usao-dc/pr/idaho-woman-sentenced-felony-and-misdemeanor-charges-actions-during-jan-6-capitol-breach.

241 Andrew Baertlein and Alexandra Duggan, "Idaho Woman Sentenced to 30 Months in Prison for Role in US Capitol Breach," KTVB7, September 13, 2023, https://www.ktvb.com/article/news/local/boise-woman-sentenced-to-30-months-in-prison-

for-role-in-us-capitol-breach-st-cyr-jan-6-idaho/277-8e208944-9f82-4cd6-8dbd-667da9195851.

242 United States of America v. Rachel Marie Powell, Government's Sentencing Memorandum, October 11, 2023, https://storage.courtlistener.com/recap/gov.uscourts.dcd.228286/gov.uscourts.dcd.228286.121.0.pdf.

243 "FBI: Clinton Staff Destroyed Devices with Hammers," CNN, September 5, 2016, https://www.cnn.com/videos/politics/2016/09/05/hillary-clinton-email-device-destuction-nr-sot.cnn.

244 Caroline Linton, "Violence Erupts in Washington in D.C. after Trump Supporters Rally," CBS News, December 14, 2020, https://www.cbsnews.com/news/washington-dc-protest-violence-trump-supporters-rally/.

245 CNN, "Reporter Asks Mom Going to Prison for Jan. 6 If She Blames Trump. Hear Her Response," YouTube, January 9, 2024, https://www.youtube.com/watch?v=Zj8Z5VHjkOM.

246 "Restoring Godly Culture," https://restoringgodlyculture.com/.

247 "See the Surveillance Video Trump Allies Are Using to Sow Doubts about Voting," CNN, November 10, 2023, https://www.cnn.com/videos/politics/2023/11/10/illegal-voting-scheme-bridgeport-connecticut-analysis-cohen-cnnmax-vpx.cnn.

248 Amelia Nierenberg, "Election Fraud Is Rare. Except, Maybe, in Bridgeport, Conn.," *New York Times*, January 21, 2024, https://www.nytimes.com/2024/01/21/nyregion/joe-ganim-john-gomes-bridgeport-mayor-election.html.

249 Josh Gerstein and Alexander Ward, "Supreme Court Has Voted to Overturn Abortion Rights, Draft Opinion Shows," *Politico*, May 2, 2022, https://www.politico.com/news/2022/05/02/supreme-court-abortion-draft-opinion-00029473.

250 "Minnesota Woman Sentenced on Felony Charge for Actions During Jan. 6 Capitol Breach," US Attorney's Office, District of Columbia, November 20, 2023, https://www.justice.gov/usao-dc/pr/minnesota-woman-sentenced-felony-charge-actions-during-jan-6-capitol-breach.

251 L A R R Y, "Cop's Body Cam Video Reveals Jan 6th Beating of Victoria White," YouTube, February 4, 2023, https://www.youtube.com/watch?v=dLyFta-RV-E.

252 Alpha News, "'I Should Be Dead': Minnesota J6 Defendant Responds to New Bodycam Video," YouTube, March 21, 2023, https://www.youtube.com/watch?v=zxskx8Xtuig.

253 Hurubie Meko, "Former N.Y.P.D. Officer Is Convicted of Taking Part in Capitol Riot," *New York Times*, March 10, 2023, https://www.nytimes.com/2023/03/10/nyregion/sara-carpenter-nypd-jan-6-guilty.html.

254 Bible Gateway, https://web.mit.edu/jywang/www/cef/Bible/NIV/NIV_Bible/PS+31.html#:~:text=A%20psalm%20of%20David.&text=In%20you%2C%20O%20LORD%2C%20I,deliver%20me%20in%20your%20righteousness.&text=Turn%20your%20ear%20to%20me,strong%20fortress%20to%20save%20me.&text=Since%20you%20are%20my%20rock,name%20lead%20and%20guide%20me.

255 United States of America v. John Herbert Strand and Simone Melissa Gold, February 5, 2021, https://archive.org/details/john_herbert_strand_and_simone_melissa_gold_affidavit_in_support_of_criminal_complaint/mode/2up.

256 Marisa Sarnoff, "Judge Sends Jan. 6 Rioter and 'America's Front-line Doctors' Founder to Jail," Law & Crime, June 16, 2022, https://lawandcrime.com/u-s-capitol-breach/judge-sends-jan-6-rioter-and-americas-frontline-doctors-founder-to-jail/.

257 "They Put Me in Prison for 32 Months for This?!?," JohnStrand.com.

258 Ibid.

259 Sean Emery, "Ex-Beverly Hills Underwear Model Gets 2 Years, 8 Months for Role in Capitol Riot," *Los Angeles Times*, June, 2, 2023, https://www.dailynews.com/2023/06/02/ex-beverly-hills-underwear-model-gets-2-years-8-months-for-role-in-capitol-riot/.

260 Stephanie Mencimer, "An Insurrectionist Underwear Model Is Finally Having His January 6 Trial," *Mother Jones*, September 22, 2022, https://www.motherjones.com/politics/2022/09/john-strand-simone-gold-insurrectionist-underwear-model-january-6/.

261 Hannah Rabinowitz, "Doctor Known for Spreading Covid Misinformation Is Sentenced to Prison for Role in US Capitol Attack," CNN, June 16, 2022, https://www.cnn.com/2022/06/16/politics/simone-gold-january-6-covid-us-capitol/index.html.

262 Daniel Dale, "Fact Check: Sotomayor Makes False Claim about Covid-19's Impact on Children," CNN, January 11, 2022, https://www.cnn.com/2022/01/11/politics/fact-check-sotomayor-mandate-covid-dinner-gorsuch/index.html.

263 "They Put Me in Prison for 32 Months for This?!?," JohnStrand.com.

264 "US Anti-Vax Doctor's Licence in the Balance," JUTA Medical Brief, February 22, 2023, https://www.medicalbrief.co.za/us-anti-vax-doctors-licence-in-the-balance/.

265 Dr. Simone Gold (@drsimonegold), X, https://twitter.com/drsimonegold/status/1751769776987222478.

266 "The Real Story of January 6, Part 1," *Epoch Times*.

267 "Babbitt Estate v. U.S.A. Wrongful Death Complaint 00033," Judicial Watch, January 25, 2024, https://www.judicialwatch.org/documents/estate-of-ashli-babbitt-and-arron-babbitt-et-al-v-u-s-a/.

268 "(WATCH) January 6th: Part 2," *Full Measure with Sharyl Attkisson*, October 17, 2023, https://sharylattkisson.com/2023/10/watch-january-6th-part-2/.

269 Abdel Jibri Omar, "Zachary Alam Biography: 13 Things about US Capitol Rioter from Centreville, Virginia," Conan Daily, September 12, 2023, https://conandaily.com/2023/09/12/zachary-alam-biography-13-things-about-us-capitol-rioter-from-centreville-virginia/.

270 "Department of Justice Closes Investigation into the Death of Ashli Babbitt," US Attorney's Office, April 14, 2021, https://www.justice.gov/usao-dc/pr/department-justice-closes-investigation-death-ashli-babbitt.

271 KUSI News, "Videos Taken by Journalist Tayler Hansen Prove Ashli Babbitt Was Not Violent Inside US Capitol," YouTube, January 25, 2022, https://www.youtube.com/watch?v=hSt2LJWo-kI0.Fhansen.

272 Philip Bump (@pbump), Twitter (now X), January 25, 2022, https://twitter.com/pbump/status/1486093426772824065?lang=en.

273 Olivia Beavers, "How Lawmakers Trapped in the House Stood Their Ground," *Politico*, January 21, 2021, https://www.politico.com/news/2021/01/21/house-capitol-riots-lawmakers-stood-their-ground-460965.

274	Mary Clare Jalonick, "'We Were Trapped': Trauma of Jan. 6 Lingers for Lawmakers," Associated Press, January 5, 2022, https://apnews.com/article/jan-6-capitol-siege-lawmakers-trauma-04e29724aa6017180259385642c1b990.

275	Katherine Tully-McManus, "Capitol Police Weapon Left Unattended in Capitol Bathroom, Again," *Roll Call*, February 27, 2019, https://rollcall.com/2019/02/27/capitol-police-weapon-left-unattended-in-capitol-bathroom-again/.

276	Susan Daniels, "Cop Who Shot Ashli Babbitt Owes IRS Big Time," *American Thinker*, December 13, 2023, https://www.americanthinker.com/blog/2023/12/cop_who_shot_ashli_babbitt_owes_irs_big_time.html.

277	WUSA 9, "'It Could Have Been Me but She Went in First,' Pro-Trump Rioter Saw Woman Shot in Capitol," YouTube, January 7, 2021, https://www.youtube.com/watch?v=eCuIxBzylyo.

278	Nick Searcy, *The War on Truth*.

279	Dennis Romboy, "Utah Activist in Capitol Riot Sold His Video to CNN, NBC for $35K Each, Court Docs Say," *Deseret News*, February 17, 2021, https://www.deseret.com/utah/2021/2/17/22287763/activist-capitol-riot-video-sold-nbc-cnn-35k-each-john-sullivan-federal-charges.

280	"Utah Man Found Guilty of Felony Obstruction and Other Charges During Jan. 6 Capitol Breach," United States Attorney's Office, November 16, 2023, https://www.justice.gov/usao-dc/pr/utah-man-found-guilty-felony-obstruction-and-other-charges-during-jan-6-capitol-breach#:~:text=John%20Earl%20Sullivan%2C%2029%2C%20of,in%20a%20restricted%20building%20or.

281	"The Real Story of January 6," *Epoch Times*.

282	"Judicial Watch: Air Force Records Reveal Tens of Thousands of Taxpayer Dollars Spent to House Ashli Babbitt Shooter and His Pet for Several Months in 'Distinguished Visitor Suite' at Joint Base Andrews," Judicial Watch, January 6, 2023, https://www.judicialwatch.org/taxpayer-dollars-spent-to-house-ashli-babbitt-shooter/.

283	"Extended Interview: Capitol Police Lt. Michael Byrd Speaks Out," NBC News, August 27, 2021, https://www.nbcnews.com/video/extended-interview-capitol-police-lt-michael-byrd-speaks-out-part-1-119645765777.

284 "Department of Justice Closes Investigation into the Death of Ashli Babbitt," the US Attorney's Office, April 14, 2021, https://www.justice.gov/usao-dc/pr/department-justice-closes-investigation-death-ashli-babbitt.

285 WUSA 9, "'It Could Have Been Me but She Went in First,' Pro-Trump Rioter Saw Woman Shot in Capitol," YouTube, January 7, 2021, https://www.youtube.com/watch?v=eCuIxBzylyo.

286 "(WATCH) January 6th: Part 2."

287 Donald J. Trump, Facebook, January 5, 2021, https://www.facebook.com/DonaldTrump/photos/i-will-be-speaking-at-the-save-america-rally-tomorrow-on-the-ellipse-at-11am-eas/101 66086351485725/?paipv=0&eav=Afa89gh13zNbw4VBss6LWc-u2AwbiW39phoCVqwFTtcVQktJcn0E8lhY8cwwzq6W45PI&_rdr.

288 Judicial Watch, "Jan 6 'Pipe Bomb' Truth with Darren Beattie," YouTube, February 15, 2024, https://www.youtube.com/watch?v=D9NdDzRgvhw.

289 A. J. Fischer, "J6: A True Timeline," Open.Ink, https://open.ink/collections/j6.

290 Betsy Woodruff Swan, Christopher Cadelago, and Kyle Cheney, "Harris Was Inside DNC on Jan. 6 When Pipe Bomb Was Discovered Outside," *Politico*, January 6, 2022, https://www.politico.com/news/2022/01/06/harris-was-inside-dnc-on-jan-6-when-pipe-bomb-was-discovered-outside-526695.

291 Kyle Cheney, Josh Gerstein, and Christopher Cadelago, "DOJ Error Highlights Jan. 6 Mystery: Where Was Kamala Harris during the Attack?" *Politico*, November 4, 2020, https://www.politico.com/news/2021/11/04/doj-kamala-harris-jan-6-519505.

292 Diana Paulsen and Ryan J. Reilly, "Ray Epps, a Jan. 6 Defendant 'Scapegoated' by Far-Right Media, Sentenced to Probation," NBC News, January 9, 2024, https://www.nbcnews.com/politics/justice-department/ray-epps-jan-6-defendant-scapegoated-far-right-media-sentenced-probati-rcna132837.

293 60 Minutes, "I Thought I Could Stop It," Facebook, April 23, 2023, https://www.facebook.com/watch/?v=1283677545867367.

294 "FBI Washington Field Office Releases Video and Additional Information Regarding the Pipe Bomb Investigation," FBI Washington Office of Public Affairs, September 8, 2021, https://www.fbi.gov/contact-us/field-offices/washingtondc/news/press-re-

leases/fbi-washington-field-office-releases-video-and-additional-information-regarding-the-pipe-bomb-investigation-090821.

295   "Mayoral Proclamation for Madison Native Karlin Younger," Mayor's Office, February 1, 2021, https://www.cityofmadison.com/mayor/blog/2021-02-01/mayoral-proclamation-for-madison-native-karlin-younger.

296   "$500,000 Reward Remains in Effect for Information about Capitol Hill Pipe Bomber," FBI Washington Field Office, January 4, 2024, https://www.fbi.gov/contact-us/field-offices/washingtondc/news/500000-reward-remains-in-effect-for-information-about-capitol-hill-pipe-bomber.

297   Michael Shellenberger (@shellenberger), "FBI and Secret Service Are Covering Up Their Role in Alleged January 6 'Pipe Bomb' Plot," X, January 20, 2024, https://twitter.com/shellenberger/status/1748707105954013404?lang=en.

298   Paul Duggan and Pierre Thomas, "McVeigh Held in Conjunction with Oklahoma City Bombing," *Washington Post*, April 28, 1995.

299   Peter Keating, "Remembering Oklahoma City, and How Bill Clinton Saved His Presidency," *New York Magazine*, April 19, 2010, https://nymag.com/intelligencer/2010/04/remembering_oklahoma_city_and.html.

300   Ken Bensinger and Jessica Garrison, "Watching the Watchmen," Buzzfeed News, July 20, 2021, https://www.buzzfeednews.com/article/kenbensinger/michigan-kidnapping-gretchen-whitmer-fbi-informant?bftwnews&utm_term=4ldqpgc#4ldqpgc.

301   Dave Boucher, "Joe Biden: 'Through Line from President Trump's Dog Whistles' to Whitmer Kidnapping Plot," *Detroit Free Press*, October 8, 2020, https://www.freep.com/story/news/politics/elections/2020/10/08/biden-trump-dog-whistles-whitmer-kidnapping-plot/5932432002/.

302   Timothy Nick, Subcommittee on Oversight Hearing, April 17, 2024, https://cha.house.gov/2024/4/subcommittee-on-oversight-hearing-three-years-later-d-c-national-guard-whistleblowers-speak-out-on-january-6-delay.

303   *The Tucker Carlson Encounter*, "Steven Sund," August 10, 2023, https://tuckercarlson.com/the-tucker-carlson-encounter-steven-sund/.

304 "Interview of Yogananda Pittman," House Select Committee, January 13, 2022, https://www.govinfo.gov/content/pkg/GPO-J6-TRANSCRIPT-CTRL0000034888/pdf/GPO-J6-TRAN-SCRIPT-CTRL0000034888.pdf.

305 Kathryn Watson, "Capitol Police Officers Give Vote of No Confidence in Leaders," CBS News, February 16, 2021, https://www.cbsnews.com/news/capitol-police-officers-give-vote-of-no-confidence-in-leaders/.

306 Nick Searcy, *The War on Truth*.

307 ChristineXP, "10 Characteristics of Mentally Strong Women," Discovery, January 16, 2024, https://discoverymood.com/blog/characteristics-of-mentally-strong-women/.

308 FBI interview, April 15, 2021.

About the Author

An independent writer and producer, Jack Cashill has written seventeen books and appeared on C-SPAN's *Book TV* a dozen times. He has also produced a score of feature-length documentaries.

Jack serves as senior editor of *Ingram's* magazine and writes regularly for *American Thinker*, *American Spectator*, and *WorldNetDaily*. He has a Ph.D. from Purdue University in American studies and a B.A. in English from Siena College.

9 798888 457757